William Roulston is Research Director with the Ulster Historical Foundation. He is a native of Bready, County Tyrone, and has researched and written on a number of aspects of the history of Ulster in the seventeenth and eighteenth centuries.

Map of Ulster from S. Lewis, *Atlas of the counties of Ireland* (London, 1837)

The Drapers' Company castle at Moneymore,
County Londonderry *(PRONI)*

Researching Scots-Irish Ancestors

*The Essential Genealogical
Guide to Early Modern Ulster,
1600–1800*

William J. Roulston

ULSTER HISTORICAL FOUNDATION

Ulster Historical Foundation is pleased to acknowledge support for the
research towards this publication from the Ulster-Scots Agency.

First Published 2005 by
the Ulster Historical Foundation.
Reprinted 2006, 2009 and 2010.
49 Malone Road, Belfast, BT9 6RY
www.ancestryireland.com
www.booksireland.org.uk

Front cover: Har headstone, Inver Church of Ireland churchyard, Larne, Co. Antrim.
Back cover: Killybegs, County Donegal, in 1622 *(PRONI)*.

Printed by Thomson Litho
Design by Cheah Design

CONTENTS

Preface

The purpose of this book is to provide a practical guide for the family historian searching for Ulster ancestors in the seventeenth and eighteenth centuries. While the book is primarily aimed at those with Scots-Irish ancestors, its breadth of coverage means that it should be of interest to anyone researching family history prior to the nineteenth century.

The need for this volume is obvious. Many people who have successfully researched their family history in the nineteenth and twentieth centuries find it difficult to take that research back before 1800. There is no denying that the loss of so many records in the destruction of the Public Record Office, Dublin, in 1922 was a catastrophe as far as historical and genealogical research is concerned. However, since 1922 the work of archivists to gather records of historical importance has resulted in a vast amount of material being available for the genealogical researcher to peruse. In addition there are other repositories in Ireland, such as the Registry of Deeds in Dublin, where the collections have survived virtually intact, as well as categories of records now available that were not in the Public Record Office in 1922 and so escaped destruction.

This book covers the sources available to researchers for the period 1600–1800. Some of these sources will be familiar to many genealogists, such as the hearth money rolls of the 1660s and the flaxgrowers' list of 1796. Others may not. In particular, much attention is given to the value of estate papers as a genealogical source. In most guides to Irish genealogy, estate papers are barely noticed and their full potential is overlooked. Part of the reason for this is that the majority of genealogy manuals have emanated from the Republic of Ireland, where the two principal repositories, the National Archives and especially the National Library, have extensive, though frequently inaccessible, estate collections. In recent times efforts have been made to improve access to these records. The Public Record Office of Northern Ireland (PRONI), on the other hand, has deployed considerable resources in cataloguing the often huge collections of estate papers in its care.

While I have tried to be as comprehensive as possible, I cannot claim to have covered every single record of genealogical interest from these centuries. Such an undertaking would require a multi-volume set rather than a single handbook. The book is undeniably skewed towards sources in PRONI, but it is here that the great majority of records relating to Ulster can be found. Nonetheless I have noted records in repositories elsewhere in Ireland and occasionally in Britain and America.

Those who wish to carry out research into family history in the period before 1800 can be divided into two categories. The first category comprises those who have already been carrying out research on family members in the nineteenth and maybe even the twentieth centuries, and who wish to extend that research by going back further generations. For others the pre-1800 period will be their starting point for the simple reason that their ancestor left Ulster prior to the nineteenth century, usually as part of the Scots-Irish emigration to Colonial America.

In Irish genealogical research it is important to know not only the name of one's ancestor, but also the area in which that person lived. The ideal is to know the townland in which the ancestor lived or, if this is not available, the name of the parish (an explanation of the administrative divisions used in this volume is given in Appendix 5). However, for many people searching for pre-1800 families – and this usually applies to those in the second category outlined above – the only information they have is that their forebear was born somewhere in Ulster, or at best they may know the name of the county in which their ancestor originated.

There are obvious difficulties to be overcome here – not necessarily insurmountable, but considerable nonetheless. Ulster is a province of nine counties, over 350 parishes and thousands of townlands. To have any chance of success it is vital that the place of origin of an ancestor can be narrowed down to a specific area. A major obstacle in trying to do this is the fact that there is no comprehensive index to names from the seventeenth and eighteenth centuries. The first census in Ireland was not held until 1821, while official registration of all births, deaths and marriages did not begin until 1864 (non-Catholic marriages were registered from 1845).

If the precise area an ancestor came from is not known, a number of nineteenth-century sources may prove helpful. The Householders Index is based on information derived from the Tithe Valuation of c.1830 and Griffith's Valuation of c.1860. It lists surnames by parish, indicating the number of occurrences of the surname in Griffith's Valuation and simply whether or not it appears in the Tithe Valuation. Using the information in the Householders Index, it may be possible to narrow down the likely area your ancestor came from. It is particularly useful if it reveals that a surname was concentrated in a small number of parishes. Copies of the Householders Index are available in PRONI, the National Archives the National Library and, for Ulster counties, on the website of the Ulster Historical Foundation (www.ancestryireland.com).

Some explanation is needed of the Tithe Valuation and Griffith's Valuation. The Tithe Valuation followed the Composition Act of 1823, which stipulated that henceforth all tithes due to the Established Church (Church of Ireland) were to be paid in money rather than in kind. This necessitated a complete valuation of all tithable land in Ireland, the results of which are contained in the tithe applotment books. The Tithe Valuation lists the names of tithe-payers. As the tithe was a tax on land these were usually tenant farmers. Landless labourers were excluded, as were usually those who lived in towns. Griffith's

Valuation lists the names of all occupiers of rateable property in Ireland. Again only the name of the head of the household is given, but it is a much more comprehensive source than the Tithe Valuation.

Having identified the likely or even possible area from which an ancestor came, it will then be possible to focus on the sources that relate to that area. This book identifies those sources and shows you how to go about using them.

ACKNOWLEDGEMENTS

I have incurred many debts in the course of writing this volume and it is only right and proper that I acknowledge at least some of these. First of all, my greatest debt is to my own family who have backed me ever since I decided to embark on a career encompassing history, archaeology and genealogy. I am grateful to the Ulster-Scots Agency for providing a grant towards the cost of conducting research for this book. For drawing my attention to some of the lesser-known sources included in this book, or who helped me to understand something of their significance, I am grateful to the following: Harry Allen, Toby Barnard, Catherine Blumsom, Terry Eakin, Simon Elliott, Bobby Forrest, Raymond Gillespie, the late John Hastings, David Hayton, Bob Hunter, Jack Johnston, Faye Logue, John McCabe, Finbar McCormick, Annette McKee, Billy Macafee, Anthony Malcomson, Ian Maxwell, Duncan Scarlett, Len Swindley and John Turner.

This book would not have been written without the assistance of the numerous archival institutions and libraries that I visited or corresponded with in the course of research for this publication. In particular I wish to acknowledge the tremendous assistance given to me by the staff of the Public Record Office of Northern Ireland. I am also grateful to my colleagues at the Ulster Historical Foundation for their encouragement and for tolerating my numerous absences from the office on research excursions. I wish to acknowledge the contribution of Fintan Mullan, Executive Director of the Ulster Historical Foundation, for giving me the necessary backing to pursue this project and for his assistance in the final production stages of the book.

I wish to record a special debt to Bill Crawford and Brian Trainor who have encouraged my interest in the history of early modern Ulster and the sources for its study. Their pioneering work has preserved many records which would otherwise have been lost and enabled countless thousands to pursue avenues of research that would have been closed to them. It is to them that this book is dedicated and offered as a token of my appreciation for their work.

ABBREVIATIONS

CI	Church of Ireland
GO	Genealogical Office
MIC	Microfilm
MOR	Moravian
NAI	National Archives of Ireland
NLI	National Library of Ireland
NSP	Non-Subscribing Presbyterian
P	Presbyterian
PRONI	Public Record Office of Northern Ireland
RC	Roman Catholic
RCB	Representative Church Body Library
RP	Reformed Presbyterian
RSF	Religious Society of Friends (Quakers)
TCD	Trinity College, Dublin
UHF	Ulster Historical Foundation

All references, unless otherwise stated, are for documents held at PRONI.

Introduction:
Ulster in the seventeenth and eighteenth centuries

The Nine Years' War (1594–1603) and the passing of the Act of Union (1800) provide appropriate brackets within which to study the history of Ulster. As a result of the former the entire island of Ireland was brought under the control of the English Crown. With the latter the Irish parliament was abolished; from then to 1922 all of Ireland would be governed as an integral part of the United Kingdom. During the intervening two centuries immense changes in the nature of Ulster society took place, which were to have profound demographic, economic, political and religious implications. This chapter provides a brief introduction to Ulster in the seventeenth and eighteenth centuries.[1]

Prelude to plantation

Ulster was the last province in Ireland to be brought under the control of the English Crown. At the end of the sixteenth century, apart from a couple of outposts at Carrickfergus and Newry, most of Ulster remained under the control of Gaelic chieftains. In the 1590s a bloody and savage conflict broke out between, on one side, a confederation of Gaelic lords led by Hugh O'Neill, earl of Tyrone, and Hugh O'Donnell, and, on the other, the forces of the English Crown. The decisive turning point was the defeat of the Gaelic lords at Kinsale in December 1601, and in March 1603 the Treaty of Mellifont, which formally ended the war, was signed. The terms granted to Hugh O'Neill were generous, but, unable to adapt to changed circumstances and with many enemies in government, he left Ireland in September 1607 along with the newly created earl of Tyrconnell, Rory O'Donnell, and almost one hundred supporters in what has become known as the 'Flight of the Earls'. O'Neill's plan to sail to Spain and seek support for further Spanish intervention in Ireland was never realised, and he died in Rome in 1616.

Plantation in Ulster

After the Nine Years' War, the government embarked upon a scheme whereby lands formerly in the possession of Irish chieftains were confiscated and parcelled out, for the most part, to new landowners of English and Scottish origin known as undertakers. Servitors (those who had served the Crown in Ireland in a civil or military capacity), 'deserving' native Irish, and institutions such as Trinity College, Dublin, and the Protestant Church were also beneficiaries of the scheme, which took three years to plan and was not implemented until 1610. Six counties were to be affected in the official plantation: Armagh, Cavan, Coleraine (renamed Londonderry), Donegal, Fermanagh and Tyrone (collectively known as the 'escheated counties'). Excepting Londonderry, which was granted to the London companies and had its own rules, a fairly uniform plan was devised for the scheme of plantation. Different obligations were placed on each of the groups, with the most significant falling on the undertakers, who were the only grantees expected to colonise, being required to plant ten families or twenty-four men for every 1,000 acres they were granted.[2]

To measure the progress of the plantation in the escheated counties, the government commissioned a series of surveys carried out between 1611 and 1622, which provide a valuable record of what was happening in west Ulster in the formative years of the plantation. The results of the first two surveys, carried out by Carew in 1611 and Bodley in 1613, showed that few of the grantees were fulfilling the requirements laid down in the conditions of the plantation, particularly with regard to the colonising and building obligations. Schemes that may have been easy to devise proved more difficult to implement, with the population on a particular proportion being determined not so much by government policy as by a combination of factors including distance from a port and the landlord's leasing policy and opportunity for profit. However, by the time of Pynnar's survey of 1618–19 and the final survey of 1622, progress was being made, with most of the uninterested grantees having sold out to men who were more prepared to invest in their lands.

By the time of the 1622 plantation survey, British settlement was well established in the Foyle valley (north Tyrone, east Donegal and west Londonderry). Other important areas of British settlement were in north County Londonderry and in mid County Armagh. Areas with smaller concentrations of British settlers included the shores of Upper and Lower Lough Erne in County Fermanagh and south and east County Tyrone. Large areas remained virtually unsettled, including most of north, south and west County Donegal, south County Armagh, most of County Cavan, mid County Tyrone and mid County Londonderry. The more mountainous areas, far from the main British settlements, remained almost exclusively Irish. In 1622, it was said of the non-resident Protestant minister in the parish of Killelagh, County Londonderry, that 'sometimes (as once in 3 months) he resorteth to the church where no man cometh at him – the whole parish consisting of Irish recusants'.[3] In the parish of Culdaff, County Donegal, it was noted in 1622 that there were no English families.

The official plantation scheme did not extend to Counties Antrim, Down and Monaghan. Private plantations in the early seventeenth century resulted in the large-scale migration of English and Scottish settlers to Counties Antrim and Down.[4] In the southern part of County Antrim, as a result of the acquisition of much of the land by English landowners such as Sir Arthur Chichester, Sir Fulke Conway and Sir John Clotworthy, much of the settlement was by migrants from England. In County Down there was a significant English settlement associated with the Cromwell estate at Downpatrick. In north-east County Down, two Scots, James Hamilton and Hugh Montgomery, acquired large estates from lands formerly owned by Con O'Neill. The British – overwhelmingly Scottish – settlement on the Hamilton and Montgomery estates was heavier than in any other part of Ulster.

Large parts of Antrim and Down remained in Irish hands in the early seventeenth century. In 1610 and 1611 most of the land in the south and west of County Down had been parcelled out in small freeholds to the native Irish Magennises. British settlement was minimal and was mainly confined to the few settler estates that did emerge. For example, the Bagenals had acquired an estate around Newry in the sixteenth century and had introduced settlers from Wales to it. Marmaduke Whitchurch and Edward Trevor also acquired estates in County Down in the early seventeenth century, the former at Loughbrickland in the parish of Aghaderg and the latter in several different areas, including part of the parish of Clonallan. The 1659 'census' reveals the level of British settlement in south and west County Down. In four parishes – Dromara, Drumballyroney, Clonduff and Drumgooland – the British population did not exceed four. In six others – Annaclone, Garvaghy, Donaghmore, Clonallan, Drumgath and Kilbroney – it did not exceed 35.

The largest land grant made in Ulster in the early seventeenth century was the grant of the greater part of the four northern baronies in county Antrim – Cary, Dunluce, Glenarm and Kilconway, an area of well over 300,000 acres – to Randal MacDonnell, a Scottish Catholic, in 1603.[5] In order to develop his massive estate, MacDonnell invited lowland Scots to settle on his lands. In 1611 it was noted that adjoining his castle at Dunluce he had founded a village, containing 'many tenements after the fashion of the Pale, peopled for the most part with Scottishmen'. To encourage Protestant Scots to settle on a Catholic-owned estate, MacDonnell contributed to the building and repair of churches.[6]

Early seventeenth-century County Monaghan differed again. Here a land settlement of 1591, which divided the county among native Irish freeholders, was re-established in 1606. There were, however, a number of settler estates in the county in the early seventeenth century, mainly based on former ecclesiastical lands. In 1575 the earl of Essex was granted almost the whole of the barony of Farney in the south of the county. Other major settler landowning families included the Blayneys and Barretts. The sale and mortgaging of Irish lands to settler landowners reduced the proportion of land in County Monaghan still in native hands to less than 40 per cent in 1641.[7]

Urban and rural settlement

Urbanisation formed a central part of the plantation scheme. In 1609 a list of 25 proposed corporate towns (i.e. towns that could send MPs to the Irish parliament) was drawn up, all but two of which were to be located at places of importance in the old Gaelic order.[8] This list was subsequently revised so that fewer towns were given corporate status. To begin with things moved slowly, and in order to give town development some momentum, it was resolved that the principal grantee near each proposed town should build houses for tradesmen who would hold their tenements from him. Incorporation would follow at a later date. At the top end of the scale were the towns of Derry, Coleraine and Strabane. Their successful development was largely due to energetic landlord involvement and favourable location for sea-borne trade. By 1630 Derry was by far the largest settlement in west Ulster, with about 500 adult British males.

Towns provided a variety of functions, economic, social and political, and their infrastructure reflected this. In this respect Strabane was very well provided for, all the more so considering that it was not even the county town of Tyrone, that distinction belonging to Dungannon. In 1622 Strabane, which by this time contained over 100 houses, was recorded as having a church, a sessions house, a market cross and a prison.[9] It was noted that the inhabitants of the town were 'very industrious and do daylie beautifie their Towne with new buildings, strong and defencible'. At the other end of the scale was the corporate town of Killybegs, which in 1622 had only seventeen British and Irish inhabitants and no public buildings.

Below the corporate towns, in terms of status though not necessarily of scale, were the villages built by the landlords on their proportions to fulfil the requirements of the plantation conditions. The more substantial villages included Lisnaskea, Letterkenny and Ramelton, all of which had 40 houses or more by 1622, which was more than many of the corporate towns. The infrastructure of these settlements varied; while most were simply collections of houses, seldom more than a dozen in number, others possessed buildings and features of importance. At Ramelton, Sir William Stewart had built a paved street between his castle and the church. In Lisnaskea Balfour had built a school, while Lowther, upon his Necarn proportion in Fermanagh, had built a market house in the estate village. By and large, however, towns in Ulster remained fairly modest in comparison with urban centres in Britain. When Bishop William Bedell first arrived in Cavan in the early 1630s, he found that 'the only considerable town in the whole county was Belturbet which yet was but as one of our ordinary market towns here in England'.[10] The settlement adjoining his cathedral was 'a mere country village'.

More than two-thirds of estates lacked a nucleated settlement.[11] Even on those estates that did possess a village, it is clear that most of the tenants lived dispersedly. The rural settlement pattern that emerged in west Ulster in the seventeenth century was one of nucleated villages and dispersed settlement, with the latter being much more prevalent. This was in direct contravention of the conditions of the plantation. The sheer impracticality of having to live in a village and travel out to one's farm every day militated against nucleated settlements on plantation proportions. This was in part due to the confines of the Irish townland system upon which the tenants' holdings were based. The settlement pattern was by no means rigid in the formative years of the plantation, and there would appear to have been considerable migration between estates.

The religion of the settlers

It can be reasonably assumed that most of the settlers who came to Ulster in the early seventeenth century were Protestants, even if only nominally so. Very few of the native population converted to Protestantism, and at various times fines were issued on those who were guilty of recusancy (not attending a Protestant church). The Church of Ireland was the established or state Church and was organised along episcopalian lines, with a hierarchy of clergy rising to the archbishop of Armagh, who was the chief Anglican cleric on the island. However, several ministers from Scotland came to Ulster in this period who dissented from this view of Church government, preferring the more egalitarian presbyterian system. To begin with such men were tolerated within the Church of Ireland, and there was no distinct Presbyterian denomination at this time.

In the 1630s the government, led by the new lord deputy, Thomas Wentworth, began to take steps to bring the Church of Ireland into closer conformity with the Church of England. This meant clamping down on the activities of ministers with Presbyterian convictions. Ministers who were not prepared to renounce their Presbyterianism were excommunicated. In 1636 some of these men, with about 140 followers, set sail in the *Eagle Wing* for America; they never reached their destination, as storms drove the ship back.[12] Other Presbyterians returned to Scotland. Here Presbyterian opposition to Charles I was also reaching boiling point. In 1638 the National Covenant was drawn up in Scotland, which declared Presbyterianism the only true form of Church government and bound the nation to the principles of the Reformation. Many in Ulster also signed the Covenant. In response Wentworth insisted that all Scots in Ulster over the age of sixteen take an oath – the infamous 'Black Oath', as it became known – abjuring the Covenant. Those who refused to take the oath could be fined and imprisoned. The result was that large numbers of Scottish settlers fled to their homeland; so many left, in fact, that in some places there were not enough people to bring in the harvest.

Catholic settlers were not entirely unknown in early seventeenth-century Ulster. There was a small but significant colony of Scottish Catholics at Strabane, under the patronage of Sir George Hamilton of Greenlaw, whose father was Lord Paisley, a prominent supporter of Mary, Queen of Scots.[13] As early as 1614 Sir George's Catholic sympathies were a source of concern for the government, and in 1622 he was described as an 'Archpapist and a great patron of them'; it was noted that all his servants were Catholics. In the late 1620s the Church of Ireland bishop of Derry became particularly agitated at the large number of Catholics he believed were living at Strabane under the patronage of Sir George Hamilton and his near relations. Among those named by the bishop were Robert and Claude Algeo, who, despite their Italian-sounding surname, were Scottish settlers. These men were probably sons of Robert Algeo, who had been Sir George Hamilton's agent or land steward. A curious stone, built into a bridge in the village of Artigarvan, bears the name Robert Algeo and the date 25 May 1625. It also features a crucifixion scene – an important Counter-Reformation symbol – and is believed to be a memorial to Algeo senior. How it got to its present location is a complete mystery.

The 1641 Rebellion

If the position for the Scots in Ulster was bad by the end of the 1630s, that of the native Irish landowners was little better. Few had been able to make the transition to a market economy and as a result many had ended up heavily in debt, forcing them either to sell or to mortgage much – or in some cases all – of their lands. Several of them conspired to rise up in rebellion against the government and take back what they believed was rightfully theirs. On the evening of 22 October 1641 the rebellion began in Ulster, plunging the province and soon the entire island of Ireland into chaos. Under the leadership of the native Irish gentry, most notably Sir Phelim O'Neill, castles and towns over much of Ulster were seized by the rebels. Notable exceptions included Belfast, Carrickfergus, Coleraine, Derry, Enniskillen and Lisburn. Initially bloodshed was limited, with a number of the rebel leaders insisting that the Scottish should not be interfered with. Soon, however, the rebel leaders lost control of the peasantry, and indiscriminate massacres of settlers began.

The numbers killed in the rebellion have been a source of contention ever since the autumn of 1641. At the time, wildly exaggerated estimates – often considerably more than the entire British population in Ulster at the time – were circulated, mainly in the English press to drum up support for crushing the rebellion. Nonetheless, thousands of settlers did die in the rebellion, at least as many from exposure and disease as from murder. Those who had the means of doing so fled to Dublin or across the Irish Sea to England and Scotland. Other sought refuge in the towns that had not been captured. At Coleraine 'the church was fitted within and without her walls and round about the churchyard with little huts "pestred" and packed with poor people'.[14]

In north-west Ulster, resistance to the rebels was organised by the Stewarts, Sir William and Sir Robert, who recruited an army from among the settlers known as the Laganeers, one of the most efficient fighting machines of the war. Additional support for the settlers came in the form of a Scottish army under the command of Major-General Robert Munro, which landed at Carrickfergus in April 1642. Soon afterwards Owen Roe O'Neill, nephew of Hugh O'Neill, earl of Tyrone, arrived at Doe Castle in County Donegal and took control of the rebel army. By this time the war had become an all-Ireland conflict, with the Old English and the Catholic Church declaring their support for the rebellion. The conflict continued for the rest of the 1640s, and it was not until Cromwell arrived in Ireland in August 1649 the island began to be brought under control. In Ulster most of the Scots supported the claims of Prince Charles, son of the recently beheaded king. Derry was briefly besieged by the Scots and in December 1649 an army of Scottish settlers was decisively defeated by a Cromwellian force at Lisburn. Owen Roe O'Neill was dead by this time, and the following summer Irish resistance had been all but crushed.

By the early 1650s order had been restored to Ulster, and within a few years there were tangible signs of recovery. The Civil Survey of 1654–6 noted that the town of Strabane was 'rebuilded upon ye ruins of ye late devastacon & repeopled with Brittish inhabbitants'.[15] In June 1665 the King wrote to the lord lieutenant of Ireland on behalf of Lord Massereene, acknowledging that 'the town of Antrim was, during the late rebellion, burned to the ground and by the trouble in that our kingdom wholly ruinated'.[16] However, since then it had been 'a good measure re-edified'.

The Cromwellian and Restoration periods

During the 1650s the remaining Gaelic landownership in Ulster was almost wiped out. Large swathes of land were confiscated from the Irish gentry as a punishment for their rebellion and granted to British settlers. For a time Scottish landowners in Ulster were also in a difficult situation, with the threat of confiscation also hanging over them for their support of the royalist cause. Eventually, however, their possessions were secured on payment of heavy fines. Cromwell died in 1658 and in 1660 the monarchy was restored. The new king, Charles II, was faced with the difficulty of having to find land for those Catholics who had remained loyal to the Crown during the previous twenty years. Several Scottish Catholics – the marquess of Antrim and the Hamiltons in Strabane barony, County Tyrone – were restored to the estates they had held prior to 1641. Apart from this there were relatively few changes to the land settlement laid down by Cromwell.

Because the land settlements did not overturn the existing estate system as far as the settlers were concerned, a significant degree of continuity prevailed. The most significant changes occurred in those areas that had been owned by Irish lords in the early seventeenth century. In County Down the main beneficiaries of confiscated native Irish land included William Waring, Colonel Arthur Hill, Sir John Magill and Sir George Rawdon. In County Fermanagh Henry Brooke, an English settler who had distinguished himself in the wars of the 1640s, was granted the massive estate owned by Conor Roe Maguire in the early seventeenth century. There were also significant changes in Counties Cavan and Monaghan. Many of those who benefited from the land settlements were men who were already established in Ulster. Relatively few of the new landowners were recent arrivals in the province.

The second half of the seventeenth century, therefore, saw the opening up and development of large parts of Ulster as manors were created, towns established and thousands of British settlers introduced to areas that had formerly been predominantly Irish. For example, Sir George Rawdon acquired two significant blocks of land in the Ballynahinch and Moira areas of County Down. When these were erected into a manor by royal patent in 1682, Rawdon was commended for having 'built a considerable town [at Ballynahinch], in the middle whereof he had set out a large market place which was paved and made fit for markets and fairs'. He had also repaired the local parish church. Meanwhile at Moira he had 'built a market town ... which was inhabited with conformable Protestants'.[17] Migration to the north of Ireland in the 1650s was encouraged by low rents in the aftermath of a decade of warfare. The Quaker Act of 1662 and the Conventicle Act of 1664 resulted in many Quakers leaving England for Ireland, and significant Quaker settlements developed around Lisburn, County Antrim, and Lurgan, County Armagh. In the 1670s migration was encouraged by the Covenanter disturbances in Scotland.

These fresh migrations were having a noticeable impact on local demographics. About 1670 Oliver Plunkett, Catholic archbishop of Armagh, noted that the city of Armagh had a population of approximately 3,000 persons, 'almost all Scottish or English, with very few Irish'.[18] This contrasted with the towns and villages in County Armagh, which, according to Plunkett, were mainly inhabited with Catholic leaseholders and peasants. In the town of Dungannon Plunkett believed that of 1,000 families barely twenty were not English or

Scottish.[19] A description of County Donegal from April 1683 noted that it was 'plentifully planted with Protestant inhabitants, especially with great numbers out of Scotland'.[20] A year earlier, in his description of the barony of Oneilland, County Armagh, William Brooke wrote that the 'few Irish we have amongst us are very much reclaimed of their barbarous customs, the most of them speaking English'. Prior to 1641 the area around Kinaird, County Tyrone, had on the whole remained in Irish hands. Following the confiscation and regranting of this land in the 1650s and 1660s, the area was opened up to British settlers. Quite quickly Kinaird, soon to be renamed Caledon, became an important settlement, necessitating the construction of a Church of Ireland church.

By the second half of the seventeenth century the Presbyterian Church had emerged as a distinct denomination and there were clear lines of demarcation between it and the Church of Ireland. On the whole Scottish settlers were Presbyterian, while English settlers were Anglican, although there were numerous exceptions to this rule. Captain John Hamilton of Cavan, near Stranorlar, County Donegal, was described as a 'most zealous Catholic ... a pious and liberal man and a great apologist for the faith', having previously been both an Anglican and a Presbyterian.[21] He later emigrated to Germany and in 1695 became a count in the Holy Roman Empire.

In County Antrim Presbyterians formed an absolute majority. In 1673 Plunkett commented that in the dioceses of Connor and Down (comprising almost all of County Antrim and north and east County Down), the Presbyterians – 'whose belief is an aborted form of Protestantism' – were more numerous than Catholics and Anglicans put together.[22] On another occasion he wrote that 'one could travel twenty-five miles in my area without finding half a dozen Catholic or Protestant families, but all Presbyterians.[23] In 1683 Richard Dobbs noted that all the inhabitants of Island Magee in County Antrim were Scottish Presbyterians.[24]

Two counties in which Presbyterianism never developed as a strong force were Cavan and Fermanagh. Although parts of both counties had been set aside for Scottish grantees in the Ulster Plantation, actual Scottish settlement was not significant. Furthermore, there was some transfer of Scottish estates to English ownership in the period before 1641. It seems, therefore, that the initial flow of Scottish settlers into these counties was arrested at a relatively early stage and that this hindered the development of Presbyterianism.[25] In Cavan and Fermanagh Protestant settlers were predominantly members of the Church of Ireland.

Large areas of Ulster continued to be sparsely planted with settlers. In 1666 Langfield parish, County Tyrone, was described as 'full of woods, mountains, bad ways ... the congregation 5 or 6, sometimes 10 or 12 might be 100, but all Irish, except some Scotch and 1 English family'.[26] The limited impact of British settlement in the northern portion of Inishowen barony, County Donegal, is confirmed in the 1659 'census', which revealed that in the parishes of Desertegny, Culdaff, Clonca, Donagh and Clonmany there were a total of eight British households. There seems to have been some increase by 1679, when Church of Ireland churches were noted in Culdaff, Clonca, Clonmany and Donagh, and in the 1680s a new church was built in the parish of Desertegny 'for the accommodation of some Protestant families'.

In areas with heavy British settlement, increased competition for land could result in the displacement of the local Catholic farming class. Even the security of a lease was not enough to prevent Catholic farmers from being moved on once the term of that lease had expired. In 1675 Plunkett wrote:

> Sometimes it happens that a parish which one year has two hundred Catholic families will not have thirty the following year, as happened in various parishes in the diocese of Armagh this year, because the Catholics being, as a rule, leaseholders, often lose their leases, which are then given to Protestants or Presbyterians or Anabaptists or Quakers. These are the dominant sects here and every time a new colony of them arrives, the poor Catholics are put aside.[27]

The Williamite War in Ulster

The accession of James II, a Catholic, to the throne in 1685 created considerable concern among Ulster's Protestants and raised hopes among the dispossessed and impoverished Catholic gentry of being restored to estates they had lost under Cromwell. The promotion of Catholics to important positions in the judiciary and in central and local government only served to heighten Protestant fears. Events in England and the Continent brought matters to a head. In 1688 William of Orange arrived in England and was declared king in what was later known as the 'Glorious Revolution'. James II fled to France, and the following year landed in Ireland with a large French army.

Protestant resistance in Ulster had already been mobilised. On 7 December 1688, as a Catholic army under the command of the earl of Antrim was on its way to Derry, a group of apprentice boys shut the gates of the city. Thus began Derry's resistance to James II. Elsewhere in Ulster, however, James's forces easily defeated any resistance and settler forces gradually withdrew to Derry. The exception was Enniskillen, where a force of mainly Fermanagh settlers known as the Inniskilling Men secured the town. On 21 March 1689 the famous 105 day siege of Derry began. As many as 30,000 settlers as well as a garrison of 7,000 men were packed into the city; it was reckoned that 15,000 of them died of fever or starvation or were killed in battle. The siege was lifted in late July and this coincided with a major defeat of the Jacobites at the hands of the Inniskilling Men at Newtownbutler, County Fermanagh. Soon afterwards a large Williamite force under the command of the Duke of Schomberg landed near Bangor, County Down, and by the autumn of 1689 James's forces had been all but removed from Ulster. As the war moved south, with important battles fought at the Boyne on 1 July 1690 and Aughrim on 12 July 1691, the province began to recover from the consequences of the conflict.

Because the military campaign was shorter in this war than it had been in the 1640s, its effects were not as severe. Nonetheless, large parts of Ulster experienced considerable devastation. In the autumn of 1691 William Waring of Waringstown, County Down, wrote to William Layfield about the condition of his estate:

> I have no hopes of getting any of it planted. The Irish natives that live on it are all fled into Connaught and the British inhabitants are wasted by warfare and sickness ... And it happened so that my house and estate about was just on the edge of that part of our country that was not wasted from here to Belfast. 16 miles was planted with Protestants, and though many of

the best sort fled, yet the generality remained in their houses ... but a mile on the other hand of me was all wasted, the Protestants all banished. The Irish would not suffer one to live amongst them in which part your estate lies.[28]

The widespread destruction of churches during the war was noted in visitations of the early 1690s, but in many parishes remedial work had already been carried out or was in the process of being undertaken.[29] Furthermore, in several parishes Church of Ireland churches were being built where they had not existed before. In his visitation of Derry diocese of 1693, Bishop William King noted that before the troubles of 1689–91 most of the inhabitants of Ballinascreen parish had been Catholics, but since then some Protestant families had settled there. In response to this the rector and conformable parishioners had built a 'very decent chappell' in that part of the parish where most of the Protestants lived. In Bishop King's opinion it would 'serve very well until the mountainy part of the parish be planted'. King also recommended that the parish church in Badoney should be rebuilt, as he believed the parish was likely to be planted with Protestants.

The aftermath of the Williamite war saw a fresh influx of thousands of Scots to the north of Ireland, encouraged by harvest crises in their native land. About 1700 Bishop King wrote that due to a fresh wave of migration from Scotland, 'the dissenters measure mightily in the north'.[30] In some places there were Presbyterian ministers where previously there had been none. In 1693 it was stated that most of the inhabitants of the dioceses of Connor and Down were Presbyterians.[31] An anonymous Jacobite tract of c.1711 noted that after 1690 'Scottish men came over into the north with their families and effects and settled there, so that they are now at this present the greater proportion of the inhabitants'.[32] Though this was an exaggeration of the overall numerical position of the Scots, it was probably the case by this time that they outnumbered English settlers by 2:1, an increase from the ratio of 1.4:1 in 1630.

The early eighteenth century
Migration to Ulster, mainly from Scotland, continued into the early eighteenth century. This was impacting on local demographics in areas where British settlement had hitherto been fairly limited. In 1714 Hugh McMahon, Catholic bishop of the diocese of Clogher, wrote that

from the neighbouring country of Scotland Calvinists are coming over here daily in large groups of families, occupying the towns and villages, seizing the farms in the richer parts of the country and expelling the natives ... The result is that the Catholic natives are forced to build their huts in mountainous or marshy country.[33]

Within the diocese of which McMahon was bishop, considerable changes were brought about by the influx of British settlers. County Monaghan witnessed a huge increase in the number of British inhabitants in the seventy years after 1660. The so-called census of 1659 recorded only 434 British households in Co. Monaghan. In the parishes in the west and south of the county there were only sixty-two British householders, fifty of whom lived in the town of Carrickmacross. In three of these parishes – Aghnamullen, Clontibret and

Tullycorbet – no British households at all were noted, while in three others the British population did not exceed four. In 1679 it was noted that in the parish of Tullycorbet there was *nemo religionis Protestantium infra parochiam* (no-one of the Protestant religion within the parish). By 1733 there was a British presence in every parish, and in some there were fairly sizeable Protestant communities.[34] In the parish of Monaghan, for example, in 1733 there were 400 Church of Ireland and 343 Presbyterian families. In the parish of Donagh there were 273 Presbyterian families, while in Galloon parish, then almost entirely within County Monaghan, there were 268 Presbyterian families.

Accompanying the growth in the number of Protestants living in County Monaghan was the increase in the number of Anglican churches and Presbyterian meeting houses. In 1715 Edmund Kaine, agent on the Barrett Lennard estate at Clones, County Monaghan, recommended to his employer, Dacre Barrett, that the local Presbyterian congregation should be given a secure lease for a plot of ground on which they were intending to build a new meeting house. Kaine's argument was that the construction of the meeting house would 'destroy the Irish and plant your estate with Protestants ... it will be a good workhouse'.[35]

Changes in settlement patterns were also discernible in parts of south County Armagh. In 1733 a number of landowners in the parish of Creggan invited Presbyterians to settle on their estates and, as an encouragement, promised to provide an income for a Presbyterian minister.[36] As a result a significant number of families of Scottish background moved to the Tullyvallen area. In 1746 one of the local landowners, Alexander Hamilton, took out a patent for a Saturday market at Newtownhamilton and two annual fairs.[37] The area around Newtownhamilton later became a parish in its own right, taking the name of the market town. Other parts of Creggan parish were also seeing an increase in the British population. The *Dublin News-Letter* of October 1737 carried the following notice about the parish: 'The Country ... is now growing every Day more and more into a peaceful and Protestant settlement, in which ... the decent repair of the Parish Church, and a good Parsonage House lately erected ... have not a little contributed'.[38] Not far away, Johnston's Bridge was described in the early 1740s as a 'small village in the middle of a wild country called the Fews, not many years ago notorious for robberies, but now civilised and free from them'.[39]

Writing about County Fermanagh some eighty years after the mid-seventeenth-century land settlements, the Reverend William Henry, rector of Killesher parish, commented:

> The partition of land among so many considerable families, the parcelling them out into convenient little freeholds, the happy independency of so many farmers, who till their own small estates, without being tributary to any, and the universal abhorrence which all have of any petty tyrant; these are the causes of the British and Protestant interest increasing so much in this county.[40]

Commentators, such as Henry, were able to differentiate between areas on the basis of the characteristics of the local inhabitants. For example, in Donegal, Henry distinguished between people of English and of Scottish descent by the way they lived and worked: 'The English planters are easily known by the neatness of their houses and pleasant plantations of trees. The Scots, on the other hand, neglected this, but made up for it through their efforts to improve the soil.'[41] Others noted the difference in speech of those of Scottish descent. When travelling through County Fermanagh in the 1740s, Isaac Butler noted that in the area to the north of Enniskillen towards Lisnarrick the people all had the 'Scotch accent'.[42] Journeying through east County Antrim c.1760, Lord Edward Willes commented that 'all the people of this part of the world speaks the broad lowland Scotch and have all the Scotch phrases. It will be a dispute between the two kingdoms until the end of time whether Ireland was peopled from Scotland or Scotland from Ireland'.[43] In the latter part of the eighteenth century the *Hibernian Magazine*, in a description of the new market house in Newtownards, County Down, noted: 'The language spoken here is broad Scotch hardly to be understood by strangers'.[44]

Catholics and Dissenters
Legislation known as the Penal Laws was passed in the Irish parliament between 1695 and 1728 by an overwhelmingly Anglican landed gentry anxious to preserve their privileged position by keeping Catholics – felt to be disloyal and untrustworthy on the basis of events in the seventeenth century – in subjection. Under the Penal Laws Catholics were forbidden to, among other things, bear arms, enter the legal profession, own a horse worth more than £5, buy land, and lease land for more than 31 years. Finally, in 1728, Catholics were denied the vote. By conforming to the Church of Ireland Catholics could avoid these restrictions; only a fraction did and these were often members of the gentry anxious to hold on to their estates. One of the most prominent converts was Alexander MacDonnell, earl of Antrim, who conformed in 1734. Laws were also passed to hinder the operations of the Roman Catholic Church in Ireland. These proved to be the most difficult to enforce: in large parts of the country priests and bishops were able to operate with impunity, while a not insignificant number of mass-houses were built with the approbation of local landowners.

Catholics were not the only religious denomination to face institutional discrimination in this period. Presbyterians also felt aggrieved at laws that restricted their rights and freedom in certain areas. For example, marriages conducted by a Presbyterian minister were not recognised by the state, and children born of such a marriage were regarded as illegitimate. In 1704 a law was passed that required persons holding public office to produce a certificate stating that they had received communion in a Church of Ireland church; this became known as the Test Act. For many members of the establishment, Presbyterians were regarded as more of a threat than Catholics, especially because of their numerical superiority over Anglicans in much of Ulster. The Test Act was never strictly enforced and in 1719, with the passing of the Toleration Act, Presbyterians were granted official recognition.[45]

In the early eighteenth century there occurred the first major dispute within Irish Presbyterianism. This was over the issued of subscription to the Westminster Confession of Faith. Those who denied the necessity of subscribing to the Confession were known as New Light Presbyterians. In 1725, for the sake of convenience, those who took this stance were placed in the Presbytery of Antrim. Other brands of Presbyterianism originating in

Scotland were established in Ulster during the course of the eighteenth century. The Seceders, as they were known because they had seceded from the Church of Scotland in 1733, soon established congregations and presbyteries in Ulster. The first Irish presbytery of the Reformed Presbyterian Church was established in 1763. The origins of this denomination went back to the National Covenant of 1638 and the Solemn League and Covenant of 1643. The Reformed Presbyterians, or Covenanters as they were also known, refused to accept that the state had any authority over the church and did not participate in parliamentary elections. Both of these denominations provided an alternative to mainstream Presbyterianism.

Rise of the linen industry

In 1759 Edward Willes, the Lord Chief Baron, commented that he had never seen 'a more beautiful country for length of way' between Monaghan and Carrickfergus. It was 'extremely well cultivated and very populous and you see the spirit of industry every step you go'.[46] Many other travellers and commentators made similar statements, reflecting the transformation of Ulster in the eighteenth century. The single most important reason for the development of Ulster in this period and its increasing prosperity was the rise of the domestic linen industry.[47] Linen had been part of the Ulster economy prior to 1700, but it was in the eighteenth century that it emerged as its most powerful element. In 1744 Walter Harris noted that the 'staple commodity of the country is linen, a due care of which manufacture has brought great wealth among the people. The northern inhabitants already feel the benefit of it, and are freed from much of that poverty and wretchedness too visible among the lower class of people in other parts of the Kingdom, where this valuable branch of trade has not been improved to advantage'.[48] In Fermanagh, Henry was in no doubt that the linen industry was the decisive factor in the increasing prosperity of the county.[49] By the end of the eighteenth century the rise in living standards was being felt at different levels of society. In 1790 it was said that the influence of industry and manufactures in County Monaghan was 'meliorating the condition of the peasant [and] improving the state of the husbandman'.[50] That is not to say, however, that many people in Ulster did not live below the poverty line.

In 1700 Ireland as a whole exported one million yards of cloth. In 1800 this had risen to 40 million yards, most of it from Ulster.[51] Why was the linen industry so successful in Ulster in the eighteenth century? Bill Crawford has suggested that 'Whereas Irish society outside Ulster evolved along traditional lines so that local craftsmen could continue to meet the demand for textiles in Ireland, Ulster society was unstable and disorganised but enterprising and ready to experiment'.[52] Ulster landlords promoted the linen industry as a means of increasing the value of their estates.

In large parts of Ulster, particularly in the east of the province, life for many families was focused on cultivating crops of flax and spinning and weaving linen. If food was grown on their holdings it was generally for subsistence rather than for sale. Linen production was their main, and for many their sole, form of income. With the increase in Ulster's population in the eighteenth century, so there was greater competition for land. In the process the size of holdings became smaller so that in areas where the domestic linen industry was most concentrated, such as north County Armagh, the average size of a holding fell to less than twelve acres. This left many families vulnerable to economic downturn, harvest crises, etc. During difficult periods, many families were reduced to poverty.

Farming, therefore, varied considerably across Ulster, depending on a range of factors such as local economics and the suitability of the terrain for agricultural production. As noted above, some areas were heavily focused on the cultivation of flax and the production of linen. In other areas the emphasis was on pastoral farming. Boho parish, County Fermanagh, was described in 1766 as 'mostly under stock or grazing, and one Papist is generally a herdsman for a whole townland'.[53] Elsewhere arable farming was important. For example, the barony of Lecale in County Down was a major grain-producing area in Ulster.

With the rise in population and an accompanying increase in the demand for land, a noticeable feature of the settlement pattern, particularly in the second half of the eighteenth century, was the expansion into previously marginal lands. Upland areas were also experiencing population increase as farming families began to settle on the mountainsides. What permitted families to survive on marginal lands was the potato, which could be cultivated on poorer quality ground and still produce a good crop.

Landlord and tenant

The picture often presented of landlordism in the eighteenth century is that of absentee landowners ruthlessly exploiting their tenantry and uninterested in managing their estates properly. This, however, is a gross distortion of the truth. Many landlords were not absentees, but lived on their estates for most of the year even if they had alternative accommodation elsewhere. Those who did not reside on their estates knew the importance of employing an effective agent to manage their lands in their absence. Much of what we know about the management of landed estates in the eighteenth century derives from the correspondence between landlords and their agents. The Abercorn estate in north-west Ulster is a prime example of this.

The basic relationship between a landlord and his tenants was governed by the lease. Leases could be issued to tenants in severalty (individually), or jointly. Under the latter arrangement several tenants took a lease for a single landholding and bound themselves jointly to pay the rent. Within this arrangement, popularly known as rundale, the tenants divided up the holding as best suited their needs. Its strength lay in its flexibility, but rundale's major weakness was its long-term viability. Eventually when it came to creating permanent boundaries on a holding that was being held in partnership, a landlord or his agent would often have to step in to ensure that this was done fairly.

Security of tenure was of major concern to the tenants, and many complained that their leases were not long enough. This was acknowledged by the earl of Abercorn's agent John McClintock, who offered the following opinion to his employer in 1749: 'I would beg leave to observe ... that nothing gives such encouragement to tenants or causes them improve with such spirits as a good tenure'.[54] Leases were frequently for 21 or 31 years, and many were for three lives. A three lives lease made a lessee a freeholder and entitled him to vote in parliamentary elections on condition that his farm was worth at least 40 shillings per annum after the rent and other fees had been paid. It is important to point out that only Protestants could be issued with a lease for lives. The maximum tenure of a Catholic lessee was 31 years. A three lives lease was extremely advantageous for a tenant farmer as it secured his tenure, so long as the lives named in the lease were alive, for perhaps half a century with no increase in rent during that period.

A common practice in many areas was for a farmer to subdivide his farm among his sons and so provide each of them with a landholding upon which to make a living. Land was also sublet by tenant farmers. In this way cottiers acquired a small patch of land on which to grow a crop of potatoes or graze a cow; farm labour supplemented their income. Attempts by landlords and their agents to curb subletting were usually unsuccessful. Instead landlords used the subdivisions to their advantage by leasing directly to the subtenants when a suitable opportunity arose. In this way the number of people with leases increased considerably towards the end of the eighteenth century. By 1800 many tenants, both Protestant and Catholic, claimed the automatic right to have new leases issued to them by their landlord on the expiry of the existing deeds. This was known as 'tenant right' or the Ulster Custom, and in the nineteenth century became a major source of contention between landlord and tenant.

Development of communications and towns
Travellers through the Ulster countryside made frequent mention of the condition of the roads. In County Fermanagh, William Henry found that 'the many fastnesses [that] made most part of the county formerly impassable' were 'now entirely removed by the indefatigable pains and public spirit which is exerted in making roads'. These roads were 'well executed by the spirit of the gentlemen and the cheerfulness wherewith the common people fulfil their statute labour'.[55] The latter remark refers to the obligation of every lessee to supply six days of free labour to mend the roads in his parish. In 1765 an act of parliament transferred the responsibility of maintaining major roads to the county grand jury. Grand juries were also allowed to finance road building by being able to impose a county cess. Later an act was passed permitting parishes to raise an extra tax to maintain minor roads, while an *Act for the making of narrow roads through the mountainous unimproved parts of this kingdom* permitted grand juries to raise money for this purpose also. The result of this legislation was a dramatic increase in the number of miles of road in the province, so that by 1800 Ulster had one of the densest road networks in Western Europe. This in turn stimulated trade and commerce, as goods were more easily transported between the places of production, sale and export.

The improvement in communications in Ulster and the rise of the domestic linen industry together contributed to the development of the new market towns as well as the revival of settlements originally founded in the seventeenth century. Landowners, such as the abovementioned Alexander Hamilton at Newtownhamilton, took out new patents for markets and fairs to encourage urban development. Public buildings, such as market houses, were constructed in ever increasing numbers in Ulster's towns. Often these were impressive edifices, designed to show off the munificence of a patron and his awareness of current architectural trends (and therefore his taste and civility). Many survive today as striking reminders of past glories. Landowners hoped to attract suitable tenants to their towns by offering them leases on advantageous terms. The agent on the Barrett Lennard estate in County Monaghan argued that offering leases for lives renewable forever in Clones 'would encourage Protestant tenants to come to the town' and that in a short time it 'would be a flourishing little town'.[56]

Not every attempt to encourage town development was successful. At Church Hill in County Fermanagh, Sir Gustavus Hume established a market and built an inn and a number of houses 'proper for tradesmen to live in' c.1714. Five years later Hume advertised his intention to establish a linen manufactory there, build a bleachyard, and provide financial backing to anyone who was prepared to carry on the business and improve the village. However, by the end of the eighteenth century this settlement had petered out.[57] Nor was it always the case that a town enjoyed the patronage of a single landowner. Writing about Omagh, County Tyrone, in 1787, Daniel Beaufort commented: 'The town is frittered among a number of landlords who give no encouragement'.[58] Thus, while it was the county town of Tyrone, with a court house and gaol, Omagh never became as important a market town for linen as neighbouring Dungannon and Strabane.

Emigration in the eighteenth century

One of the historical processes most closely associated with eighteenth-century Ulster was the large-scale emigration to the American colonies.[59] Although Presbyterians were not the only grouping to leave in this period, they were by far the most numerous. Emigration to America had been taking place for some time prior to 1718 – the year in which it began in earnest – but on a small scale.

The factors encouraging emigration in this period were numerous and complex; debate has focused on the economic motivation of the migrants set against the issue of religious freedom. Both were clearly at play. In 1718 Edmund Kaine, agent on the Barrett Lennard estate, noted that one hundred families had passed through his town in the past week heading for New England, adding that those departing 'complain most the hardship of the tithes makes them all go, which is true, for the clergy is [sic] unreasonable'.[60] On the other hand, when the Rev. Isaac Taylor, minister of Ardstraw Presbyterian church, came before the presbytery of Strabane in July 1720 asking for permission to leave his flock and emigrate to America, he cited financial hardship as the principal motivating factor.[61] Despite considerable reluctance on the part of the presbytery, permission was given, though Taylor stayed only two years in America before returning to Ardstraw. Seven years after this Taylor shocked the local Presbyterian community by joining the Church of Ireland, becoming a curate in the parish of Ardstraw.

The departure of so many of their tenants was a cause of considerable concern to the Ulster landlords, as they feared that it would lower the value of their estates. They were also worried that vacated farms would be taken by tenants of lower calibre than their predecessors. Realistically, there was little that landowners could do to prevent tenants from leaving their farms. Robert McCausland advised William Conolly in November 1718 that if there was any decree from the government forbidding people from emigrating, 'it would make them the fonder to go'.[62] He set out his own position on the matter: 'all I would have done, if it were possible, to oblige these "rougs" who goes of[f] to pay their just debts before they go, and then let all go when they please who are inclined to go'.

Others were concerned that emigration was draining Ulster of its Protestants and would harm the nascent linen industry. The Rev. John Wilson, Church of Ireland minister in Lettermacaward parish, County Donegal, wrote in 1766 of the 'apparent decay of the Protestant religion in this whole country, & of the prosperous growth of popery'.[63] Wilson attributed this to 'Papists supplanting Protestants in their land, whereby numbers of families were forced of late years to flee to other Kingdoms for shelter'. That year, Wilson reckoned, eighteen of the seventy-two Protestants in Lettermacaward 'will certainly go abroad, so that it is to be feared, that in a few years, there will be few or none to cultivate that religion for which our ancestors gloriously and virtuously laid down their lives'. In the event the concerns raised by clerics and landowners were not realised. The number of people emigrating was not constant, with variations depending on economic conditions in Ireland as well as other external factors. Emigrants were frequently the return cargo on ships bringing flax seed to Ulster's ports. The outbreak of the American war of independence in the 1770s all but halted emigration, but once peace had been signed in 1783 it resumed.

Popular protest, the 1798 rebellion and the Act of Union

Popular protests, many emanating from agrarian grievances, had been a recurring feature of eighteenth-century Ulster. In the early 1760s and the early 1770s movements known, respectively, as the Hearts of Oak and Hearts of Steel protested against such things as local taxes, rent increases and tithes due to the Church of Ireland. In some areas there was considerable animosity between the ministers of the Church of Ireland and the local Presbyterian population. In 1766 the Rev. Charles Humble, rector of Killeeshil parish, County Tyrone, described those involved in recent Hearts of Oak protests in his area as 'the Spawn of Scottish Covenanters, avowed enemies to all Civil and Religious Establishments, and the most violent and furious persecutors of the Established clergy during the late troubles in the North of Ireland'.[64]

Influenced by the American and French Revolutions, some began to consider more radical solutions to what they believed were Ireland's problems. The Society of United Irishmen was founded in Belfast on 18 October 1791. Soon afterwards clubs were founded in Dublin and a number of other places. The Belfast United Irishmen were overwhelmingly Presbyterian and middle class. The aims of the Society were parliamentary reform and the elimination of English interference in Irish matters. Following efforts to suppress it, the Society reorganised itself as a secret organisation and began to prepare for rebellion. Following a failed French expedition in December 1796, the repressive measures taken by the government in 1797 severely weakened the United Irishmen in Ulster. Rebellion began in Leinster in late May 1798. On the night of 6–7 June it spread to Ulster when a party of United Irishmen advanced into Larne and forced a contingent of government troops back to their barracks. Soon afterwards Ballymena and Randalstown were taken, but at Antrim Town the rebels were defeated. In County Down following an initial success at Saintfield the rebels were roundly defeated at nearby Ballynahinch on 11 June, and the rebellion in Ulster was all but finished. There followed a series of executions; one of the last to be hanged was the most famous Ulster rebel of them all, Henry Joy McCracken, on 17 June.

Even before the rebellion had been fully suppressed, the government in London sent Lord Cornwallis to Ireland, delegating to him responsibility for forcing legislation through the Irish parliament to effect a union between Britain and Ireland. There was considerable opposition to this from the Irish elite, but eventually, after much lobbying, the act of union was passed in 1800, coming into effect on 1 January 1801. It was a defining moment in Irish history, though at the time one that meant little to the majority of Ulster's people, still recovering from the effects of the rebellion.

Case studies of Ulster families

The following case studies examine two families in Ulster in the seventeenth and eighteenth centuries with Scottish connections and show how it is possible, using a range of different sources, to build up a profile of these families and the part they played in their wider communities.

Case study 1: The Hamiltons of Lisdivin, County Tyrone
The story of one seventeenth-century Ulster family of Scottish background can be illustrated by examining the Hamiltons of Lisdivin, County Tyrone. In the early seventeenth century, under the patronage of the earl of Abercorn and his relatives, Strabane became one of the main areas of Scottish settlement in Ulster. Among the earliest settlers on the earl's estate was Hugh Hamilton of Lisdivin, the son of John Hamilton of Priestfield in Blantyre, who was apprenticed to a William Nisbett in Edinburgh in 1603.[65] In the early stages of the plantation, he, together with his brother William, moved to Strabane barony, where he combined his mercantile dealings with the acquisition of freehold land. By a deed dated 1 January 1615, he was granted the townland of Lisdivin in the parish of Donagheady in fee farm (that is, in perpetuity) by the earl of Abercorn.[66] For this he was to pay either £6 or 'one hogshead of Gascoign wine, one pound of good pepper, four pounds of loaf sugar and a box of marmalade containing at least two pounds of the preserve'. This would seem to indicate that Hamilton's mercantile activities involved the importation of luxury foodstuffs; it is remarkable to think that there were sufficient people in Strabane barony in the early seventeenth century to justify such a trade. An early port book of the city of Londonderry records that Hugh Hamilton imported from Scotland in 1614 goods to the value of around £34.[67]

In July 1616, as Hugh Hamilton of 'Loughneneas' – a freehold he had acquired from Sir George Hamilton of Greenlaw in the neighbouring proportion of Cloghogall – he received a grant of denization.[68] By 1622 he had built a stone house at Lisdivin.[69] As well as this house, Hamilton owned four houses in the town of Strabane.[70] He also acquired an interest in the former monastic lands of Grange in Donagheady parish, which, together with his merchant business and his other properties, must have him one of the richest men in the barony. In addition, Hamilton engaged in the political life of Strabane, being listed as one of its first burgesses in 1612 and serving as provost in 1624–5.[71] He married Marion, sister to James Gibbs, himself provost of the town in 1629–30, and they had six sons: George, Hugh, Frederick, John, William and Robert.[72] He died in 1637.[73] His lands passed to his eldest son, George.

George Hamilton, whose son Hugh died in 1642, died before June 1652, when administration of his estate was granted to his brother Robert.[74] The Civil Survey of 1654–6, however, records that Lisdivin and Loughneas were in the possession of George's younger brother, Hugh.[75] The Civil Survey also names this Hugh Hamilton as the proprietor of former monastic lands at Grange, though they were actually in the possession of James Galbraith through his wife Elizabeth by virtue of a jointure from her first husband, the abovementioned George Hamilton.[76] Hugh Hamilton also acquired lands at Tullydowey in the parish of Clonfeacle, County Tyrone, and he was resident here according to the hearth money roll of 1666.[77] He moved back to Lisdivin some time after this.

In his will, dated 11 October 1689, he requested that he be buried in the 'Church of Grange', referring to the graveyard surrounding the old monastery.[78] His lands at Lisdivin, Loughneas and Grange were left to the use of his 'loving & dutiful' wife for the rest of her life. These lands were then to pass to his eldest son, James. His younger son, John, was to receive £60, which was to be paid to him by his older brother. Hugh's daughters, Elizabeth and Margaret, were bequeathed, respectively, £100 and £40. The Hamilton family continued to own Lisdivin and Grange throughout the eighteenth century, and played a prominent role in local affairs.

Case study 2: The Reas of Magheraknock, County Down
While the above study looked at an Ulster family of Scottish background in seventeenth-century west Ulster, this study considers a family in east Ulster in the eighteenth century: the Reas of Magheraknock, near Ballynahinch, County Down.[79] The first member of the family known to have lived at Magheraknock was David Rea. Of major assistance in disentangling this family was the discovery that a copy of David Rea's will, dated 2 February 1754, was available in the Registry of Deeds in Dublin.[80] In his will David Rea appointed two of his sons, Matthew and Hugh, to be his executors. He refers in it to 'my last wife's children she had to me', named as Debro, James, Jane and Robert – clearly David Rea had been married more than once. The lands of 'Kelein' belonging to the testator, at that time in the possession of undertenants John and Robert Granger, are mentioned – these lands were to be equally divided between the children of his second marriage – as are the holding in Ballycreen and the mill of Magheraknock, both of which were held from Mr Onsley (Annesley). The will was registered by Debro Armstrong, 'otherwise Rea, now the wife of John Armstrong of Magheranock, Co. Down, farmer', who, it is reasonable to assume, was the aforementioned daughter of David Rea.

One other interesting item in this will was the request by David Rea that he be buried in the churchyard at Saintfield. A search through volume three of the County Down *Gravestone Inscriptions Series*, edited by R. S. J. Clarke and published by the Ulster Historical Foundation, revealed that a memorial to David Rea was erected and has survived.[81] The Rea gravestone provides information on three generations of the Rea family. David Rea died in 1754 aged 82, meaning that he must have been born in 1672 or thereabouts. The gravestone additionally records the death of David Rea's son Hugh in 1759, and also Hugh's son David, who died in 1770 in his early teens. Hugh's wife Elizabeth, whose maiden name was Jackson, and the wife of Matthew Rea, Catherine, née Barnett, are also commemorated. They died in, respectively, 1779 and 1781.

Although the *Guide to Church Records* compiled by the Public Record Office of Northern Ireland lists the earliest Presbyterian registers from Ballynahinch as dating from no earlier than 1820, recently some very early registers have come to light.[82] These relate to what is now 1st Ballynahinch Presbyterian Church and cover the period from 1696 to 1735. The baptisms of the following children of David Rea are listed:

John bapt. Thursday 12 July 1705
John bapt. Sunday 16 April 1710
Hugh bapt. 26 June 1715
David bapt. 12 December 1717
David bapt. December 1719
Elizabeth bapt. 23 December 1722
Debora bapt. 4 April 1725
James bapt. 23 March 1729

For whatever reason, Matthew was not listed among the children. Clearly two of the children died young, hence the duplication of the names John and David (a practice that can often be a source of confusion for present-day genealogists). The finding of these early registers is remarkable and highly valuable as far as the Rea family is concerned. Unfortunately, the registers do not name the mother of the baptised child. In the case of the Rea family, it is clear, from David Rea's will, that at least two of the children – Debora and James – were born to his second wife.

The name of David Rea's first wife has not survived, but that of his second is revealed in a mortgage of 29 October 1739 of the 'quarterland' of Killeen – the 'Kelein' of David Rea's will – in the parishes of Holywood and Dundonald for £100.[83] In this deed David Rea's wife is named as Elizabeth Martin. A second deed, dated 11 September 1742, also a mortgage of Killeen, this time for £200, refers to David Rea's wife as formerly Martin and identifies one of the parties to the mortgage as John Magill of Ballycroon, a linen weaver, who is stated to have been her eldest son by her former marriage.[84] We can take from this that Elizabeth Rea had been previously married to a man by the name of Magill (by whom she had children) and that Martin was her maiden name. A later deed of 5 July 1810 refers back to a lease of 2 July 1694 by which James Ross of Portavoe, County Down, leased to David Martin of Killeen the Quarterland of Killeen in as ample a manner as Ross had held it from the Earl of Clanbrassil. On the basis of this deed it may be assumed that David Rea held Killeen through his wife Elizabeth Martin, who was possibly the daughter of David Martin.

Two of the sons of David Rea (d. 1754) went on to play important roles in the emigration trade in the mid-eighteenth century. John Rea emigrated to South Carolina *c.*1729–30 as a young man. From there he actively encouraged individuals and families from Ulster to emigrate to Colonial America. His brother Matthew remained in Ireland and worked as an emigration agent.[85] In 1776 Edward Moore, the agent on the Annesley estate in County Down, described Matthew Rea as a man who had 'made money in exporting our Protestants to America to people the lands of a brother of his and others who went there some time ago, and for whom he was a sort of slave factor [the word 'agent' has here been crossed out]'.[86] Two deeds from the 1770s throw some light on Matthew Rea. The first, dated 22 December 1774, involved on the one hand Margaret Rea, widow, and David Rea, farmer, both of Killeen, and on the other hand Mathew Ryan [sic] of Drumbo, gent.[87] The deed was an assignment of a rent charge of £20 per annum arising out of the lands of Killeen in the possession of Margaret and David Rea and their under-tenants, John Murray and Thomas Mayne. The deed stated that Margaret was the widow and David the eldest son and heir of the late James Rea of Killeen.

This James Rea was the son of David Rea of Magheraknock; his father's will had named him as one of the heirs of the lands of 'Kelein'. The second deed, dated 9 November 1776, was a transfer of the rent charge from Matthew Rea to Robert Stevenson of Belfast, surgeon and apothecary, and it recited much of the information in the first deed.[88] By this time, therefore, there were two branches of the Rea family, one living at Magheraknock and the other at Killeen. James Rea was married to Margaret, but we do not know her maiden name. From the Ballynahinch registers we know that James Rea was born in 1729. We have no record of when he died, but clearly it was before December 1774. At this stage David Rea of Killeen would have been a fairly young man – he may not even have reached majority (i.e. twenty-one years). This would explain why his mother was party to the deed with his uncle Matthew. There is no record of when Matthew Rea died – curiously he is not named on the family gravestone in Saintfield – but it seems to have been *c.*1800.[89] The Reas continued to live at Magheraknock and Killeen well beyond the end of the eighteenth century.

Notes

1   For a more detailed consideration of the province in this period see Jonathan Bardon, *A History of Ulster* (Belfast, 1992, reprinted 2005). See also the chapters by Raymond Gillespie, 'Continuity and change: Ulster in the seventeenth century' and W. H. Crawford, 'The political economy of linen: Ulster in the eighteenth century' in C. Brady, M. O'Dowd and B. Walker (eds), *Ulster: An Illustrated History* (London, 1989).

2   For a general background to the plantation see P. Robinson, *The Plantation of Ulster* (Dublin and New York, 1984).

3   PRONI DIO/4/23/1/1.

4   Settlement in Antrim and Down is considered in Raymond Gillespie, *Colonial Ulster* (Cork, 1985).

5   M. Perceval-Maxwell, *The Scottish Migration to Ulster in the Reign of James I* (London, 1973), p. 48.

6   *Calendar of the State Papers relating to Ireland, 1625–32*, p. 607.

7   P. J. Duffy, 'The evolution of estate properties in south Ulster, 1600-1900' in William J. Smyth and Kevin Whelan (eds), *Common Ground. Essays on the Historical Geography of Ireland* (Cork, 1988), p. 96.

8   R. J. Hunter, 'Ulster plantation towns', in D. Harkness and M. O'Dowd (eds), *The Town in Ireland: Historical Studies XIII* (Belfast, 1981), p. 55.

9   V. W. Treadwell, 'The survey of Armagh and Tyrone, 1622', *Ulster Journal of Archaeology*, 3rd series, xxvii (1964), pp. 140–1.

10 Quoted in Raymond Gillespie, 'Faith, family and fortune: The structures of everyday life in early modern Cavan' in Raymond Gillespie (ed.), *Cavan. Essays on the History of an Irish County* (Blackrock, 1995), p. 113.

11 Robinson, *Plantation of Ulster*, p. 158.

12 Bardon, *History of Ulster*, p. 133.

13 William Roulston, 'The evolution of the Abercorn estate in north-west Ulster, 1610–1703', *Familia*, 15 (1999), pp. 56–7.

14 T. Fitzpatrick, *The Bloody Bridge and Other Papers relating to the Insurrection of 1641* (Dublin, 1903), p. 262.

15 R. C. Simington (ed.), *The Civil Survey III* (Dublin, 1937), p. 373.

16 *Calendar of the State Papers relating to Ireland, 1663–5*, p. 599.

17 NAI Lodge Mss, viii, 130–1.

18 John Hanly (ed.), *The letters of Saint Oliver Plunkett, 1625–1681* (Dublin, 1979), p. 74.

19 Ibid., p. 75.

20 TCD Ms 883/1.

21 Hanly, *Letters*, p. 226.

22 Ibid., p. 394.

23 Ibid., p. 530.

24 PRONI D/162/8.

25 Alan Gailey, 'The Scots element in North Irish popular culture' in *Ethnologia Europaea*, viii (1975), pp. 8–9.

26 J. B. Leslie, *Derry Clergy and Parishes* (Dundalk, 1937), p. 248.

27 Hanly, *Letters*, pp. 454–5.

28 Private possession.

29 PRONI T/505/1.

30 PRONI DIO/4/29/2/1/2, no. 10.

31 PRONI DIO/4/5/3, no. 23.

32 Gillespie, 'Continuity and change', p. 125.

33 P. J. Flanagan, 'The diocese of Clogher in 1714' in *Clogher Record*, i (1954), p. 40.

34 PRONI DIO/4/24/2/1.

35 PRONI T/2529/6/370.

36 W. H. Crawford, 'The reshaping of the borderlands, 1700–1840' in Raymond Gillespie and Harold O'Sullivan (eds), *The Borderlands. Essays on the History of the Ulster-Leinster Border* (Belfast, 1989), p. 95.

37 Ibid., p. 99.

38 *Dublin News-Letter*, 25–8 October 1737, quoted in E. McParland, *Public Architecture in Ireland, 1680–1760* (New Haven, CT and London, 2001), p. 19.

39 Armagh Public Library, Physico-Historical Society papers.

40 PRONI T/2521/3/1, p. 3.

41 NAI M2533, fo. 408.

42 I. Butler, 'A Journey to Lough Derg', *Journal of the Royal Society of Antiquaries of Ireland*, xxii (1892), p. 135.

43 J. Kelly (ed.), *The Letters of Lord Chief Baron Edward Willes to the Earl of Warwick, 1757–62* (Aberystwyth, 1990), p. 36.

44 John Stevenson, *Two Centuries of Life in Down, 1600–1800* (1920, reprinted Dundonald, 1990), p. 244.

45 Bardon, *History of Ulster*, pp. 168–74.

46 Kelly, *Letters*, pp. 30–31.

47 For more on the linen industry see W. H. Crawford, *The Impact of the Domestic Linen Industry in Ulster* (Belfast, 2005).

48 W. Harris, *The Antient and Present State of the County of Down* (Dublin, 1744), p. 108, quoted in Crawford, 'Political economy of linen', pp. 137–8.

49 PRONI T/2521/3/1.

50 E. M. Johnston-Liik, *History of the Irish Parliament* (6 vols, Belfast, 2002), ii, p. 308.

51 Crawford, 'The political economy of linen', p. 135.

52 Ibid.

53 PRONI T/808/15266.

54 PRONI T/2541/1AI/1D/49.

55 PRONI T/2521/3/1.

56 Martin Dowling, *Tenant Right and Agrarian Society in Ulster, 1600–1870* (Dublin, 1999), p. 136.

57 Graeme Kirkham, '"To pay the rent and lay up riches": economic opportunity in eighteenth-century north-west Ulster', in R. Mitchison and P. Roebuck, *Economy and Society in Scotland and Ireland, 1500–1939* (Edinburgh, 1988), p. 97.

58 TCD Ms 1019.

59 The best introduction to this subject remains R. J. Dickson, *Ulster Emigration to Colonial America* (London, 1966).

60 PRONI MIC/170/2.

61 PRONI CR/3/26.

62 PRONI T/2825/C/27/2.

63 PRONI T/808/15266.

64 Ibid.

65 G. Hamilton, *A History of the House of Hamilton* (Edinburgh, 1933), pp. 716–17.

66 PRONI D/623/B/13/2a.

67 R. J. Hunter (ed.), *Plantation in Ulster in Strabane Barony*, 1600–41 (Londonderry 1982), p. 54.

68 *Calendar of the Irish Patent Rolls of the Reign of James I*, p. 306.

69 Cambridgeshire Record Office, Kimbolton Mss, ddM 70/35.

70 PRONI T/808/6461.

71 Hunter, *Plantation in Strabane Barony*, p. 31.

72 Hamilton, *House of Hamilton*, p. 717.

73 PRONI T/808/6461.

74 Hamilton, *House of Hamilton*, p. 717.

75 Simington, *Civil Survey*, p. 398.

76 Ibid., p. 401.

77 PRONI T/307A.

78 PRONI T/581/2, p. 247.

79 For a fuller look at the Rea family see William Roulston, 'Reconstructing an eighteenth-century Ulster family: the Reas of Magheraknock and Killeen, County Down', *Familia,* 20 (2004), pp. 85–94.

80 P. Beryl Eustace, *Registry of Deeds, Dublin. Abstracts of Wills*, ii (Dublin, 1954), pp. 256–7. The actual reference to the will is 302.571.202079.

81 Some 50,000 gravestone inscriptions have now been made available by the Ulster Historical Foundation on the Internet at www.historyfromheadstones.com.

82 A computerised copy of these registers was presented to the Ulster Historical Foundation. They are also available online at http://freepages.genealogy.rootsweb.com/~rosdavies/WORDS/BallynahinchPresbyterianIndex.htm

83 Registry of Deeds, Dublin, 99.17.67715.

84 Ibid., 109.88.75088.

85 Dickson, *Ulster Emigration*, pp. 164–73.

86 PRONI D/2309/4/3.

87 Registry of Deeds, Dublin, 305.477.203064.

88 Ibid., 314.77.210257.

89 The will of a Matthew Rea of Ballycreen was probated Dromore diocese in 1800.

1. Some general sources

1.1 Guides to sources

Before starting out on Irish family history research, it is extremely advisable to consult the multi-volume guides to sources compiled under the editorship of Richard Hayes. *Manuscript Sources for the History of Irish Civilisation* (Boston: G. K. Hall, 1965) includes four volumes on persons, two each on subjects, places and dates, and a single volume containing a list of manuscripts. Places are arranged alphabetically within counties. Estate records and maps are also listed by county. Five years later *Sources for the History of Irish Civilisation: Articles in Irish Periodicals* (Boston: G. K. Hall, 1970) was published. This included five volumes on persons, three on subjects and a single volume covering places and dates. After a further nine years there appeared the *First Supplement, 1965–75* (Boston: G. K. Hall, 1979) in three volumes. Copies of Hayes's guides are available in many libraries and repositories across Ireland and beyond. Another book worth checking is *British Sources for Irish History, 1485–1641*, compiled and edited by Brian Donovan and David Edwards (Dublin: Irish Manuscripts Commission, 1997), which acts as a guide to manuscript material in repositories in England, Scotland and Wales.

1.2 Personal Names Index, PRONI

When the Public Record Office of Northern Ireland opened in the early 1920s there was an ambitious project to index the personal names in all the documents that were taken into its care. The sheer volume of material brought into PRONI meant that this could not continue, though individually numbered items continued to be indexed. The result is a card index running to tens of thousands of names. The indexed items include many early estate rentals and leases. This source is well worth consulting prior to delving into the original sources themselves. The early *Reports of the Deputy Keeper of the Records (NI)* included listings of these indexed names, though unfortunately without precise references.

1.3 International Genealogical Index (IGI)

The International Genealogical Index (IGI) was created by the Latter Day Saints (Mormons). It is available on microfiche in PRONI (MF/1) and at Mormon family history centres around the world. The IGI contains information on family history drawn from a variety of sources, including church registers. While there may be doubts as to the reliability of some of the information listed, particularly for the pre-1800 period, an examination of the IGI might nonetheless throw up something of relevance to a researcher and is always worth consulting. There is a complete alphabetical index to entries relating to Ireland, and the Irish material is also arranged by county.

1.4 Internet

There is no denying that the advent of the Internet has revolutionised genealogy. A vast amount of information relating to Irish family history is now available on the World Wide Web, though, as with the IGI, there are reservations as to the veracity of some of it. To list all websites with genealogical material relating to Ulster would be impossible and has not been attempted in this book. A website with numerous links to Irish genealogical websites is www.cyndislist.com/ireland.htm. Some websites focus on a particular county and contain extensive lists of digitised sources, while others contain information on a specific family. Probably the best way of finding potentially relevant information on the Internet is to use a search engine such as Google (www.google.com) to look for specific items or names.

2. Church records

If one is researching ancestors prior to the introduction of civil registration of all births, deaths and marriages in 1864 (non-Catholic marriages registered from 1845), the main sources of information on family history are the registers kept by local churches. Unfortunately, many of these survive from no earlier than the nineteenth century. The loss of over 1,000 Church of Ireland registers in 1922 created an enormous gap. Poor record-keeping and the accidental loss of other registers has further contributed to the paucity of church records from the seventeenth and eighteenth centuries. Nonetheless, enough has survived to provide many people with information on their forebears.

PRONI has a vast collection of microfilms and photostat copies of church records, as well as some original material, relating to all denominations in Ulster. Surviving records pre-dating 1800 are listed in full in Appendix 1. These show Church of Ireland registers to be the best represented, with only a handful of Roman Catholic registers surviving from this period. Proper use of the records is dependent on an understanding of their limitations. Three categories of church records are of most use to the researcher.

Baptismal registers.
The basic information provided in a baptismal register is the name of the child, the name of the father and the date of baptism. The mother's name will usually be given, as will a specific location. The occupation of the father and the date of birth of the child may also be provided. Roman Catholic registers will normally give the names of the sponsors of the child. Occasionally the order of the child in the family (i.e. whether it was the firstborn, second or third in line) will be given.

Marriage registers.
Prior to the standardisation of marriage registers after 1845 for non-Catholics and 1864 for Catholics, these gave in their simplest form the date of the marriage and the names of the bride and groom. The residence and the name of the father of each party may be provided. The names of the witnesses might also be given.

Burial registers.
Burial registers can be fairly uninformative, with the name of the deceased, the date of

burial (not the date of death) and occasionally the occupation and age at death given. The deaths of children will usually include the name of the father, while the burial of a married woman may include her husband's name. Rarely will the cause of death be provided. Many Catholic 'burial' registers are actually registers recording payments made at the funeral of the deceased.

2.1 The Church of Ireland

The Church of Ireland is an episcopal church with a hierarchical system of church government and services that follow an accepted liturgical form and structure. From 1537 until 1870 the Church of Ireland was the state church in Ireland, and was therefore often referred to as the Established Church or simply the Church. Because of its close links with the Church of England, it was also known as the Anglican Church. Because of its official position, the Church of Ireland enjoyed privileges denied to other denominations. Despite its standing, however, the Church of Ireland never enjoyed the support of more than a minority of the population of Ireland, probably no more than 10% during the eighteenth century. In Ulster it was strongest in the areas where English settlement had been heaviest during the seventeenth century: south Antrim, north Armagh and north-west Down.

The basic administrative unit in the Church of Ireland is the parish. In the main the Church of Ireland continued with the existing network of medieval parishes it inherited from the pre-Reformation Church. Occasionally parish boundaries were altered and new parishes created. Moira parish in County Down, for instance, was created in 1722 by detaching a number of townlands from the parish of Magheralin. Clogherny parish in County Tyrone was created out of Termonmaguirk parish in 1732. Parishes are grouped together to form dioceses, each of which is headed by a bishop. Again, the medieval network of dioceses was continued. Ulster is divided into eight dioceses – Armagh, Clogher, Connor, Derry, Down, Dromore, Kilmore and Raphoe – which form part of the province of Armagh headed by the archbishop of Armagh. Within the Church of Ireland the archbishop of Armagh is the most senior churchman and is known as the Primate of All Ireland.

By the middle of the eighteenth century the Church of Ireland had a physical presence in the form of a church building in a majority of parishes in Ulster. Members of the Church of Ireland in parishes without a church would attend a church in a neighbouring parish. This may have been purely for convenience or it may have been because there was an ecclesiastical union of parishes. For example, in the eighteenth century the parishes of Ballyhalbert, Ballywalter and Inishargy in County Down were grouped together for ecclesiastical purposes, with the place or worship for all three at Balliggan in Inishargy. This was a reflection of the low numbers of Anglicans living in these mainly Presbyterian parishes.

From 1634 the Church of Ireland was required to keep proper records of baptisms, marriages and burials. For a handful of parishes there are records dating from the seventeenth century. In date order of surviving baptismal register, these are: Blaris (Christ Church cathedral) (1637), Templemore (St Columb's cathedral) (1642), Inishmacsaint (1660 – extracts), Drumglass (1665), Enniskillen (1667 – extracts), Culdaff (1668),

Errigal Truagh (1671), Seagoe (1672), Shankill (1681), Clones (1682), Comber (1683), Hillsborough (1686), Tynan (1686), Magheralin (1692), Derriaghy (1696), Donaghcloney (1697), Donagheady (1697), and Inishkeel (1699). Not all of these registers run continuously from the earliest date, and there are frequent and often lengthy gaps in the records. If there are no early registers for a particular parish it may be because there was no church in the parish in the period being researched. Important churches also drew people from a wider area than the parish in which they were situated. The seventeenth-century register of St Columb's cathedral in Derry includes references to people from far beyond the bounds of Templemore parish.

Analysis of Church of Ireland registers has shown that many people who belonged to other denominations frequently appear in these records. There are various reasons for this. For instance, before 1782 it was not legal for Presbyterian ministers to perform marriages, and until 1844 they could not perform 'mixed marriages', i.e. marry a Presbyterian to a member of the Church of Ireland. For this reason many marriages of other denominations, especially those classed as Dissenters, are recorded in the Church of Ireland registers. Marriages between Protestants and Catholics may also be found. For example, the marriage register of Donagheady parish in County Tyrone includes a record of the marriage of Alexander Sterling and Ann Kelly on 11 August 1707 with the comment that they had been 'formerly married by a popish priest, [and] remarried by the Chancellor's order' (MIC/1/35).

Occasionally additional information of interest is recorded in a Church of Ireland register. In the case of Ballyphilip Church, Portaferry, records can be found of victims of shipwrecks who were washed up on the surrounding coastline. In the register for baptisms, marriages and burials for 1745–94 (MIC/583/17–18) the following entry appears:

> George Vachell (Captain of the Wolf Sloop of War which was wreckt on Carny point on Fryday night being the 30th of December 1748) was buried in the Church Yard of P'ferry on Monday the 2d Day of January following & the same Day forty-five of the Crew belonging to the sd Sloop were Buried in the Church Yard of Slans & on the next Day being Tuesday the 3d of the sd Month Charles Bowden Lieutenant of the sd Sloop was buried in the Church Yard of P'ferry & in a few days after that at Different Times twenty one persons more of sd Crew were buried in the Church Yard of Slans, so there were in all Sixty Six persons Buried in the last mentioned Church Yard.

The entry includes a list of those whose names were known.

2.1.1 Vestry minute books

The vestry was an assembly of parishioners who met to consider parochial business, and took its name from its meeting place – the vestry, or room in the church in which the minister's vestments were kept. In theory membership of the vestry was open to all those who were liable to parish taxes. In practice, however, judging from the number of signatures and marks in the surviving vestry minute books, it would appear that most meetings of vestry were attended by the rector or his curate, who presided, and the leading parishioners – the landowners, if resident in the parish, and the principal farmers or merchants if the parish contained a significant urban settlement. At the more important meetings, such as those to decide whether or not to build a new church, attendance was much higher. At one meeting in the parish of Knockbreda, County Down, in 1733 around 300 persons were present.

The officers of the parish in both civil and ecclesiastical matters were the churchwardens. There were two to a parish and they were elected on an annual basis, although one man could hold the post for several years at a time. To help the churchwardens many parishes appointed assistants known as sidesmen. The vestry could levy taxes for the maintenance of the church and the payment of parish officers such as the sexton and the parish clerk. The vestry could also raise funds for local services such as poor relief, parish constables, road repair, the organisation of education and the provision of recruits for the army.

The names appearing in the vestry books include those of the churchwardens and sidesmen, those attending vestry meetings, persons appointed to oversee the repair of roads, masons and craftsmen employed to work on the parish church, and persons appointed to care for the elderly and infirm or abandoned children. Taken together, these names can run to a considerable number. For example, the Donagheady vestry book, covering the period 1697–1723, names over 220 different individuals from all denominations and walks of life.

Often lengthy lists of names may appear in vestry books. These may be the names of those liable to parish taxes or even a list of the seatholders in the church. The latter can provide an indication of the relative standing of a family in a parish. Those of wealth and status sat in the grandest seats at the front of the church, with the poor standing or sitting on plain benches at the back, and the 'middling' people in between. Other lists of names include poor lists recording those who were given alms by the parish to help them in their need. In the Kilrea vestry book there is a loyal declaration by the inhabitants of Kilrea and Tamlaght O'Crilly, dating from 1745–6, the time of the Jacobite rising in Scotland, which includes over 130 names (MIC/1/55). Lists of confirmations feature regularly; those for Christ Church cathedral in Lisburn survive back to 1667. Vestry minute books sometimes contain some baptism, marriage and burial entries, particularly in the period covered by this book. The vestry book of Killygarvan parish, County Donegal, is one such example (MIC/1/166D/1).

2.1.2 Information on clergymen

A Church of Ireland clergyman with responsibility for looking after a parish or group of parishes was usually known as a rector, though occasionally the title 'vicar' was applied. A clergyman assisting a rector or vicar was known as a curate. For those seeking information on Church of Ireland ministers, the best sources are the *Clergy and Parishes* volumes meticulously complied on a diocesan basis by Canon J. B. Leslie. Through years of research Leslie was able to compile brief biographical notes on nearly all ministers in the Church of Ireland from the early seventeenth century through to the early twentieth century. He gathered a vast amount of information from sources, such as wills, which were destroyed in 1922. For the north of Ireland the following volumes were published: *Armagh* (1911),

Clogher (1929), *Derry* (1937), *Down* (with H. B. Swanzy) (1936), *Dromore* (with H. B. Swanzy) (1933), *Raphoe* (1941), and *Supplement to Armagh* (1948). The Ulster Historical Foundation has published *Clergy of Connor* (1993) based largely on unpublished succession lists drawn up by Canon Leslie, and in single volumes has issued reprints of *Down and Dromore* (1996) and *Derry and Raphoe* (1999). A reprint of *Clogher* is planned for the near future.

It must not be thought that all Anglican ministers were of English background. Many Church of Ireland ministers in the seventeenth and eighteenth centuries were Scots or had Scottish ancestry. For example, William King, successively bishop of Derry (1690–1703) and archbishop of Dublin (1703–29), was born to Scottish parents in County Tyrone about 1650. Many of these Scottish ministers were vehemently opposed to Presbyterianism and used their position to stifle nonconformity. The inscription on the memorial to John Sinclair (d. 1703), the Scottish-born rector of Camus-juxta-Mourne and Leckpatrick parishes in County Tyrone, praises him for his efforts in suppressing Dissenters. Occasionally native Irishmen served in the Church of Ireland pastorate. In Inishowen, County Donegal, in the late seventeenth century two McLaughlin brothers were ministers: one Church of Ireland, the other Roman Catholic.

2.1.3 Visitation books

Bishops regularly carried out inspections of their dioceses; the results of these investigations are contained in visitation books. The information is fairly limited for genealogists, but the names listed can include those of the rector, curate, churchwardens, parish clerk and parish schoolmaster. Occasionally some items of interest about individual parishioners may turn up. For example, in a visitation of Armagh diocese of 1700 Mary Beston of Tandragee, wife of William Beston, was reprimanded for being a 'lewd woman' and for keeping a 'bawdy house' (DIO/4/29/2/1/2).

2.2 The Presbyterian Church

From the middle of the seventeenth century the Presbyterian Church has been the dominant Protestant denomination in Ulster. Presbyterianism emerged in Scotland in the late sixteenth century. It is characterised by worship services where reading the Bible and preaching have greatest importance and where there is a lack of emphasis on ritual and liturgy. In terms of church government it is democratic rather than hierarchical: every minister is considered equal, and to assist him each congregation will appoint a number of 'elders'.

In the early seventeenth century, with the influx of large numbers of Scottish settlers, a number of clergymen with Presbyterian convictions arrived in Ulster from Scotland. To begin with they were accommodated within the Church of Ireland and were allowed a certain amount of freedom to practise their beliefs. Presbyterianism did not exist as a distinct denomination at this time. However, in the 1630s there were moves to bring the Church of Ireland more closely into line with the Church of England. A number of clergymen who held to Presbyterian beliefs were expelled for refusing to accept the changes.

In 1642 an army from Scotland landed at Carrickfergus to defend Scottish settlers from attacks from rebellious Irish. Accompanying this army were a number of Presbyterian ministers, and here the first Irish presbytery was founded (see below for more information on the role and function of a presbytery). In the 1650s, during the Cromwellian regime, there was considerable freedom of worship and many ministers in Ulster were Scottish Presbyterians. Following the Restoration of 1660, ministers who refused to conform to the teachings and government of the newly reinstated Church of Ireland were dismissed. Despite periods of persecution, Presbyterians began to form congregations and build their own churches from the 1660s. Numerically they were far superior to Anglicans, and this was a major source of concern for both the government and the Established Church.

Each Presbyterian congregation kept registers of baptisms and marriages. In general, Presbyterian registers start later than those of the Church of Ireland. There are a number of early Presbyterian registers, however, including Drumbo (baptisms from 1692), Killyleagh (baptisms from 1693 and marriages from 1693), Lisburn (baptisms from 1692 and marriages from 1688), and Portaferry (baptisms from 1699). Additional Presbyterian records available for consultation at PRONI include session books, communicant rolls and pew rent books. Because Presbyterians rarely kept burial registers, gravestone inscriptions provide valuable information that cannot be found elsewhere. It is also worth looking at Church of Ireland registers for baptisms, marriages and burials involving Presbyterians, for reasons outlined in Chapter 2.1 above.

The Presbyterian Historical Library is located at 26 College Green, Belfast. The library has many manuscripts relating to Presbyterian families and baptismal and marriage records of Presbyterian churches throughout Ireland. Presbyterian records copied by PRONI are available under MIC/1P and CR/3. In addition to registers of baptisms, marriages and burials, there are other categories of records relating to the Presbyterian Church that are worth consulting for the information they contain on individuals and families.

2.2.1 Session records
The session was composed of the ministers and elders in a particular congregation. Session records cover a range of matters, many of which relate to the internal discipline of members of the congregation for a variety of misdemeanours. Occasionally they may contain baptisms and marriages. Only a handful of session records from the seventeenth and eighteenth centuries have survived; those that are available for consultation are included along with the pre-1800 church registers listed in Appendix 1.

2.2.2 Presbytery records
The presbytery was the middle layer of government in the Presbyterian Church, above session and below Synod. It comprised the ministers and ruling elders of the congregations affiliated to the presbytery. It dealt with matters that could not be settled at the level of session, either because there was a dispute of a nature that could not be resolved without recourse to a higher authority or because the issues related to more than one congregation. Presbytery meetings were held on a regular basis. Presbyteries were frequently reorganised.

In addition, individual congregations could change presbytery if it meant that a dispute would be resolved.

The presbytery of Strabane, for example, was formed in 1717 and when originally constituted included the congregations of Strabane, Ardstraw, Urney, Donagheady, Ballindrait, Derg, Omagh, Badoney and Pettigo. The surviving minute book, covering the period 1717–40, reveals that the presbytery dealt with a variety of matters relating to the members of the congregations within its bounds (CR/3/26/2/1). For instance, those planning to emigrate would often petition presbytery for a certificate testifying to their credentials as good Presbyterians. This would enable them to join a Presbyterian congregation in America without having to undergo a rigorous examination of their character and religious beliefs. In December 1718 John Alison came before Strabane presbytery desiring such a testimonial as he was preparing to emigrate. Presbytery decided not to issue him with one until just before he was ready to leave, and then only conditional on his continued good behaviour. In 1730 Strabane presbytery rebuked John Patterson and Mary Atchison for marrying without making sure that Atchison's former husband, who had emigrated to America, was definitely dead.

Original and duplicate copies of presbytery minute books and related records in PRONI are as follows.

Antrim presbytery, 1654–8 – CR/5/5E/2; D/1759/1A/1
Antrim presbytery, 1671–91 – D/1759/1A/2
Biographical notes on ministers and reports on meeting in Antrim presbytery,
   1681 – D/1759/1A/3
Bangor presbytery, 1706–23 – D/1759/1D/21
Bangor presbytery, 1739–74 – CR/5/5E/2
Bangor presbytery, 1739–1842 – D/1759/1D/15
Down presbytery, 1706–15 – CR/5/5E/2
Down presbytery, 1707–15, 1785–1800 – D/1759/1D/16
Killyleagh presbytery, 1725–32 – D/1759/1D/10
Laggan presbytery, 1672–95 – CR/5/5E/2; D/1759/1E/1–2
Route presbytery, 1701–5 D/1759/2A/13
Strabane presbytery 1717–40 – CR/3/26/2/1

2.2.3 Synod of Ulster records
The Synod of Ulster was the highest authority in the Presbyterian Church in Ulster. It met once a year, usually in June, and was composed of representatives from every congregation in each of the presbyteries. The records of the Synod of Ulster meetings for the period 1690–1820 were published in three volumes by the Presbyterian Church in 1891. A typescript index in three volumes is available for consultation in the library at PRONI. Much of the minutes deals with matters of a fairly routine nature. Occasionally, however, an item of real value will be recorded. For example, at the Synod of 1738 a petition was presented from a section of the Drummaul (Randalstown) congregation who wanted to be disannexed from Drummaul and united to the congregation at Ahoghill. The commissioners representing the disaffected members of Drummaul were Jon Nisbet and Wm Wining and, usefully, the names of those signing the petition were listed in the

minutes of Synod (vol. 2, p. 240). This list distinguished between heads of families and young people, as follows.

Heads of families	Young people
Jas Walker	Adam Glass
Jas Ker	Jno Ker
Jas Bankhead	Jno Nisbet
Thos Doel	Samuel Stuart
Jon Wallace	Jno Stuart
Mort Gallaway	Saml Wilson
Hugh Reny	Jno Wilson
Wm Gallaway	Jas Lemon
Christy Nelson	Wm Craig
Saml Thomson	Wm Anderwood
Robt Adair	Alex Dumbar
Jos Thomson	Wm Graham
Robt Lyamon	
Jas Henderson	
Saml Agnue	
Jno Hillis	
Jno Forbes	
Jas Winning	
Stephen Harper	
Alexr Muron	
Jno Marshall	
Jno Thomson	
Wm Carson	
Jas Craig	
Jas Gillespie	
Andr Clerk	
Jas Montgomery	
Jas Willson	

2.2.4 *Information on congregations*

An indispensable guide to the Presbyterian Church in Ireland is the *History of Congregations* published by the Presbyterian Historical Society in 1982. It provides brief sketches of each of the congregations, mainly focusing on the succession of ministers. It is particularly useful in determining when a particular congregation came into being. *A Supplement of Additions, Emendations and Corrections with an Index* was published in association with the Ulster Historical Foundation in 1996.

2.2.5 *Information on Presbyterian ministers*

Biographical information on Presbyterian ministers was published as *Fasti of the Irish Presbyterian Church, 1613–1840* compiled by James McConnell and revised by his son Samuel G. McConnell (Belfast: Presbyterian Historical Society, 1951). The biographical sketches are fairly succinct, but can include the name of the father and possibly mother of the minister, his own family details, where he was educated and where he served.

Publications, if any, may also be noted, and perhaps something exceptional about his career.

2.3 The Secession Presbyterian Church

The Secession Church was a branch of Presbyterianism that emerged following a split in the Church of Scotland in 1712 over the issue of official patronage. Before long it had gained a foothold in Ulster. Essential reading for an understanding of the Secession Church in Ulster is David Stewart's *The Seceders in Ireland: With Annals of Their Congregations* (Belfast, 1950). In the nineteenth century nearly all of the Secession churches were received into the Presbyterian Church in Ireland. Therefore, in the list of surviving pre-1800 church records, congregations that originated as Secession churches – Tyrone's Ditches in Ballymore parish, County Armagh, being one example – will be found listed as Presbyterian churches. Synod and presbytery records relating to the Secession Church available in PRONI include the following.

> Typed copy of the minutes of the Associate Presbytery of Moira and Lisburn, 1774–86 – D/1759/1D/22
> Typed copy of minute book of Associate Synod, 1788–1818 – D/1759/1F/1
> Typed copy of extracts from the minute book of the Secession Synod, 1736–82 – D/1759/1F/3
> Extracts from Monaghan Secession records, 1777–1820 – D/1759/2A/12

2.4 The Non-Subscribing Presbyterian Church

The origins of the Non-Subscribing Presbyterian Church go back to a dispute within the Presbyterian Church over the issue of subscription to the Westminster Confession of Faith, the statement of doctrine of the Presbyterian Church. Those who denied the necessity of subscribing to this work were known as 'New Light' Presbyterians or 'Non-Subscribers'. In 1725, in an attempt to deal with the situation, ministers and congregations of the 'New Light' persuasion were placed in the presbytery of Antrim (this did not mean that all the congregations were in County Antrim). About 100 years later the issue of subscription again became a source of contention within Presbyterianism, and in 1829 a small section of the Presbyterian Church withdrew and formed what was known as the Remonstrant Synod. Along with the presbytery of Antrim, this group became the core of the Non-Subscribing Presbyterian Church. Some of the early Non-Subscribing Presbyterian Church records, created before the split, are in fact Presbyterian records: for example, the early records of Scarva Street Presbyterian Church in Banbridge are to be found in Banbridge Non-Subscribing Presbyterian Church records. For a brief background to this denomination see *A Short History of the Non-Subscribing Presbyterian Church of Ireland* by John Campbell (Belfast, 1914).

2.5 The Reformed Presbyterian (Covenanter) Church

The Covenanter or Reformed Presbyterian Church was composed of those who adhered most strongly to the Covenants of 1638 and 1643 and who rejected the Revolution Settlement of 1691 in Scotland. The National Covenant of 1638 was a reaction against the attempts by Charles I to bring the Scottish Church into closer conformity with the episcopal Church of England and to introduce greater ritual and a prescribed liturgy to services. It firmly established the Presbyterian form of church government in Scotland, and bound the people to uphold the principles of the Reformation. The Solemn League and Covenant of 1643 was composed on similar lines and affected England and Ireland as well as Scotland. During the reigns of Charles II (1660–85) and James II (1685–8) there was considerable persecution of Covenanters, and many were executed or banished. This ended with the accession of William III. In 1691 Covenanters refused to accept the Revolution Settlement as it gave the government a role in the running of the Church of Scotland. Covenanters, therefore, stood apart from mainstream Presbyteriansism in Scotland.

Of the early history of the Covenanters in Ireland very little is known, save that the denomination was small and scattered. It was not until the latter part of the eighteenth century that congregations began to be organised and ministers were ordained. Very few Reformed Presbyterian records have survived from the eighteenth century. This can be partly explained by the paucity of ministers at this time; many baptisms and marriges were performed by visiting ministers from Scotland and there is little evidence of proper records being kept of these events. Congregations were divided into societies, composed of several families living within a short distance of each other. Records belonging to these societies – if any were kept – have not survived from the pre-1800 period.

A minute book of meetings of the Reformed session of Antrim (the congregations of Kellswater and Cullybackey) for the period c.1789–1802 is available and is revealing of the principles of the church at this time (CR/5/9A/1). For example, because the Covenanters refused to accept the political status quo, they did not participate in elections. In 1792 the Reformed session of Antrim was forced to deal with Robert Nickol. It was alleged that Nickol had accepted a bribe to leave the town of Antrim during an election, presumably so that he would not have voted. Shortly afterwards Nickol was summoned to appear before a court in Dublin to give evidence in a trial arising from this allegation. There he had sworn in an 'idolatrous way'. Afterwards he had returned to Antrim and taken an active part in the election there. He was publicly rebuked by session for his actions.

There are a number of eighteenth-century records in the Reformed Presbyterian Theological College in Belfast, including session and committee minutes, but these are not accessible to the general researcher at present. Moves are afoot to have much of this early material transferred to PRONI. For background information on this denomination see *The Covenanters in Ireland: A History of the Reformed Presbyterian Church of Ireland* by Adam Loughridge (Belfast, 1984). For information on ministers in the Reformed Presbyterian Church see *Fasti of the Reformed Presbyterian Church of Ireland* compiled and edited by Adam Loughridge (Belfast, 1970).

2.6 The Methodist Church

In 1738 John Wesley and his brother Charles started the movement that soon acquired the name of Methodism. John Wesley made his first visit to Ulster, where the movement had already established itself in many of the major towns, in 1756. He visited Ulster regularly for the rest of his life. The majority of Methodists were members of the Established Church and they remained members of their own local churches even if they attended separate meetings to hear Methodist preachers. Therefore, they continued to go to the parish church for the administration of marriages, burials and baptisms. It was not until the early nineteenth century that Methodists began to keep their own records of baptisms and marriages. For those who think their eighteenth-century ancestors may have sympathised with Methodism, the best place to look for them is the local Church of Ireland register.

2.7 The Moravian Church
The Moravian Church is a Protestant denomination that originated in what is now the Czech Republic and was introduced to Ireland in the middle of the eighteenth century. It is formally known as the Unitas Fratrum or Unity of the Brethren. Occaionally Moravians are referred to as the United Brethren (not to be confused with the Plymouth Brethren). Principally through the missionary work of John Cennick, congregations were established at a number of places in Ulster, including Gracehill in County Antrim, Gracefield in County Londonderry and Kilwarlin in County Down. The most successful Moravian community was that at Gracehill, where a planned village was laid out with the church as its focus. The Moravians were very good record-keepers, and the information recorded extended to a wide range of their activities. For the Moravian church at Gracehill, in addition to baptisms, marriages and burials, there are elders' conference minutes beginning in 1755, congregational committee minutes beginning in 1788, and a register of members, 1755–91, with an index.

2.8 The Religious Society of Friends
The Religious Society of Friends, also known as 'Quakers' or 'Friends', was founded by George Fox in England in the mid-seventeenth century. Soon afterwards the Quaker movement was brought to Ireland by William Edmundson when he established a business in Dublin in 1652. A few years later he moved north to Lurgan, County Armagh, and by the 1660s a Quaker settlement was firmly established there. The Quakers were particularly strong in the Lagan Valley and north Armagh – areas particularly associated with English settlement – with further congregations established at Ballyhagen, Cootehill, Hillsborough, Lisburn, Richhill and elsewhere.

From the beginning Quakers were among the best record-keepers of any denomination. Monthly meetings contain registers of births (Quakers do not practise baptism), marriages and deaths, minutes of meetings, accounts of sufferings and charity papers. As a result, Quaker records contain a great deal of information about local affairs. A Quaker library at the Friends Meeting House, Railway Street, Lisburn, County Antrim, contains records dating from the seventeenth century covering Ulster. Many records have been copied by PRONI and were originally given the reference T/1062. These copied records can now be consulted under MIC/16. An excellent introduction to Quaker records is *Guide to Irish Quaker Records, 1654–1860* by Olive C. Goodbody with a contribution on Northern Ireland records by B. G. Hutton (Dublin, 1967). This volume includes a section listing surnames extracted from Quaker registers (pp. 193–207). A useful book about Quaker emigration is A. C. Myers's *Immigration of the Irish Quakers into Pennsylvania, 1682–1750* (privately published, 1902).

Surviving Quaker records for local meetings are listed in the church records section at PRONI under the prefix RSF (Religious Society of Friends). The following records relate to the Ulster province/quarterly meetings.

Minutes of province/quarterly meetings, 1674 – MIC/16/1A–1B
Women's minutes of province/quarterly meetings, 1792–1801 – MIC/16/4
Ministers' and elders' minutes of province/quarterly meetings, 1758–64 – MIC/16/4
Marriage certificates, 1731–86 – MIC/16/6
Book of sufferings, 1748–1809 – MIC/16/6
Register of tithe sufferings, 1706–11 – MIC/16/7

2.9 The Roman Catholic Church

The Reformation in Ireland did not result in the conversion of more than a fraction of the native population to Protestantism; nearly all continued to look to Rome for supreme authority in matters ecclesiastical. At an institutional level, however, the Roman Catholic Church suffered considerably as a result of the disruption caused by the plantations and wars of the late sixteenth and seventeenth centuries. Legislation in the form of the Penal Laws in the early eighteenth century also had an impact, though in spite of these laws Catholic priests and bishops operated freely in most areas. In the course of the eighteenth and nineteenth centuries the Roman Catholic Church was able to establish new parochial structures, based in the main on local demographics. Catholic parishes, therefore, do not follow the same pattern as civil and Church of Ireland parishes, and it is important for researchers to take this fact into consideration.

For the historical reasons briefly outlined above, very few Roman Catholic registers pre-date 1800. Among the earliest are those for Clonleigh and Camus, straddling the border between Counties Donegal and Tyrone, and Castlerahan and Munterconnaught, Castletara, Killinkere, Lurgan and Mullagh, all in County Cavan, all of which have registers starting before 1780 (but no earlier than 1750). PRONI has microfilm copies for Catholic registers of parishes in Ulster (MIC/1D). The National Library of Ireland also has copies of Catholic registers. For background reading on Catholics and Catholicism in Ulster see Marianne Elliott, *The Catholics of Ulster* (London, 2000) and Oliver P. Rafferty, *Catholicism in Ulster 1603–1983: An Interpretative History* (London, 1994).

2.10 Huguenots

Strictly speaking, the Huguenots in Ulster were not a denomination in their own right, but were the French Protestant refugees who left France mostly after the revocation of the edict of Nantes in 1685. Significant numbers of Huguenots came to Ireland, with the most important colony in Ulster at Lisburn, County Antrim. The names of many of the early Huguenot settlers in Lisburn appear in the registers of Christ Church cathedral and several of them have surviving memorials in the adjoining churchyard. About 1700 a 'French church' catering for the spiritual needs of the Huguenot colony was built in Lisburn. It was demolished *c.*1830 and, unfortunately, its registers have been lost. E. Joyce Best, *The Huguenots of Lisburn* (Lisburn, 1997), includes biographical sketches of Huguenot families who settled in the area.

2.11 Marriage licence bonds

During the seventeenth and eighteenth centuries, when it was illegal for 'dissenting' ministers to perform marriages, some Roman Catholic and Presbyterians chose to be married in the Church of Ireland. To do so they would ask the minister to publish banns or purchase a licence from the bishop of the diocese. Before the licence was granted the couple had to enter a bond at a diocesan court. These bonds included the names of the bride and groom and their ages and place of residence. Most of the bonds and licences were destroyed in the Public Record Office, Dublin, in 1922, but indexes to many of them have survived. These indexes contain the names of the bridegroom and bride and the date of the bond. Marriage licence bonds issued by the Prerogative Court in Dublin are available from *c.*1625 under T/932.

The following marriage licence bonds are available on microfim at PRONI for Ulster dioceses:

Armagh, 1727–1845 – MIC/5B/1–3
Clogher, 1709–1866 – MIC/5B/4
Down, Connor and Dromore, 1721–1845 – MIC/5B/5–6

An index to Kilmore and Ardagh marriage licence bonds, covering the period 1697–1844, is available online at http://freepages.genealogy.rootsweb.com/~adrian/ColKilm.htm. For the diocese of Raphoe see Rosemary ffolliott, *Index to Raphoe Marriage Licence Bonds, 1710–1755 and 1817–1830* (Dublin, 1969, supplement to *The Irish Ancestor*).

3. Gravestone inscriptions

The value of gravestone inscriptions for ancestral research has long been recognised. The discovery of a single gravestone may provide more information on the history of a family than could be gleaned from documentary sources. Prior to 1864, when official registration of deaths began in Ireland, a gravestone inscription may provide the only record of someone's death. Before embarking on systematic research in the archives, a search for the family gravestone or gravestones is strongly recommended.

3.1 Graveyards

Finding out which graveyard your ancestors may have been buried can be far from straightforward. Usually the deceased will be buried in a graveyard in the parish in which they lived. However, this was not always the case. In the 1750s the Reverend George Bracegirdle, rector of Donagheady in County Tyrone, complained that the inhabitants of the neighbouring parish of Cumber were using a graveyard in his parish because the burial fees were lower. On many occasions the deceased was taken back to the parish of his birth for burial even if he was living somewhere else at the time of his death. Wills frequently include instructions from the testator regarding his preferred place of burial. While these requests were not always followed, a will can assist with identifying the burial place of an ancestor (see Chapter 8 for more information on wills).

In graveyards founded before the sixteenth-century Reformation, all denominations can usually be found. There may be demographic or other reasons why a pre-Reformation graveyard was used by people from only one denomination. For example, in the early seventeenth century the pre-Reformation graveyard in the parish of Faughanvale, County Londonderry, was not used by the Protestant settlers in the area because it had been used for the burial of unbaptised infants and persons who had committed suicide. In many parishes there will be more than one graveyard dating from before the Reformation. One will usually be the site of the parish church and the other the site of a subsidiary chapel of ease or a monastery. In 1698 the Irish parliament passed a law that forbade burial in the vicinity of a disused monastery. This law was universally ignored by both Protestants and Catholics.

At the Reformation most parish churches were taken over by the Church of Ireland. The existing church was either repaired or demolished and built afresh. However, even though the church may have belonged to the Church of Ireland, the graveyard attached to it was used by all denominations. Many Church of Ireland churches still stand on pre-Reformation sites. Quite often the Church of Ireland did not use the pre-Reformation site, but built a new church on a new site. If this occurred in the early seventeenth century, the graveyards will generally have been used by Protestants of any denomination, but not Catholics. To further complicate the picture, if the new Anglican church was built after the 1660s, when Presbyterianism began to emerge as a distinct denomination, the graveyard will generally only have been used by members of the Church of Ireland. In these instances Presbyterians buried their dead in the local pre-Reformation graveyard.

It was generally not until the late eighteenth century that Presbyterians began to lay out their own graveyards in the vicinity of their meeting houses. However, relatively few Presbyterian graveyards pre-date 1800. The same is true of Catholic graveyards. As always, there are exceptions to these rules. For example, Drumbo Presbyterian church, County Down, is built on a pre-Reformation site, as is Kinawley Roman Catholic church, County Fermanagh. Other denominations founded their own graveyards in this period, including the Quakers and Moravians. Some Quaker graveyards were founded in the late seventeenth century, but the practice of erecting headstones was not permitted until the mid-nineteenth century. The earliest Moravian burial ground in Ulster is at Gracehill, near Ballymena, County Antrim, which was opened in the late 1750s. Clifton Street graveyard in Belfast was opened in the late 1790s by Belfast Charitable Society, making it the oldest burial ground in Ulster not connected with a religious denomination.

3.2 Inscriptions

Memorials from the seventeenth and eighteenth centuries frequently communicate more information about the departed than do more recent headstones. Information about the deceased's life, occupation and place of residence will often be recorded. Some inscriptions incorporate a mini-biography of the deceased. The inscription on the monument to Sir Richard Hansard (d. 1619) in Clonleigh parish church, Lifford, County Donegal, informs us that Hansard was born in Biskerthorpe in Lincolnshire, was educated at Cambridge, came to Ireland as a soldier where he distinguished himself in the Nine Years' War and rebellion of Sir Cahir O'Dogherty, and was subsequently granted the town of Lifford and the lands around it. It continues by providing details of the bequests in Hansard's will.

Translated from Latin, the inscription to Alexander Sandirson (d. 1633) in Desertcreat Church of Ireland church, County Tyrone, records that he was a born in Scotland, served as a foot-soldier in Belgium, was a cavalry officer in Poland, before coming to Ireland where he was a justice of the peace and high sheriff. The monument to Henry Savage of Rock Savage (d. 1797) in Ardkeen Church of Ireland church, County Down, records that he was 'late Major in the 16th Regt of Foot. After having distinguished himself in the service of his country, both in the German and American wars, he returned to fulfil the social duties of domestic life. He was a just magistrate, steady friend and most excellent husband.'

While there was a direct correlation between the wealth of the deceased's family and the elaboration of the memorial, it must not be thought that gravestones were entirely the preserve of the elite. From the late seventeenth century an increasing number of headstones were erected by people from the middling strata of society. In Counties Fermanagh and Monaghan there are hundreds of headstones from the late seventeenth and eighteenth centuries. Most of them bear native Irish names and are presumably to Catholics. These people could have been no more than tenant farmers. Interestingly, almost without exception the inscriptions are in English.

Occasionally the circumstances in which the person died will be recorded. One of the few inscriptions referring to the 1641 rebellion can be read in Drumbeg Church of Ireland churchyard in County Down: 'Capt William Stewart, son of Lord Garlies, was killed at Kilcullin Bridge, he & his escort cut into pieces by a party of Roman Catholicks in 1641'. A number of memorials also allude to the 1798 rebellion. In Whitechurch graveyard in Ballywalter, County Down, a stone was erected in memory of Hugh and David Maxwell of Ballywalter 'whose bodies are here interred. They fell in an attack made on the town of Newtownards the 10th of June 1798.' In coastal areas graveyards abound in memorials to mariners. Occasionally an eighteenth-century gravestone will refer to individuals lost at sea. In Saul Church of Ireland churchyard, Country Down, a headstone featuring a carving of a woman mourning over a tomb commemorates Ambrose Lennon, who 'foundered in a hurricane in the West Indies on board his Majesty's ship Barbadoes with all the crew in the year 1780'. The memorial was erected by their son, Captain John Lennon.

The following inscription from Derg Church of Ireland churchyard in Castlederg, County Tyrone, indicates the Scottish origins of the deceased:

HERE LIETH INTERRED THE
BODY OF CORNET ARCHB
ALD JOHNSTON DECEND
ED OF THE ANCIENT F
AMILY OF LODERHAY IN
ANANDEAL IN THE KIN
GDOM OF SCOTLAND W
HO DECEASED THE [-] OF
MAR 167[-] AND ALSO MA
RGRET HIS WIFE DECEN
DED OF THE ANCIENT
FAMILY OF GRAHAMS
OF MUL WHO DECEASED THE
(abruptly ends here)

3.3 Gravestone symbolism

The symbols carved on memorials from this period also have much to tell us of the mental worlds in which our forebears lived. The most popular emblems were mortality symbols, which could include a combination of a skull, crossed bones, hourglass, coffin, bell, Bible and sexton's tools. These symbols represented visually what *memento mori* – 'remember you must die' – communicated in words. Although mortality symbols are found on the memorials of individuals from all backgrounds, they are most frequently met with in the seventeenth century on the gravestones to Scottish settlers. One of the earliest is the gravestone to Thomas Goodlate (d. 1624) in Killyman Church of Ireland graveyard, which depicts a skull clenching a longbone in its teeth.

The use of mortality symbols continued into the eighteenth century, but by the close of the 1700s had more or less died out as funerary symbolism began to reflect hope and the resurrection, rather than death. Masonic symbols also appear, such as the late eighteenth-century Hannan gravestone in Cranfield graveyard, County Antrim, which depicts an arch and a representation of Pythagoras' theorem.

Symbols associated with the trade of the deceased were also carved on memorials. This occurred far less frequently in Ulster than it did in Scotland. The stone to William Stennors (d. 1626) in Bangor Abbey church, County Down, has representations of the symbols associated with the deceased's occupation of mason carved on it. The gravestone in Friar's Bush graveyard in Belfast to John Gibson (d. 1777) features shears, suggesting that the deceased may have been involved in the cloth trade. Symbols associated with a seafarer, including cannons, sextant and anchor, appear on the gravestone to Captain George Colvill in Bangor Abbey graveyard. Colvill was the commander of the private ship of war *Amazon* which was wrecked near Bangor on 25 February 1780.

Another interesting memorial is the headstone to Alexander McCormick (d. 1781) in Ballyhalbert graveyard, County Down, which features a well-carved figure of a Volunteer at the top, on one side of which is a flag with a harp on it, and on the other side a small cannon and a drum. The inscription records that McCormick was an 'Echlinvale Volunteer' and that 'His Hon. Captain & Companie did him honour at his death & he was buried with ye honours of war' when he died aged just fifteen.

3.4 Locating inscriptions

While many old graveyards in Ulster are well maintained by those charged with their responsibility, a number are not. In a neglected graveyard it may be impossible to identify a particular gravestone in the undergrowth. Even if the graveyard is properly looked after, the family burial plot may be within railings that are impossible to get behind or squeeze between. An added problem is that many of the older memorials are largely if not completely illegible. Generally the inscription on a slate gravestone will have a much better survival rate than one on a sandstone memorial. Inscriptions carved in false relief will often survive better than incised inscriptions.

The gravestone inscriptions from a large number of graveyards in Ulster have been transcribed and published. Since 1967 the Ulster Historical Foundation has published twenty-one volumes of graveyard inscriptions for County Down, four for Belfast and four for County Antrim. The Ulster Historical Foundation also holds recordings of gravestone inscriptions for many other graveyards in Ulster. These inscriptions are available for purchase on its *History from Headstones Online* website (www.historyfromheadstones.com). Inscriptions recorded by Irish World Ltd are also available for purchase online (www.irishgenealogy.ie). Many Ulster inscriptions appeared in the *Journal of the Association for the Preservation of the Memorials of the Dead in Ireland*, published in thirteen volumes between 1888 and 1937. These recordings are particularly useful if the gravestone can no longer be traced. A guide to the graveyards in Northern

Ireland featured in this series is Ian Forsythe, 'An index to the *Memorials of the Dead*', in *Directory of Irish Family History Research* no. 15 (1992). In addition, the inscriptions from a large number of other graveyards in Ulster have been published in the journals of local historical societies such as *Clogher Record, Donegal Annual* and *Breifne*.

4. Seventeenth-century records

4.1 Fiants of the Tudor sovereigns, 1521–1603

Fiants were a documentary series unique to Ireland. These documents preceded the issue of royal grants. The term 'fiant' derives from the first word of the usual form of *Fiant literae patentes*, meaning 'Let letters patent be made'. The preliminary fiants prepared in Ireland provide far fuller information about individuals than the actual letters patent issued in London. The uniqueness of the information contained in the fiants encouraged the staff in the newly established Public Record Office of Ireland to publish calendars of these fiants. Ingeniously, they got the calendars published as appendices in the steady stream of annual reports published by the office in the years 1875–90 (Reports nos 11–13, 15–18 of the Deputy Keeper of the Public Records of Ireland). The attention of the scholarly world was drawn to the quality of the information available in the fiants by the publication of reprints of these calendars of Irish fiants for the years 1521–1603 in four volumes, including a comprehensive index, by Edmund Burke in 1994. These serve as very adequate substitutes for the original records destroyed in the Public Record Office of Ireland. When Irish chiefs were granted pardons under the 'surrender and regrant' policy they often listed scores of members of their extended families as well as gallowglasses (mercenary soldiers), horsemen and yeomen, husbandmen, tenants and even, on occasion, cottiers. Individuals were identified with their full names, often with specific locations.

4.2 Plantation records

Although by no means the first project of colonisation introduced to Ireland, the scheme for the plantation in Ulster was by far the most ambitious. More than two years in planning, it eventually came to embrace six Ulster counties: Armagh, Cavan, Coleraine (later renamed Londonderry), Donegal, Fermanagh and Tyrone. The government commissioned four surveys between 1611 and 1622 to investigate the progress being made in the Ulster Plantation. These surveys and where they may be found are as follows.

> 1611 – A survey carried out by Sir George Carew: *Calendar of the Carew Manuscripts, 1603–24*, pp. 68–9, 75–9, 220–51.
>
> 1613 – A survey carried out by Sir Josias Bodley: Historical Manuscripts Commission, *Hastings Mss*, iv (London, 1947), pp. 159–92.

1618–9 – A survey carried out by Captain Nicholas Pynnar. This survey is printed in full in George Hill, *An Historical Account of the Plantation of Ulster at the Commencement of the Seventeenth Century* (Belfast, 1877).

1622 – A survey carried out by commissioners appointed by the government. The official reports for each county were published as follows:

Armagh: V. Treadwell in *Ulster Journal of Archaeology* 3rd series 23 (1960)
Cavan: P. O Gallachair in *Breifne*, vol. 1 (1958)
Donegal: V. Treadwell in *Donegal Annual*, vol. 2 (1951–4), vol. 3 (1954–7)
Fermanagh: P. O Gallachair in *Clogher Record*, vol. 2 (1958)
Londonderry: *Calendar of the State Papers relating to Ireland*, 1615–25
Tyrone: V. Treadwell in *Ulster Journal of Archaeology* 3rd series, vol. 27 (1964)

In addition to the published reports there is a significant amount of original documentation relating to the 1622 survey in the National Library of Ireland under Ms 8013–8014 and to a lesser extent in the Cambridgeshire Record Office in the Kimbolton Manuscripts under DD/M. This material includes many of the original certificates presented by the undertakers or their agents. These certificates give considerably more information on the estates than the official report. Names of tenants, often distinguishing between freeholders and leaseholders, are provided as well as information on the buildings on the estate and who had built them. An edition of the 1622 papers has been prepared by Victor Treadwell and will be published by the Irish Manuscripts Commission.

4.3 Calendars of patent rolls from the reigns of James I and Charles I

The original Irish patent rolls, recording, among other things, grants of land or pardons issued, were destroyed in the Public Record Office, Dublin, in 1922. Fortunately, some of the material had been published in calendar form. Printed calendars have survived for the patent rolls of James I and the early part of the reign of Charles I. The *Calendar of the Patent Rolls of the Reign of James I* was prepared under the direction of the Irish Record Commission prior to 1830 and was printed before the Commission closed. The Irish Manuscripts Commission published a facsimile of the printed calendar in 1966, but this publication is now out of print. Unfortunately no personal and place name index to this calendar has as yet been published. The *Calendar of the Patent and Close Rolls of Chancery in Ireland, of the Reign of Charles the First: First to Eighth Year, Inclusive* edited by James Morrin (Dublin, 1863), does have the advantage of an index.

4.4 Denization and naturalisation records

The abovementioned calendars of patent rolls include the names of Scots in Ulster who were given grants of denization. As a denizen, a Scot occupied an intermediate position between an alien and a native-born subject. It meant that he was able to purchase land and was to his family's benefit in matters of inheritance. By acquiring a grant of denization, the individual concerned was usually indicating a desire to stay in Ireland and protect his possessions using the existing legal safeguards. Naturalisation, on the other hand, placed an alien in the same position as a native-born subject. The Reverend David Stewart, a

Presbyterian minister and a very active local historian, extracted the names of about 1,000 Scots who were recorded as having been granted denization and naturalisation from the printed calendars, and published his findings in pamphlet form as *The Scots in Ulster: Their Denization and Naturalisation* (Belfast, 1954). In this Stewart provides a historical background to the processes of denization and naturalisation. The pamphlet was reprinted as an article in *Familia* in 1995 (this edition is now out of print). A database of these names is available on the Ulster Historical Foundation's website (www.ancestryireland.com). See also William A. Shaw (ed.), *Letters of Denization and Acts of Naturalisation for Aliens in England and Ireland*, 1603–1700, Publications of the Huguenot Society of London, xviii (Lymington, 1911), which includes lists of Irish denizens from 1605.

4.5 Calendars of state papers
State papers concerning Ireland are preserved in The National Archives (formerly the Public Record Office) in London under SP/63. The documents concern the administration of Ireland in this period of enormous change. There is much information of interest about the Ulster plantation and also the management of the Conway (later Hertford) estate in south County Antrim from the 1650s onwards. Calendars of the papers covering the period 1509–1670 were published in 24 volumes by the Public Record Office between 1860 and 1911, under the title *Calendar of the State Papers relating to Ireland*. After 1670 Irish material may be found in the *Calendar of the State Papers, Domestic Series*, also published by the Public Record Office; this series continues until the end of the reign of Queen Anne in 1714. Each volume has a comprehensive index. Typescript copies of the original papers in London after 1714 and up to 1780 are available in PRONI. The volumes covering the sixteenth century contained, in the main, brief abstracts of the original records.

An initiative by the Public Record Office and the Irish Manuscripts Commission to produce fuller versions of the sixteenth-century Irish state papers has so far resulted in the publication of one new volume: *Calendar of State Papers: Ireland: Tudor Period 1571–1575*, edited by Mary O'Dowd (Kew and Dublin, 2000). Also worth consulting for early material on the administration of Ireland is the *Calendar of the Carew manuscripts: Preserved in the Archiepiscopal Library at Lambeth*, edited by J. S. Brewer and William Bullen (6 vols, London, 1867–73), covering the period 1515–1624. A complete set of these volumes is in the Main Library of Queen's University, Belfast; others may be found in the National Library of Ireland and in the Reading Room at PRONI. Microfilm copies of the original State Papers, covering the period 1509–1782, can be found in PRONI (MIC/223). Home Office papers, beginning in 1782, containing material relating to Ireland can also be viewed at PRONI (MIC/224).

4.6 Ulster Inquisitions
If the government wanted information on particular estates in the seventeenth century, it assembled juries composed of local men who investigated such matters as landownership, inheritance and leasing policy. The findings of these juries were published in summary form in the *Inquisitionum in officio rotulorum cancellariae Hiberniae asservatarum*

repertorium, published in two volumes in the 1820s. Volume 2 covered Ulster. Many of the summaries are printed in an abbreviated form of Latin, though it is usually possible to get the gist of what is being said. The Ulster Inquisitions is a valuable source as it can name many of the tenants on individual estates. The following example is from the estate of Sir William Hamilton of Manor Elieston in County Tyrone, and dates from 4 May 1631:

> Bryen Roe McConmoy houldeth the balliboe of land called Tireamaddan for the term of two years from Andrew Hayes who houldeth the same from said Sir William. Morrise O'Ternan houldeth the balliboe of Litterbrett and Dorgragh from the said Sir William 'till the feast of all saints next, and dooth, plough, pasture and grass upon the same. Shane Roe O'Devin houldeth the 1/2 balliboe of Nonihicannon ... from James Hamilton who houldeth the same from the said Sir William, and doe plough, pasture and grass the same 'till hallowtide next. Bryen McCrener and Rory O'Quyn hould the balliboe of Aghnacree from the said James Hamilton in manner aforesaid. Patrick Groome O'Devin hould the balliboe of Leath ... from Thomas Petticreive whoe houldeth the same from the said Sir William, and doe plough, pasture and grass the same. The said Patrick houldeth 1/2 the balliboe of Loughes, in manner as aforesaid. Owen Modder McConmoy houldeth the ballebo of Gorten from the said Sir William, and also the balliboe of Leanamoor, in manner as aforesaid.

4.7 Summonister rolls

Summonister rolls record, among other things, the names of people fined for non-attendance at quarter sessions (courts that dealt with less serious crimes – similar to today's civil courts). Other offences are also recorded. For example, Henry O'Finnoghan in County Londonderry was fined for plowing his land with horses fixed to the plow by their tails (T/808/15130). In the Tenison Groves collection of genealogical notes there are transcripts from several counties of the names in these rolls. Most date from the early seventeenth century. These provide the names and residences of hundreds of individuals. In date order they are as follows:

> Counties Cavan, Londonderry and Tyrone, 1610–24 – T/808/15131
> County Londonderry, 1611–69 – T/808/15130
> County Tyrone, 1615–38 – T/808/15090
> County Tyrone, *c.*1615–21 – T/808/15126
> County Tyrone, *c.*1618–38 – T/808/15120
> Counties Londonderry and Tyrone, *c.*1637–40 – T/808/15132
> Counties Londonderry and Tyrone, *c.*1640–70 – T/808/15133
> Counties Londonderry and Tyrone, 1656–62 – T/808/15134
> Counties Londonderry and Tyrone, 1623–38 – T/808/15135
> Counties not specified, *c.*1620–84 – T/808/15139

4.8 Muster rolls

A muster roll was a list of able-bodied men who were capable of military service. They were armed at their own expense. Several muster rolls survive for Ulster counties from the early seventeenth century (later muster rolls are noticed in Chapter 11). They are usually arranged by estate and consist in the main of a list of names with perhaps the weapon, if any, possessed.

County	Date	Source
Antrim	1618	D/1759/3B/5 (Mss copy extracts)
Antrim	1631	D/1759/3C/3
Armagh	1631	T/934/1
Cavan	1618	D/1759/3B/5 (Mss copy extracts)
Cavan	1631	T/934
Donegal	1618	D/1759/3B/5 (Mss copy extracts)
Donegal	1631	D/1759/3C/2
Down	1630	D/1759/3C/1
Fermanagh	1618	D/1759/3B/5 (Mss copy extracts)
Londonderry	1618	D/1759/3B/5 (Mss copy extracts)
Monaghan	1618	D/1759/3B/5 (Mss copy extracts)
Tyrone	1618	D/1759/3B/5 (Mss copy extracts)
Tyrone	1631	T/934

See also:

A list of the men and arms of Sir Thomas Phillips and Sir Robert MacClelan [McClelland],
  County Londonderry, 1611–16 – T/1080/1
Muster roll of Coleraine and Londonderry, 1622 – printed in *Londonderry and the London*
  Companies, edited by D. A. Chart (Belfast, 1928), pp. 52–4

The 1630 muster roll for Donegal was published in *Donegal Annual*, vol. 10 (1972),
pp. 124–49.

4.9 Depositions of 1641

The depositions are the collected accounts of witnesses to the atrocities that took place, or
were reputed to have taken place, during the rebellion that broke out in October 1641.
Eight Protestant clergymen, led by Henry Jones, Dean of Kilmore, were empowered to
take evidence during two commissions in December 1641 and January 1642. In 1652,
following Cromwell's subjugation of the country, a High Court of Justice was established
to collect evidence for the trials of those who had risen against the settlers. The depositions
are deposited in the library of Trinity College, Dublin. Most of the witnesses were English
settlers and their occupations ranged from 'gentleman' to 'tanner', 'tailor' and 'inn keeper'.
They named their attackers or those rumoured to have taken part in the rising, and the
depositions provide rare documentary evidence of the native Irish families who had once
dominated the country. Copies of the 1641 depositions are available at PRONI, reference
D/1923, T/2706/8 and MIC/8. Many transcribed depositions were published in M.
Hickson, *Ireland in the Seventeenth Century* (2 vols, London, 1884). An index to the 1641
rebels from County Monaghan recorded in the depositions appeared in *Clogher Record*, 15
(1995) and for County Fermanagh in *Clogher Record*, 19 (2004).

The following is a copy of a deposition relating to County Fermanagh (MIC/8/2):

Hugh Stokes of Tawnategorman in the parish of Clownesse [Clones], barony of Clankelly and
county of Fermanagh gent being duly sworn before us deposeth and saith that the 23th [sic]
day of October last he was robbed rightfully possessed of his goods and chattels and estate vizt

in cows, horses and other cattle to the value of 110 pounds, in corn in his hagard worth 20 pounds, in household stuff worth 20 pounds and seized of freehold land worth 70 pounds per annum, and that the day aforesaid Edmund Carragh Maguire, Ross McGilpatrick Maguire, Cormk Roe Maguire, Turlagh McHugh McArt Maguire, Patrick Magill Duff Maguire accompanied with divers other rebellious persons came unto and forceably entered into this deponent's mansion house and possessed themselves of the same, and of all his goods and chattels aforesaid disseised him of his said lands and that this deponent hardly escaped from them with his life and that they have ever since so forceably withheld the same.

And that they and others of the said rebels the same day murdered and killed divers of this deponent's neighbours and tennants as namely Thomas Sergeant, Thomas Aston, Thomas Seaton, Miles Acrigg, Sebastian Cottingham and divers others to the number of 30 persosn that were well known to the deponent. And he heard some of them say that they had a commission for their so doing.

Sworn 7th January 1641 before Henry Brereton and William Aldrich.

4.10   Records relating to the Cromwellian and Restoration land settlements

When order was restored in Ireland in the early 1650s following the turbulence of the previous decade, the Cromwellian regime began a process of land confiscation and redisitribution which continued during the reign of Charles II. Several categories of record relating to the confiscations survive which can be useful to researchers. These are outlined below.

4.10.1   Civil Survey, 1654–56

The Civil Survey was carried out under the Cromwellian administration in Ireland. It began in 1654 and continued until 1656. The information contained in the Civil Survey is set out in columns and includes for each denomination of land the name of the proprietor, the extent of profitable and unprofitable acres and the value of the lands in 1640. The proprietor was not always the outright owner of the land, as freeholders and leaseholders were also included under this column. The ethnic background and religion of the proprietor is usually given, and occasionally additional information about him. Will More, a freeholder in the parish of Clogher, was a 'horseman at the Seidge of Derry'. This was a siege that took place in 1649 when an army of Presbyterians, angry at the execution of Charles I, briefly encamped around Derry before dispersing.

Supplementary information is also provided, such as details of tenure and rents paid by individuals leasing the lands from the proprietors. In County Donegal several leases were issued by the bishop of Raphoe in 1636 which included the proviso that the tenant was to pay a specified sum of money – in one case £250 – towards the cost of building the bishop's castle. An edition of the Civil Survey for Counties Donegal, Londonderry and Tyrone was published by the Irish Manuscripts Commission in 1937 under the editorship of R. C. Simington. For each of the baronies in the three counties there is a personal name index, with an index to lands at the end of the volume.

4.10.2   Books of survey and distribution

The books of survey and distribution were compiled in the course of the Restoration land settlement of the 1660s and 1670s. They record the transfer of land ownership from forfeiting Irish landowners to new patentees who had been granted the confiscated lands by the crown. The information in the books is given in tabular form by county. The name of the landowner in 1641 is stated, together with a list of the lands in his possession, as well as their value and extent. The name of the new owner is also given. A set of the books of survey and distribution can be found in the Annesley collection in PRONI under D/1854/1 and MIC/532.

4.10.3 Land grants and other sources

Printed abstracts of the land grants made at this time may be found in the *Reports of the Commissioners Appointed ... Respecting the Public Records of Ireland*, 11th–15th Annual Reports (Dublin, 1825). Also included in this volume is an index to the certificates of the Court of Claims, indexes to Adventurers' and soldiers' certificates and an index to adjudications in favour of the 1649 officers. The Court of Claims was initially established in 1661 to hear and deliberate on claims presented by Catholics attempting to prove their innocence of any wrongdoing in the previous twenty years and have their lands restored to them. The Adventurers were individuals who, in the 1640s, subscribed money towards the war effort in Ireland in return for which they were promised grants of land. The 1649 officers (or '49 Officers) were settlers who had supported the royalist cause in Ireland, mainly between 1648 and 1650, and who, to compensate them for their sufferings, were to receive grants of land. The abstracts of the land grants in the aforementioned Reports were based on the Lodge Manuscripts in the National Archives of Ireland (available in PRONI under MIC/600). Guides to the manuscript material relating to the land settlements of this period may be found in the 55th and 56th *Reports of the Deputy Keeper of the Public Records in Ireland*. Of particular interest are the following:

'Alphabetical list of persons to whom certificates were granted by the Court of Claims' – NAI Ferguson Collection

'An alphabetical list or repertory of the decrees to Innocents' – NAI Ferguson Collection

'List of claims of innocents, to be heard by Act of Settlement Commissioners for trial of innocents', 1663 – Armagh Public Library

'A rentroll of the forfeited houses, lands and tenements assigned towards satisfaction of the arrears of the commissioned officers who served in Ireland before the 5th June 1649, set for one year determining the 25th of March 1662, reserved thereon' – Rawlinson Mss B.508, Bodleian Library, Oxford

4.11 Census of Ireland *c.*1659

The census of 1659 is not a census in the true sense of the word, as it contains only the names of individuals termed 'tituladoes' (mainly those with title to land) and the total number of English and Irish resident in each townland (Scots were usually counted with English). An edition of the census by Seamus Pender entitled, *A Census of Ireland circa 1659, with Supplementary Material from the Poll Money Ordinances*, was published in 1939 by the Stationery Office, Dublin, on behalf of the Irish Manuscripts Commission (recently reprinted). This includes a breakdown of the figures for each county and an index of both personal names and place names. The 'census' is available for every county in Ulster with the exceptions of Cavan and Tyrone.

4.12 Poll books, *c*.1662

Only a few parishes in Ulster have surviving poll books, all of them in County Tyrone. These date from the 1660s and list the names of those liable for the poll tax. The names are arranged by townland with the occupation of the taxpayer – usually farmer, servant or yeoman – noted and the amount payable. Poll tax was paid as follows: a gentleman 4 shillings, a yeoman or farmer 2 shillings, a servant or labourer 1 shilling, with the sum doubled if the individual was married. Some caution should be exercised, however, regarding these designations. Patrick Crossle, who transcribed the poll tax roll for Aghaloo parish, commented: 'Although parties are entered as labourers, this is not a true description of their social standing – it was done principally to evade the tax'.

Comparisons with subsidy rolls (see below) reveal that many people classed as labourers or yeoman in the poll books paid a higher subsidy tax on their goods than some who were styled 'gentleman' or 'esquire'. It also seems to have been the case that the grown-up children of yeomen and gentry were classified as servants so as to avoid paying the higher tax. For example, in Ardugboy (present-day Mountcastle) townland in the parish of Donagheady, Archibald Galbraith and wife were classified as gentry, while a Christian Galbraith was listed as a servant. In all likelihood, however, Archibald was Christian's father.

Parish	Source
Aghaloo	T/458/8
Donagheady	T/1365/1; J. Rutherford, *Donagheady Presbyterian Churches and Parish* (Belfast, 1953), pp. 106–9
Termonmaguirk	Earl of Belmore, *A History of Two Ulster Manors* (London and Dublin, 1903), pp. 305–9
Urney	T/1365/1; T/808/15089

4.13 Hearth money rolls, 1663–9

In the 1660s the government introduced a tax on hearths as a means of raising revenue. The returns, arranged by parish and usually with townland locations, list the names of all householders paying this tax; they survive for half the counties in Ireland, with coverage most complete in Ulster. The hearth money rolls cannot be taken as a complete record of every household in the areas covered. There seems to have been considerable evasion, while for many houses of a less permanent nature occupied by Irish families no hearth tax was paid. The original hearth money rolls were destroyed in Dublin in 1922, but copies, in many cases typescript versions, had been made of many of them prior to this. Most counties have more than one hearth money roll, but in some cases the hearth money roll is incomplete, with only a few parishes covered. Appendix 3 should be consulted to see whether or not a particular parish has a surviving hearth money roll. There is no hearth money roll for County Down.

County	Year	Source
Antrim	1666	T/3022/4/1; S. T. Carleton (ed.) *Heads and Hearths* (Belfast, 1991)
Antrim	1669	T/307/A; S. T. Carleton (ed.) *Heads and Hearths* (Belfast, 1991)
Armagh	1664	T/604
Armagh	1665	(incomplete) T/808/14950
Cavan	1664	(incomplete) T/808/15142, 15143 (Urney, Cavan borough, Annagelliff, Templeport, Killeshandra, Annagh, Kildallan); Breifne, vol. i, no. 3 (1960), pp. 247–62 (Killeshandra, Kildallan, Templeport, Tomregan, Killinagh); *Breifne*, vol. vii, no. 25 (1987), pp. 489–97 (Lurgan, Crosserlough, Castlerahan and Munterconnaught, Killinkere)
Donegal	?1663	T/808/15003
Donegal	1665	T/283D; T/307D
Fermanagh	1665, 1666	(incomplete) T/808/15042; *Clogher Record*, ii (1957), pp. 207–14
Londonderry	1663	T/307A
Monaghan	1663, 1665	T/808/15156; published in D. Rushe, *History of Monaghan* (Dundalk, 1921), pp. 291–338
Tyrone	1664	(incomplete) T/458/8, T/1365/3
Tyrone	1666	T/307A

Heads and Hearths, edited by S. T. Carleton (Belfast, 1991), provides a detailed analysis of the hearth money roll of County Antrim, matching 1669 townlands with those from the present day and identifying where two or more parishes have been listed under one heading. It also lists names from the 1666 hearth money roll of County Antrim not found in the 1669 roll. The volume is particularly useful when dealing with the barony of Toome, where parishes are not named. Unfortunately, the book was published without an index. There is, however, an index to the hearth money rolls of Antrim, Londonderry and Tyrone under T/307A.

4.14 Subsidy rolls, 1662–6
Subsidy rolls list the nobility, clergy and laity who paid a grant in aid to the crown. The surviving lists are made up of those of means in the community who were subject to the payment of subsidies, which then formed the government's main method of direct taxation. They include the amount paid and the status of the person. Because they include only the wealthier members of society, they are less useful than hearth money rolls.

County	Year	Source
Antrim	1666	T/808/14889
Cavan	1662	T/808/15142
Donegal	1662	T/808/14998

Donegal	1669	T/808/15003
Down	1663	T/307A
Fermanagh	1662	T/808/15068 (Enniskillen town only)
Londonderry	1662	D/4164/A/14; T/716/4, 15; T/1592/19
Tyrone	1664	T/283/D/1; T/808/15092
Tyrone	1668	T/808/15097

4.15 Excommunications in Derry diocese, 1667

In 1667 a significant number of people in Derry diocese were excommunicated by the Established Church, mostly for nonconformity. According to the order for their expulsion, nonconformity was defined as 'not only absence from church, but baptising by unlicensed ministers'. A number of individuals were excommunicated for refusing to contribute to the repair of the Church of Ireland church in their parish. Another excommunicant, John Boyd of Ardstraw, was further charged with ploughing on Christmas Day and condemning the ecclesiastical government. The parishes in question were Ardstraw, Balteagh, Bodoney, Cappagh, Clondermott, Clonleigh, Cumber, Donagheady, Donaghmore, Drumachose, Dungiven, Faughanvale, Tamlaght Finlagan and Termoneeny. The names of those excommunicated were transcribed by Canon J. B. Leslie and can be found in PRONI under T/552.

4.16 Franciscan petition lists, Armagh diocese, 1670–71

These lists relate to a dispute between the Franciscans and Dominicans beginning in the 1640s over the rights to such things as the collections of alms or donations. Most of the clergy and laity in Ulster sided with the Franciscans. The following is an extract of the petition for the parish of Creggan, County Armagh:

> Here followeth the names of the parishioners of parish of Creggan, by their one consent and humble request drawn, against certaine Dominicans pretending to intrude unjustly upon them, and severall others, commonly begging at their alters to their same and unhability etc. being unable (God help them) to maintaine their one clergy booth secular and regular, as their predecessors did, which is enough for them, I pray God they may do it.

The complete lists for the diocese of Armagh were published by P. J. Campbell in *Seanchas Ardmhacha*, vol. 15, no. 1 (1992). The parishes from which petitions emanated were as follows.

> County Armagh: Armagh, Creggan, Derrynoose, Drumbruchuis (thought to have been part of Keady), Kilclooney, Killevy, Kilmore, Loughgall, Loughgilly, Mullaghbrack, Tanathly (Ballymore), Tynan
> County Tyrone: Aghaloo, Errigal Keerogue, Termonmaguirk

4.17 Names of those attainted by James II, 1689

In 1689 an 'Act for the Attainder of Divers Rebels, and for Preserving the Interest of Loyal Subjects' was passed in the Irish parliament. It listed the names of Irish Protestants considered by the government of James II to be disloyal to the king. Most of those listed were members of the landed gentry or freeholders. The names of those attainted (i.e. found guilty of treason) were published in *The State of the Protestants of Ireland under the late King James's Government* by William King (Dublin, 1713). A photocopy of the relevant pages from this book is available on the open shelves of the Public Search Room at PRONI. A list of those attainted in County Monaghan appears in Denis Carolan Rushe, *History of Monaghan for Two Hundred Years, 1660–1860* (Dundalk, 1921), while the names of those attainted in County Armagh can be found under T/808/14985.

4.18 Records relating to the siege of Derry, 1689
For information on those who were involved in the siege of Derry in 1689 and events during the Williamite War in general, the best single source is W. R. Young, *Fighters of Derry, Their Deeds and Descendents, Being a Chronicle of Events in Ireland during the Revolutionary Period, 1688–91* (London, 1932). This lists the names of some 1,660 individuals who defended Derry or were associated with William of Orange; for many of them brief biographical sketches are provided. This book provides a real insight into settler society, particularly in north-west Ulster, in the late seventeenth century. Young has also compiled a list of 352 Jacobites, again with biographical sketches for many of them.

4.19 Collectors' accounts
Several collectors' accounts may be found among the papers in the Groves collection of manuscripts in PRONI. These date from 1689 to 1692 and are mainly concerned with the collection of excise duties.

Collectors [?] accounts for Coleraine, naming individuals and amounts paid, 1689–91 – T/456/1

Collectors' accounts naming person who owed arrears, Lisburn, Glenavy, Hillsborough, Antrim and Ballymena Walks, 1690, over 500 names arranged by place – T/808/14903

Collectors' accounts naming persons owing arrears for Lisburn Walk, 1691, over 400 names arranged by place – T/808/14904 (T/808/14902 is an alphabetical list of the names in this source)

Collectors' accounts, County Londonderry, 1692 – T/808/15137

4.20 Records relating to the Williamite land settlement, 1691–1703
Following the end of the Williamite War in 1691, there was a major redistribution of land in Ireland. Lands that had been confiscated from Jacobites were vested with the Trustees for the Sale of the Forfeited Estates. Sir Francis Annesley was one of the Trustees and played a major role in the deliberations over the sales. A large collection of depositions, minute books, accounts, etc., relating to the work of the Trustees has survived among the Annesley estate archive in PRONI under reference D/1854. For more on the background to these documents see www.proni.gov.uk/records/private/annesley.htm. The information in this collection is less extensive for Ulster than for other provinces in Ireland. This was due to the fact that in Ulster most of the land had already passed to British landlords by the 1680s as a result of the Plantation scheme of the early seventeenth century and the Cromwellian and Restoration land settlements of the 1650s–70s.

Of particular interest is a volume entitled *Printed rentals and particulars of sale of forfeited lands exposed for sale in Dublin with manuscript additions detailing the sales by cant giving purchasers names, addresses, date of sale, purchase price, method of sale etc.* (D/1854/2/29a). Most of the sales took place in 1703 and we can assume that the rentals must have been drawn up shortly before this. The volume includes a rental of the manor of Strabane owned by the earl of Abercorn (the Catholic 4th earl had been a prominent supporter of James II). Names of tenants from a number of smaller estates owned by Jacobites are also given. The following extracts provide examples of the type of information listed.

Loghtee barony, County Cavan

Denomination	Late proprietor	Tenant	Description
One tenement in the east side of Cavan	Bryan McCabe	Rob Johnson	This house stands in the market-place in the Town of Cavan, built of timber, and in good repair, the back part being newly built, containing 30 foot in front, backward 420 foot, and 60 foot broad in the garden.

Kinelarty barony, County Down

Denomination	Late proprietor	Tenant	Description
Ballymaglane Itragh with a tuckmill	John O'Hara	William Scott	In the parish of Magredrill [Magheradrool], distant from the parish church one mile, Downe and Hillsborough each 8 miles, Belfast 15. On it 5 farm-houses, with barns, stable and a small orchard; the land is arable, meadow and course shrubby pasture.

There are numerous handwritten annotations providing the name of the purchaser of the property and the amount of money paid for it. The parishes in the province of Ulster affected are as follows.

County Antrim: Ballintoy, Ballymoney, Ballyrashane, Derrykeighan, Dummaul, Killead, Layd, Loughguile, Racavan
County Armagh: Creggan, Killevy, Loughgilly, Tynan
County Cavan: Enniskeen, Urney

County Donegal: All Saints
County Down: Ardglass, Ballyphilip, Bright, Magheradrool, Newry
County Londonderry: Ballinderry
County Monaghan: Muckno
County Tyrone: Ardstraw, Camus-juxta-Mourne, Urney

It should be acknowledged that, with a few exceptions, the number of townlands in each parish affected was fairly small; the number of names of tenants will vary.

Another volume of interest is *A list of the claims as they are entered with the Trustees: at Chichester House on College Green, Dublin, on or before the tenth of August, 1700* (Dublin, printed by Joseph Ray and are to be sold by Patrick Campbell bookseller in Skinner-Row, 1701). The *List of the claims* runs to 355 pages and provides details on the names of the claimants, what they were claiming for, its value and where it was located as well as the name of the forfeiting proprietor. The book was apparently never made available to the public because of the alarm expressed by the claimants over its contents. The government was forced to destroy the entire impression with the exception of copies already given to the Trustees. Only a few copies survive; they can be found at such places as Queen's University Library, Belfast, the National Library of Ireland and the National Archives of Ireland. See also a detailed list of lands forfeited by supporters of James II in County Antrim, 1690s (D/207/15/30). Abstracts of the land grants made in this period may be found in the *Reports of the commissioners appointed ... respecting the public records of Ireland*, 11th–15th Annual Reports (Dublin, 1825).

5. Eighteenth-century records

5.1 Records of the Irish parliament

The *Journals of the House of Commons of the Kingdom of Ireland, 1613–1800* were published in 41 volumes between 1763 and 1900. The *Journals of the House of Lords, 1634–1800* were published in eight volumes between 1779 and 1800. A wide variety of information is included in these volumes, ranging from petitions from individuals or bodies to information on law and order, road-building projects and industrial ventures. The appendices to volume 7 include the names of individuals transported from Ireland between 1735 and 1743 for various crimes ranging from being a felon or vagabond to forgery and sheep-stealing. This information, including names from every county in Ulster, was published as Frances McDonnell, *Emigrants from Ireland to America, 1735–43. A Transcription of the Report of the Irish House of Commons into Enforced Emigration to America* (Genealogical Publishing, 1992). The appendices to volume 17 of the House of Commons journal, published in 1798, include schedules of prisoners brought to trial in each of the Ulster counties in 1797–8, as well as lists of prisoners still in gaol. This is followed by a list of JPs appointed since 1 June 1789 and a list of JPs superseded (i.e. dismissed or retired) in the same period. Unfortunately the indexes to these volumes are not sufficiently comprehensive to allow a search for a specific name.

5.2 'A view of the archbishopric of Armagh', 1703

Although this source properly belongs with the Armagh Church of Ireland diocesan archive, the original is closed on grounds of preservation, and instead a photostat version is available for consultation (T/848). The 'View' is a survey of the extensive lands owned by the archbishop of Armagh at the beginning of the eighteenth century. These lands were mainly to be found in Counties Armagh, Londonderry, Louth and Tyrone, with smaller portions in Down and Meath. The name of the tenant is given together with the names of his subtenants. Information is provided on the extent of the holdings and the buildings then standing.

5.3 Convert rolls, 1703–1838

The Convert Rolls list those converting from Roman Catholicism to Protestantism (limited to the Church of Ireland). Following the 'Act to prevent the further growth of popery' of 1703, a Catholic converting to the Church of Ireland had to provide proof of conformity. By conforming to the Established Church a Catholic was freed from the legal disabilities affecting property rights and membership of certain professions etc., in force under the Penal Laws. By 1800 over 5,000 enrolments had taken place, most of them in the period 1760–90. The original rolls were destroyed in Dublin in 1922, but not before they had been calendared and recorded. The Convert Rolls were published by the Irish Manuscripts Commission in 1981 under the editorship of Eileen O'Byrne. The information provided is fairly limited. In addition to the name and address of the convert and the dates of conformity and enrolment, the status or occupation of the individual is occasionally given.

5.4 Lists of the nobility and gentry in each county, c.1731

Lists of those 'generally esteemed' to be worth more than £100 per annum were compiled for each county c.1731. These lists show that the denominational bias was overwhelmingly in favour of the Church of Ireland, followed some distance behind by Presbyterians, with Catholics coming in third. Over 500 individuals are named in the lists, usually without indicating where they lived. The breakdown by county is as follows:

County	Church of Ireland	Presbyterian	Roman Catholic
Antrim	36	8	1
Armagh	54	3	0
Cavan	63	2	4
Donegal	64	1	1
Down	79	10	1
Fermanagh	44	3	1
Londonderry	34	1	0
Monaghan	67	4	0
Tyrone	49	9	0
Total	490	41	8

5.5 The 'census of Protestant householders', 1740

What has generally been termed a 'census of Protestant householders' was compiled in 1740. The returns were made by the collectors of the hearth money and it is likely that the names were taken from this list. Furthermore, for the barony of Loughinsholin in County Londonderry, it seems that both Protestants and Catholics were included. The 'census' is no more than a list of names arranged by county, barony and parish and, reflecting its supervision by the inspector responsible for collecting hearth money, it is occasionally divided into 'walks'. The original records of this survey were destroyed in Dublin in 1922 but copies survive for part of the survey in transcripts prepared by the genealogist, Tenison Groves. Copies are held by PRONI (T/808/15258) and the National Library of Ireland (Ms 4173). A bound typescript copy is available on the open shelves of the Public Search Room at PRONI.

The parishes or areas covered in each county are as follows.

County Antrim – Ahoghill, Armoy, Ballintoy, Ballymoney, Ballywillin, Billy, Culfeightrin, Derrykeighan, Drummaul, Duneane, Dunluce, Finvoy, Kilraghts, Kirkinriola, Loughguile, Ramoan, Rasharkin and Rathlin
County Armagh – Creggan, Derrynoose, Loughgall, Mullaghbrack, Shankill and Tynan
County Donegal – Clonmany, Culdaff, Desertegny, Donagh, Fahan, Moville and Templemore
County Down – Kilbroney, Seapatrick and Loughbrickland Walk
County Londonderry – all parishes
County Tyrone – Derryloran and Kildress

5.6 The religious census of 1766

In March and April 1766, Church of Ireland rectors were instructed by the government to compile complete returns of all householders in their respective parishes, showing their religion: Church of Ireland (Episcopalian), Roman Catholic (termed 'Papists' in the returns) and Presbyterians (or Dissenters), and giving an account of any Roman Catholic clergy active in their area. Some of the more diligent rectors listed every townland and every household, but many drew up only numerical totals of the population. All the original returns were destroyed in the Public Record Office in 1922, but extensive transcripts, again made by Tenison Groves, survive. Three bound volumes of these returns can be found on the shelves of the Public Search Room at PRONI. The parishes in Ulster covered in these volumes are as follows.

County Antrim – Ballymoney
County Armagh – Creggan
County Cavan – Kinawley (partly in Fermanagh), Lurgan and Muntercconnaught
County Down – Kilbroney, Seapatrick
County Donegal – Inch, Leck
County Fermanagh – Derryvullan, Devenish, Kinawley (partly in Cavan), Rossorry
County Londonderry – Artrea, Ballynascreen, Bovevagh, Cumber, Desertlynn, Desertmartin, Drumachose, Magherafelt
County Tyrone – Aghaloo, Artrea, Carnteel, Clonfeacle, Derryloran, Donaghenry, Drumglass, Kildress and Tullyniskan

Copies of the 1766 Householders List can also be found at the Linen Hall Library, Armagh Museum, RCB (Ms 23); National Archives of Ireland (M 207/8; M 2476); and the National Library of Ireland (Ms 4173). Some originals and transcripts are available at the Genealogical Office (GO 537). In many cases these are the same as the returns in PRONI, though there are a few extra. Additional returns are as follows.

County Antrim – Ahoghill (NAI M 2476), Ballintoy (NLI Ms 4173)
County Donegal – Donaghmore (NAI M 207/8), Raphoe (NAI M 2476)

5.7 Hearts of Steel memorials, 1771–2

The Hearts of Steel was a Protestant movement of agrarian protest that originated on the Donegall estate in County Antrim over the general reletting of the farms in 1770. The movement spread to other parts of Ulster over the following two years, with the protests concentrating on rent levels, evictions and local taxation. Frequently these protests were violent and included the burning of houses and the maiming of cattle. In response to the outrages, the inhabitants of a large number of towns and parishes as well as a few townlands drew up memorials declaring their abhorrence of the activities of the Hearts of Steel. Many of these memorials, usually accompanied by a list of names, were published in the *Belfast Newsletter*. The following is an extract from the memorial drawn up by the inhabitants of Magherafelt, County Londonderry:

> We, the inhabitants of the town of Magherafelt, sensible of the danger of that spirit of riot and outrage which has so amazingly spread itself in this neighbourhood, and desiring to contribute all that in us lies to the preservation of order and the authority of the laws, do agree to each other not only to shun all such combinations and lawless practices ourselves, but also to take care that all under our influence shall also abstain from them.

The names from some twenty memorials were published in the *Belfast Newsletter* in 1771 and 1772. Many more memorials were submitted to the editor of this newspaper, but unfortunately these were printed without the list of names. The areas for which the names of signatories are available, together with the edition of the *Belfast Newsletter*, are as follows.

County Antrim
Ahoghill – 14 April 1772
Ballyeaston [Ballycor parish] – 11 October 1771
Ballymoney – 7 April 1772
Ballynure – 25 October 1771
Dunaghy – 17 March 1772
Island Magee Presbyterian congregation [Island Magee parish] – 21 April 1772
Lisburn [Blaris parish] – 24 March 1772
Killead – 10 April 1772
Larne [probably including Inver], Kilwaughter and Raloo – 7 April 1772
Magheragall (the tenants of James Watson of Brookhill) – 22 May 1772

County Armagh
Lurgan [Shankill parish] – 11 December 1772

County Down
Ballyhalbert – 10 April 1770
Ballykeel in Dromore parish – 27 March 1772
Ballynahinch [Magheradrool parish] – 31 March 1772
Cluntagh in Annahilt parish – 3 April 1772
Drumlough in Dromore parish – 31 March 1772
Killinchy – 31 July 1772
Moneyrea Presbyterian congregation [Comber parish] – 3 April 1772
Saintfield – 25 August 1772

County Londonderry
Magherafelt – 17 March 1772
Tamlaght O'Crilly – 14 April 1772

5.8 Petitions of Protestant Dissenters, 1775

The petitions of Protestant Dissenters are lists of names of Dissenters (or Presbyterians) on either a parish or a congregational basis that were submitted to the government in October and November 1775 in response to proposed discriminatory legislation. Only names are given, not locations. Transcript copies are located on the shelves of PRONI and under reference T/808/15307. The congregations and parishes for which there are petitions with names are set out below.

> County Antrim – Antrim Borough; Old Antrim; Ballyclare town and neighbourhood; Ballymena town and neighbourhood; Belfast parish and town; Carnmoney parish; Carrickfergus town and county; Donagore, Kilbride and Nilteen; Dunmurry congregation in Drumbeg parish; Larne, Raloo, Carncastle, Kilwaughter, Glenarm & Ballyeaston; Lisburn town and neighbourhood
> County Armagh – Armagh parish; Clare congregation in Ballymore parish
> County Down – Ballee congregation; Comber parish; Dundonald parish; Dromore parish; Drumara parish; Drumballyroney and Drumgoolan parishes; Drumgooland; Killileagh parish
> County Londonderry – Coleraine and Killowen parishes; Londonderry City
> County Tyrone – Benburb town and neighbourhood; Coagh; Cookstown congregation; Dungannon barony; Dungannon town and neighbourhood; Strabane town and neighbourhood

5.9 Catholics migrating from Ulster in 1795–6

Due to considerable unrest in Ulster, and in particular in north County Armagh, in the 1790s many Catholic families left Ulster. Many of them ended up in County Mayo. The background to this episode, together with a list of names, may be found in Patrick Tohall, 'The Diamond fight of 1795 and the resultant expulsions' in *Seanchas Ardmhacha*, vol. 3 no. 1 (1958), pp. 17–50. The information provided includes the name of the individual (or householder) concerned and the parish, and in many cases the townland, from which they originated. The counties covered are Antrim, Armagh, Down, Londonderry, Monaghan and Tyrone. See also 'Petition of Armagh migrants in the Westport area' in *Cathair na Mart*, vol. 2, no. 1 (1982).

5.10 The flaxseed premiums of 1796

In 1796, as part of a government initiative to encourage the linen industry in Ireland, free spinning wheels or looms were granted to farmers who planted a certain acreage of their holdings with flax. The names of over 56,000 recipients of these awards have survived in printed form, arranged by county and parish. Nearly two-thirds of the names relate to Ulster. The only copy of the book listing the names of these recipients known to exist until recently was held in the Linen Hall Library, Belfast. Another copy has now been acquired by the Irish Linen Centre in Lisburn Museum. The Ulster Historical Foundation has indexed this source and it is available as a searchable database on the UHF website (www.ancestryireland.com). A copy is available on the shelves of the Public Search Room at PRONI, and a microfiche copy of the printed volume with an index is available at PRONI (MF/7/1). The number of names by county is as follows.

County	Names
Antrim	1,185
Armagh	3,161
Cavan	2,467
Donegal	7,455
Down	3,028
Fermanagh	2,345
Londonderry	5,144
Monaghan	4,555
Tyrone	7,049
Total	*36,389*

It is clear that there was considerable variation between counties as to the number of premiums claimed. Donegal and Tyrone head the list with over 7,000 claimants each, but the large and populous county of Antrim lags some distance behind.

5.11 Records relating to the 1798 rebellion

The most important source of information on the United Irishmen and the 1798 Rebellion is the 'Rebellion Papers' in the National Archives in Dublin. Search aids are available in the National Archives. For an online survey of the 'Rebellion Papers', see www.nationalarchives.ie/topics/rebellion/rebpapers.htm. In PRONI there are also numerous items that can be consulted. These include the 'Black Book of the Rebellion of the North of Ireland' (D/272/1), which contains the names of some 200 individuals who were members or suspected to be members of the United Irishmen and some details of their appearance and activities. For example, James Maxwell of Monaghan was described as 'about 40 years of age, brown hair, but not very short & was once a prisoner in the Artillery Barracks'. There are also lists from 1798–9 of persons confined by order of the government in Belfast, Carrickfergus and the prison ship, *Postlethwaite*, and affidavits of United Irishmen (D/272). See also a notebook containing notes on the 1798 rebellion (D/3300/5/1).

In the National Library of Ireland there are returns of those who suffered losses in the rebellion in Counties Antrim and Down (NLI JLB 94107). These provide names, addresses and occupations of *c.*140 individuals from County Antrim and *c.*180 individuals from County Down. See also *List of persons who have suffered losses in their property in the county of Down, and who have given in their claims on or before the 6th of April, 1799, to the Commissioners for enquiring into the losses sustained by such of his Majesty's loyal subjects as have suffered in their property by the rebellion* (Dublin, 1799).

Numerous books and articles have been written about the 1798 rebellion. Two excellent publications of recent years are A. T. Q. Stewart, *Summer Soldiers: The 1798 Rebellion in Antrim and Down* (Belfast, 1995) and Harry Allen, *Men of the Ards* (Ballyhay Books, 2004). The bibliographies of these books should be consulted for additional published and unpublished material.

5.12 Petitions relating to the Act of Union, 1799–1800

The Act of Union was passed in 1800 and came into force on 1 January 1801. The Irish parliament was abolished and henceforth Irish MPs represented their constituents at Westminster. During the debates associated with this, petitions both for and against the Act of Union were drawn up across Ireland. Some of these petitions were county-based, while others were from parishes or manors. Several were published in the *Belfast Newsletter* in 1799–1800, as follows.

County Antrim – 27 December 1799
County Armagh – 14 January 1800
County Donegal – 27, 31 December 1799 and 3, 7, 17 January 1800
County Londonderry – 27 September 1799
County Tyrone – 3, 6, 13 December 1799
City of Londonderry – 24 September 1799
Borough of Antrim – 11 October 1799
Manors of Richhill and Mullalelish, County Armagh – 20 December 1799
Roman Catholic inhabitants of Lower Creggan, County Armagh – 17 January 1800
Parish of St Andrews (Ballyhalbert), County Down – 31 January 1800
Parish of Bangor, County Down – 28, 31 January 1800
Landholders and inhabitants in and about Tandragee, County Armagh – 11 February 1800

5.13 The agricultural census of 1803

Although, as the date suggests, this source post-dates the period covered by this book, its importance and scope means that it cannot be overlooked. The threat of an invasion of Great Britain and Ireland by Napoleonic France recurred periodically during the late 1790s and the early years of the nineteenth century. The government in London made plans in 1797 and 1798 to abandon coastal areas and introduced new legislation for the defence of the realm. This legislation required the lord lieutenant for each county to make returns, especially from maritime parishes, enumerating livestock (farm animals) and the wagons and horses available for transport, and giving the quantity of dead stock (crops stored). There are extant returns for some southern counties in England. During a scare in 1803 about an invasion of Ireland, resulting from the planned but abortive insurrection of that year, similar returns were made under the same legislation, which, after the Act of Union, applied to Ireland. The surviving returns relate to many parishes in County Down and the northern parishes of County Antrim.

The returns for County Down were made to the 1st marquess of Londonderry. Presumably he received returns for each parish, although it is clear from those that have survived that there was considerable variation in their content. Most information is listed in various categories of livestock and dead stock, but in some returns the information also includes numbers of 'cars and carts', of people 'able to drive cattle and load carts' or those 'willing to serve the Government gratuitously or for hire', which underline the concern about a possible invasion. The returns for the agricultural census of 1803 are included in the Londonderry Papers of the 1st marquess, held in PRONI. The PRONI reference for the census returns is D/654/A2/1–37A–C. A detailed analysis of the returns for County Down is provided by Duncan Scarlett in *Researching Down Ancestors*, published by the Ulster Historical Foundation in 2004. The surviving returns for County Antrim are available as a database on the Ulster Historical Foundation's website (www.ancestryireland.com).

6. Landed estate records

The documents generated by the management of landed estates are among the most valuable records for the local and family historian. Until the late nineteenth and early twentieth centuries Ulster was a province of landed estates. These estates ranged in size from over 100,000 acres to under 1,000. There were thus considerable variations in the wealth and lifestyles of landowners, and to regard them as forming a homogeneous group would be wrong. The largest landowners were usually titled and often owned estates in other parts of Ireland and in Britain. Their homes were generally built on a grand scale and were set within extensive demesnes. They exerted considerable control over representative politics in their respective counties. The smaller landowners lived more modestly and in many cases were on the same level as many of the more substantial tenant farmers. One thing that most landowners shared in the eighteenth century was membership of the Church of Ireland. Only a small number of landowners were Presbyterians, and even fewer were Roman Catholics (see Chapter 5.4 above).

6.1 Locating estate papers

The best collection of Irish estate papers is housed in PRONI. This comprises not only collections of estate papers for Northern Ireland, but also many for the Republic of Ireland, notably for County Monaghan. What makes the records in PRONI stand out is the fact that most of them have been expertly catalogued so that it is relatively easy to discover whether the records for a particular estate are available. A two-volume *Guide to Landed Estate Papers* is available for consultation in the Public Search Room. It is arranged by county, with the estate collections listed alphabetically according to the name of the landowning family. A brief synopsis of what is available is provided for each estate collection along with references.

Because of the way in which the records have been calendared it is usually possible for the researcher to identify reasonably quickly the records of potential value. For many of the larger collections, detailed introductions have been prepared. Most of these introductions, which are now available to read on the PRONI website, were written by Dr A. P. W. Malcomson and describe the history of the landowning family concerned as well as the way in which the collection has been organised (www.proni.gov.uk).

6.2 Identifying the relevant estate

Before delving into estate papers, it is first of all necessary to establish which estate, if any, your ancestor lived in. If searching in the nineteenth century, the easiest way to identify the name of a landowner is to examine Griffith's Valuation of *c.*1860 for the relevant townland and note the name of the immediate lessor. For the researcher working on the eighteenth century there are clearly limitations in the usefulness of this. Although the landowning family in 1860 was often the same as in 1760, and occasionally in 1660, in many cases it will not be. Sometimes this will not be a problem, as the records of successive owners will be found in the one collection in PRONI. One possible solution is to examine the books of survey and distribution of the later seventeenth century (see Chapter 4.10.2 above for more information on these). Another would be to consult the Quit Rent Rolls. These record the names of those who paid quit rent to the Crown on the basis that they owned their lands outright.

Even after trying all these possibilities, it may be impossible to identify the appropriate estate collection. It must also be acknowledged that the records of many estates are not available for inspection in PRONI. Some were destroyed in the disturbances of the early 1920s; others were lost in the more recent troubles, such as the papers relating to the Stronge estate in County Armagh. Still others were burnt by their owners, who felt that they had no more use for them or wanted to clear some space. A few collections, some of which are fairly extensive, remain in private custody. The records of the smaller estates, those in and around the 1,000–3,000 acre range, are especially poorly represented in PRONI.

6.3 The range of records

Some categories of estate papers are more useful to genealogists than others. Title deeds are concerned with the legal ownership of an estate, and are generally of limited value to genealogists. The same can be said of mortgages. Wills and marriage settlements usually refer only to the members of the landowner's family. However, rentals, leases, lease books, maps and correspondence can all be extremely useful to those searching for their ancestors within landed estate records. When examining the contents of a particular estate archive in the appropriate calendar displayed on the shelves of the Public Search Room, it is worth looking for lists of tenants that may have been compiled for various reasons by the local landlord. For example, among the records of the Londonderry estate is a copy of a rent roll for the Comber estate for the year 1684, which is also available in typescript form in the calendar.

6.3.1 *Rentals*

Rentals, rent rolls or rent books record rent payments made by a tenant to his landlord. They are generally arranged by year (rents were usually paid half-yearly) or with several years covered by the same volume. The information provided will usually be limited to the name of the tenant, the extent and location of his holding and the rent payable by him. Occasionally rentals are annotated and may contain additional details such as a change in occupancy and the reason for it.

6.3.2 *Leases*

A lease granted by a landlord to a tenant gave him the right to occupy the property for a specific period of time. Two copies of the lease were usually prepared; the original lease was signed by the landlord and kept by the tenant. The counterpart was signed by the tenant and kept by the landlord. A lease was usually for a term of years, 21 or 31 being quite common, but leases for three lives were in fairly widespread use. A three-life lease expired when all the three persons named in the lease died.

Three-life leases are very useful for genealogists because a tenant often named members of his family as the lives. Frequently young relatives were named as the lives in the hope that at least one of them would survive for many years. Depending on the terms on which the lease was issued, a three-life lease could be renewed at the fall of each life by inserting a new name on payment of a renewal fine. The renewable three-life lease was therefore in reality a grant in perpetuity so long as the tenant wished to renew it. When new lives were inserted details of age and relationship were often included, and it is possible to work out when the old life died. Tenants often sub-let the property, or part of it, to a third party; this was known as a sub-lease. The third party became an undertenant, paying rent to the tenant, who continued to pay rent to the landlord. For some information on the workings of this system see 'The lives lease system and emigration from Ulster: an example from Montgomery County, Pennsylvania' by Peter Roebuck, *Directory of Irish Family History Research* 18 (1995), pp. 75–7.

The following extracts are taken from a lease for a farm in County Tyrone (D/476/21):

> This indenture made the twenty-first day of November in the year of Our Lord, one thousand seven hundred and eighty three between the Right Honourable Thomas, Lord Baron Welles of Dungannon, in the County of Tyrone, of the one part, and Joseph Dickson of Mullaghbawn in the Parish of Donaghmore in the County of Tyrone aforesaid of the other part.
>
> Witnesseth that the said Thomas, Lord Baron Welles, for and in consideration of the yearly rents and covenants hereinafter reserved and expressed, hath demised, granted, set and to farm let unto the said Joseph Dickson all that part and parcel of land in the townland of Dristernan formerly in the possession of James McGinnis and partners and now in the actual possession of the said Joseph Dickson containing by Henry Long's survey thirty-six acres English Statute measure appertaining, situate, lying and being in the townland of Dristernan, parish of Donaghmore, barony of Dungannon, and county aforesaid.
>
> To have and to hold all and singular the said demised premises with the rights, members and appurtenances unto the said Joseph Dickson his heirs, executors, administrators and assigns, for and during the natural life and lives of the three following persons, and the survivors and survivor of them and each of them, to wit, the life of the said Joseph Dickson, part to these presents, Samuel Dickson, now aged about six years, and Mathew Dickson, now aged about two years, both sons of the said Joseph Dickson, commencing from the first day of November, one thousand seven hundred and eighty three from thenceforth fully should be complete and ended.
>
> Rent of 13 shillings per acre every year. Additional covenants concerning payment of duties, non-payment of rent, covenant by tenant to build a house, tenant to make enclosures, tenant bound to grind at the landlord's mill, tenant to plant an orchard, landlord's promise to tenant of quiet enjoyment of the premises.

6.3.3 Lease books

Lease books can be among the most useful of estate papers as far as genealogy is concerned. They record in condensed form the same sort of information contained in the original leases, such as the name of the lessee, the location and extent of the holding and the rent payable on it. Generally covering an entire estate, they can be a much quicker way of finding information on a tenant farmer than searching through several bundles of leases.

6.3.4 Maps

Maps form an important element in most estate collections. These show the property of the landlord, who employed a surveyor to illustrate the extent of his land and the more important features on his estate. Maps come in all shapes and sizes, and can be coloured or roughly etched in black and white. The earliest surviving detailed estates maps for Ulster are those prepared by Thomas Raven of the lands of the London companies in County Londonderry in 1622. These provide the names of the householders in the settlements founded by the companies. For example, the named householders in the village of Bellaghy founded by the Vintners' Company in the parish of Ballyscullion were:

> Sir Baptist Jones; William Deard; Robert Stevenson; Tho. Jone; Thomas Lewin; Ellis Okes; Thomas Sparry; Eustace Bell; Robert Kinge; William Coxe; Thomas West; Thomas Hutchin; and Henry Prettie.

These maps and the names of householders were published in *Londonderry and the London Companies*, edited by D. A. Chart (Belfast, 1928). Coloured replica drawings of the originals are in PRONI (T/510). In 1625 Raven prepared detailed maps of the Hamilton estate in County Down. Copies of these are available in PRONI (T/870).

Early estate maps were often pictorial and included representations in relief of houses and other landscape features. Later, as surveying methods became more precise, such features usually disappeared from maps. For genealogical purposes, maps that name tenants and pinpoint the location of their farms are the most useful. The value of such maps lies in the fact that they enable a researcher to identify the location of the farm in which an ancestor lived perhaps 100 years before Griffith's Valuation. Occasionally estate maps have an accompanying 'terrier' that includes detailed information about each farm.

6.3.5 Surveys and valuations

A landlord keen to improve his estate to maximise his income from it would periodically carry out a survey or a valuation of it. Often these surveys contain little of genealogical interest, as they concentrate on land quality and use. For example, William Starrat of Strabane worked extensively as a surveyor in west Ulster in the first half of the eighteenth century, but there is little in his surveys of value to the family historian. Nonetheless, while not containing the sort of information that will allow the family tree to be constructed, such surveys can provide a glimpse into the world of our forebears.

Other surveys and valuations do, however, contain much of interest to the genealogist. The following extract is from a valuation of the Ironmongers' estate in County Londonderry by John Hood in 1765, and relates to the townland of Ballinuntagh:

James Collins an aged and infirm man whose ancestors has [sic] held a considerable deal of land in the proportion since the first settlement of Protestants in Ireland implores the compassion of the Governor and Company as he is unable to pay more rent than he at present pays (MIC/145/8).

6.3.6 Correspondence

The correspondence between a landlord and his agent can be of immense genealogical value. Not only does it include details of the day-to-day running of the estate, but mention is often made of those who worked on the estate.

The most serious drawback to using estate correspondence is the fact that it will almost certainly not be indexed. Furthermore, much of it lies unsorted in boxes. The best collection of eighteenth-century estate correspondence relates to the Abercorn estate in west Tyrone and east Donegal. Typescript copies of the great majority of the letters are available for inspection in calendar form in the Public Search Room of PRONI. Most of the letters were written by the 8th earl of Abercorn and his estate agents, John McClintock, Nathaniel Nisbett, John Colhoun, John Sinclair, John Hamilton and James Hamilton. The 8th earl was an absentee landlord who lived most of his life in London and only rarely visited his Irish estates. However, few absentee landlords can have known so much about their estates as the 8th earl knew about his. The letters cover a broad range of subjects and relate to all aspects of the estates' management. The lives of the tenants are recorded in the minutest detail, as the following excerpt from a letter of November 1767 from John Hamilton to the 8th earl shows.

Patrick Biglay, late of Brownhill [Leckpatrick parish], had three sons, Patrick, Thomas and George. Patrick, who was the eldest got the half of his father's land several years ago. Thomas was taught the weaver trade and maintained in his father's house, notwithstanding would not leave his father or give up his claim to the land till George, who laboured the land and supported his aged father, was obliged to pay him five guineas upon which his father gave an article of the land to George, reserving some little part to himself. Patrick the father was a papist and his wife being a Protestant, all the sons went to church with the mother. Thomas never satisfied that George should get the land. To ingratiate himself into his father's favour returned to Mass, and the father upon that takes him again into his house and dispossess [sic] George. The father on his death bed made a will and left it to be divided equally between them. Now as Thomas has a trade and in good circumstances and George quite destitute, who made a fair bargain with the father, I think ... that George has the best right (D/623/A/37/105).

The following letters relate to the Erne estate in County Fermanagh, and highlight why it may be necessary to read two or more letters in order to grasp the full story of a particular incident. On 19 May 1770, William Veaitch wrote to Lord Erne:

I am apprehensive that the lives of Kinoghtra lease are now extinct by the death of James Morton of Belturbett. John, James and George Lawrence, and George's son called George are all dead.

On 30 May 1770, Hume Jones to Lord Erne:

> I had a letter from Mr Veaitch by which he gives me to understand that your Lordship is informed my lease of Kenotrah is expired and that your Lordship is kind enough to give me liberty of treating with you for a renewall for which I am extreamly obliged to you, but I do assure your Lordship on my word and honour I never untill I gott Mr Veaitches note heard of George Lawrence's death nor do I yet believe he is dead as I think it nearly impossible he shoud be dead withoute my hearing of it as he is a relation of mine and lives in Dublin; he is the only life I now have of it, if he is dead my lease is certainly expired. If your Lordship would give yourselfe the trouble of ordering one of your servants to call at the lying in Hospitall his mother is a housekeeper there and he can readily find out whether he is living or not.

6.3.7 Accounts

Frequently found in estate collections are sets of accounts. Often these are of limited genealogical value and relate primarily to expenditure by members of the landowning family. Occasionally, however, an item of real interest will turn up. Among the Perceval Maxwell of Finnebrogue papers are accounts from the 1770s recording workmen's wages. One from 1774 lists the names and wages of workmen employed in weeding oak in 'Portilogh'. The names of the 31 workmen employed were:

Wm Pake	Fellmey McCrisshan
Wm Gibpson	Henry McGraw
James Law	Henry McLay
John Law	John McLay
James McMullen	Hugh Meglainen
John McMullen	Hugh Meglanen junior
James McComb	Nickles Flanigan
James Calwal	James Cochren
Edward Monen	John Dornan
John Melvin	Hugh Cochren
Wm Richey	Patrick Fichpatrick
Nickles Richey	Brine Dorragan
John Whisker	James Meglanen
James McCation	Archey Boyd
Daniel Casmey	Daniel Blaney
George Nelson	

Although no residences are given for these men, it may be assumed that they lived in the Finnebrogue area.

6.3.8 Manor court records

Under the Plantation scheme of the early seventeenth century, the newly created estates were given the status of manors by royal patent. This converted a landowner into a landlord with power over his tenants. The manor provided the basic legal framework within which an estate could be managed, and was vital to its successful development. The lord of the manor was enabled to hold courts leet and baron to regulate the affairs of his estate. The courts also provided an arena where tenants could settle their disputes.

The court leet, also known as a 'view of frank-pledge', was originally a meeting of the freeholders of the manor called to exercise criminal jurisdiction. With the development of the criminal justice system and the rise of the magistracy, the importance of the court leet declined so that it became an administrative body. The court baron dealt with a range of civil actions including small debts, trespass and claims for damages. Usually a limit of 40 shillings was placed on the claims that the court could deal with. However, if a landlord wished to extend the power of his court he could have it made a 'court of record', which could deal with larger claims. The courts were under the control of an official called a seneschal who was appointed by the lord of the manor.

Only a relatively small number of manor court records have survived. The best collection is found in the Antrim estate papers (D/2977). A good introduction to these records is Ian Montgomery, 'The manorial courts of the Earls of Antrim', in *Familia* no. 16 (2000), pp. 1–23, which discusses the range of manor court records and the function of these courts. The surviving manor court records in Ulster are listed under the respective estate to which they belong.

.

7. Registry of Deeds

The Registry of Deeds was established by an act of parliament in 1708. The aim of the act was to provide one central office in Dublin 'for the public registering of all deeds, conveyances and wills, that shall be made of any honours, manors, lands, tenements or hereditaments'. The Registry of Deeds is located in a large Georgian building in Henrietta Street, Dublin. The main entrance for vehicles is off Constitution Hill. The Registry is open Monday to Friday, 10.00 a.m. to 4.30 p.m., and a small fee is charged for accessing the records. A member of staff will be on hand to offer help and advice.

7.1 Registration

Registration was not compulsory to begin with, and the number of deeds registered varied from place to place. The deeds registered include leases, mortgages, marriage settlements and wills. This can provide the researcher with names, addresses and occupations of the parties involved as well as the names of those who acted as witness. During registration, which often took place years after the original transaction, a copy of the deed called a memorial was made. The details of the memorial were then copied into a large bound volume. It is these transcript volumes that are available for public inspection.

7.2 Using the indexes

Each registered deed was given its own individual reference number. In the indexes to the deeds, the volume and the page are also given. For example, the reference 18.236.8764 means that this particular deed is on page 236 of volume 18 and is deed number 8764. This referencing system was used until 1832. After that the reference number includes the year in which the deed was registered.

Two indexes are available to the researcher: the Index of Grantors and a Lands Index. The format of the Index of Grantors has changed over the years. Before 1832 the Index gives the surname and the Christian name of the grantor, the surname of the grantee and the reference number. There is no indication of the location of the property concerned. After 1832 the Index is more detailed and includes the county in which the property is located.

The Lands Index is arranged by county, with one or more counties per volume. The entries are arranged alphabetically, but only with regard to initial letter. Each entry gives the surnames of the parties, the name of the denomination of land, and the reference number. After 1828 the Lands Index is subdivided by barony. The Index of Grantors and the Lands Index are available on microfilm at the National Library. PRONI has microfilms of both the indexes and the deeds (MIC/7 and MIC/311).

Corporate towns differed from other urban centres in that they were able to return two members to the Irish House of Commons in Dublin. Deeds relating to corporate towns are indexed separately from the rest of the deeds for a particular county. Frequently the index will provide a more precise location for a property in a corporate town than for a rural landholding, including for example the name of the street, or the names of the occupiers of neighbouring tenements.

7.3 The range of documents registered
Any type of document concerned with the transfer of legal title to land could be registered. The main categories are set out below.

7.3.1 Sales/conveyances
The legal jargon used in the deeds means that it is often impossible to identify an outright sale of a piece of property. Furthermore, many 'sales' were conveyances of property held under long-term lease. Nonetheless, such deeds can provide a great deal of useful family history information. A deed of July 1763 relating to Strabane, County Tyrone, serves as a good example. The parties to the deed were as follows.

> Elizabeth Hunter, formerly Tredennick, of Omagh, widow, eldest daughter of George Tredennick, late of Strabane
> Robert Baird and George Baird of Strabane, husband and son to Jane Tredennick, second daughter of the aforementioned George Tredennick
> John Orr of Strabane, merchant, and Martha, his wife, third daughter of the aforementioned George Tredennick
> Samual Gormaly, then in America, and Margaret, his wife, of Strabane, fourth daughter of the aforementioned George Tredennick
> John Vance of Strabane, merchant

The property in question was a tenement in the town of Strabane which, according to the deed, had been granted to Edward Tredennick, father of George Tredennick, by the 6th earl of Abercorn in 1704. George had presumably inherited the tenement from his father Edward and he in turn must have bequeathed it jointly to his daughters. It therefore required the consent of all his daughters and their husbands before the property could be conveyed to John Vance. The reference to one of the parties being in the American colonies is also interesting. Occasionally deeds referring to emigrants will be found.

7.3.2 Leases
The value of leases to the genealogist is explained in Chapter 6.3.2. Only leases for longer than three years could be registered at the Registry of Deeds.

7.3.3 Marriage settlements

A marriage settlement was the agreement made between the families of the prospective bride and groom prior to their wedding. The main aim was to provide financial security to the woman should she outlive her husband. The information in this type of deed varies, but can include the names and addresses of a large number of people from the two families involved. Occasionally the more detailed settlements include lists of names of tenants living on the lands of the groom's family. The marriage settlement of 1734 involving Lord Mountjoy included a list of tenants on his Newtownstewart estate in County Tyrone (this list was published in the 2001 edition of the *Directory of Irish Family History Research*).

The marriage portion or dowry included in a marriage settlement provides an idea of the wealth of the bride's family. The marriage portion could be paid in one lump sum or in stages. Registered in February 1745 was the marriage settlement of John Walker of Terconnelly, Donagheady parish, County Tyrone, a Presbyterian tenant farmer, and Mary Gillaspy of Minlougher, County Donegal (117.232.80596). Under the terms of the settlement the bride's parents, Thomas and Elizabeth Gillaspy, agreed to pay an initial marriage portion of £50 with an additional £25 to be paid on each of their deaths.

7.3.4 Mortgages

In the era before banks were widespread, mortgages were commonly used as a ready means of raising capital, particularly by merchants and those seeking to buy land. They are not always easy to identify and their genealogical value can be fairly limited. Rent charges were annual payments issuing from nominated lands and were used to pay off debts or provide for family members without an adequate income.

7.3.5 Wills

A large number of wills were registered. A will was usually registered if there were concerns that it was going to be contested. The genealogical value of wills is discussed in Chapter 8. Abstracts of over 2,000 wills registered between 1708 and 1832 were published in three volumes by the Irish Manuscripts Commission (P. B. Phair & E. Ellis (eds), *Registry of Deeds Dublin: Abstracts of wills*, 1954–88).

7.3.6 Bills of discovery

Bills of discovery were issued against Catholics holding lands on terms forbidden under the Penal Laws. The Protestant filing the bill was able to claim the lands affected. In many cases the bill was filed by a Protestant friend of the Catholic concerned in order to pre-empt a less sympathetic discovery. The following deed makes reference to a bill of discovery relating to lands in County Fermanagh.

Volume 107, page 297, memorial number 73998
A memorial of an assignment bearing date the 27th day of April 1742 between Rowland Kane of Desertmartin, in the County of Londonderry, gent., and Hugh Montgomery of Derrygonnelly, in the County of Fermanagh, Esq.; reciting that the said Rowland Kane hath exhibited his bill in his Ma[jes]ties Couty of Exchequer in Ireland on or about the 16th day

of February last past against Hugh O'Donnell of Mullaghbane in the County of Fermanagh aforesaid, Esq., and John Cole of Florence Court within said County, Esq., as a Protestant Discoverer to be decreed to the benefit of a lease or term of years of the town and lands commonly called & known by the names of Aghagilgulman [there follows a long list of place-names] situated in the barony of Glenawley & County of Fermanagh aforesaid made by the said John Cole to the said Hugh O'Donnell who is disabled to take such lease term or int. by the laws and statutes inforce in this kingdom. [Kane then assigned the lands in question to Montgomery for the sum of 5 shillings.]

7.4 The value of research in the Registry of Deeds

A popular misconception of the Registry of Deeds is that it is of little value for those searching for Presbyterian ancestors. Two recent publications on Irish genealogy claim that 'very few deeds made by dissenting Protestants are registered' and 'Ulster Presbyterians tended to steer clear of registered deeds'. These statements are simply not true. Intensive research into the deeds has shown that, right from the beginning of registration, a significant number do refer to Presbyterian tenant farmers and merchants. Furthermore, these deeds constitute a broad range of document types.

For example, for the manor Ardstraw in County Tyrone, held by the McCausland family in the early eighteenth century, there are over a dozen registered leases from the 1720s containing the names of about 100 tenant farmers. Information on the occupiers of churchlands in the eighteenth century is usually very hard to come by, making this collection all the more valuable. The names from most of these leases were published in the 2001 edition of the *Directory of Irish Family History Research*. The same editon of the *Directory* contained a list of the names of over 120 individuals, the majority of them almost certainly Presbyterians, which were extracted from fourteen leases relating to the corporate town of Strabane. The fourteen leases represent only a fraction of the total number of eighteenth-century leases for Strabane.

Nor is it true that ordinary Catholic tenant farmers are excluded altogether from the memorials in the Registry of Deeds. The following slightly abridged deed relates to County Armagh.

Volume 36, page 4, memorial number 20880.
A memorial of an indenture dated 24 December 1719 between Roger o fferan of Tonnywalton, County Armagh, yeoman, of the one part, and Bryan o ffearan of the said town and county of the other part.

Whereby the said Roger fferan to farm let to the said Bryan Fearan that parcel of the townland of Tonnywalton containing 34 acres as also another parcel part Pagan's farm containing 20 acres, 22 roods and 3 perches, likewise another parcel of land part of Barkley's farm containing 10 acres, 3 roods, all situate in the Manor of Clare, County Ardmagh, to hold to the said Bryan o ffearan from November 1 last past for the term of 31 years at the yearly rent of £11 5s. 4d. above all taxes.

Said lease witnessed by Cornelius Calter of Cornescribe, County Ardmagh, Arthur Devlin, John McGrune and John FitzPatrick, all of Tavanawalton, County Ardmagh. This memorial witnessed by Cornelius Calter aforesaid and by Bryan Rogers of Portadown, County Ardmagh.

Cornelius Calter swears as to the witnessing on 26 May 1722 at Richhill, County Ardmagh, before Andrew Charleton in the presence of J. Richardson and Andrew Charleton, JPs.

Although the layout of the building can be confusing, the arrangement of the records somewhat haphazard and the transcript volumes heavy and cumbersome, the Registry of Deeds is unlike any other archive in Ireland and is well worth a visit, if only for the experience of having used it.

8. Wills and testamentary records

Wills are among the most important sources for the genealogist. A single will can provide the names of the testator's wife, children, grandchildren, siblings, cousins, friends and neighbours. Details on the testator's possessions, both personal belongings and land, can be recorded. Family members living abroad, for example in America, might be mentioned. For these reasons, it is worth paying careful attention to all the information contained in a will.

8.1 The information in a will

Wills generally followed a standard format. The testator usually began by committing his soul to God. These expressions were often formulaic, but occasionally it is possible to discern a genuine religious devotion on the part of the testator as he or she prepared for death. The preferred place of burial was often stated. This could be more specific than the name of the church or churchyard. For example, in 1717 Walter Dawson of Armagh left instructions in his will that he was to be buried in the cathedral of Armagh 'in the south aisle in the grave where my d[ea]r daughter Ann Dawson lies, it joining my dear father and son Walter Dawson' (D/3053/1/2/3).

Some form of provision would usually be made for the testator's wife. This might be an annual sum of money to be paid to her by the principal beneficiary of the will. The family home or part of it might be left to the wife and any unmarried daughters in the family. If the testator was on good terms with his children, all of them could expect to receive a bequest from him, unless they had already been provided for. If the testator was a farmer he would usually leave the farm to his eldest son. Even if he did not own the land outright he could still leave the 'interest' in the farm to his son. Unless the testator was in possession of several landholdings, the other children usually received bequests of money. The testator's personal possessions, such as clothing, riding equipment, books or watch, were divided out among family members.

Other beneficiaries of the will included the testator's servants – a will may be the only mention anywhere of the existence of such people. In 1634 Sir Marmaduke Whitchurch of Loughbrickland left his servant Pdk Madden McRathy 'two cows & a garron [horse] & an old doublet & hose of mine' (D/765/1). The will of George Macghee of Strabane, dated 25 October 1741 includes bequests to the following poor people: Widow O'Quin, Widow

Mackroddian, Mary Robison alias Widow Monroe, Meve the lame woman, 'Bigg Margret' and Jos Dowler (LPC/1325). The executors appointed to carry out the instructions in a will were often close family members. The names of witnesses should also be noted, for even if there is no apparent relationship, this may be revealed with further searching.

It must be remembered that only a fraction of the population left wills. Even for many individuals who were comfortably off, there is no evidence that they left a will. In some families the question of inheritance was settled without the need to make a will. Many people, of course, possessed so little that there was little point in making a will. On other occasions death came so suddenly that there was no time to make a will.

The will of Charles McKenna of Tandergee, County Tyrone, provides a particularly detailed insight into the circumstances of one farming family in rural Ulster at the end of the eighteenth century, and is quoted here in full.

> In the Name of God, Amen, I, Charles McKenna, of Tandergee, parish of Pomeroy and County of Tyrone, being frail in body and calling to mind my state of mortality do make and publish this my last will and testament in maner following: first I leave and bequeath my soul to God who gave it and my body to be buried in a Christian maner in the church yard of Donaghmore; secondly I leave and bequeath to my grandson, Charles McKenna, second son of Patrick McKenna of said Tandergee now deceased the full half of the farm in said Tandergee which half I now possess, my daughter-in-law, Sarah McKenna, possessing the other half as her husband, my son, and I was [sic] joyned in lease equally for said farm; also to Charles my grandson my old dwelling house which is now made a barn of with my pot, crock, & tongs; also I will to my daughter Alis [Alice?] McKenna, otherwise Donaghy, one shilling sterling. Lastly I nominate and apoint Thomas Kinaghan of said Tandergee executor of this my will in trust to see it executed according to the true intent and meaning of it, making void all other wills made or done by me.
>
> In witness whereof I have put my hand an seal this twenty second day of Aught in the year of our Lord eighteen hundred 1800.
>
> Signed sealed & delivered in presence of being first duly read, Henry Long, Kennedy Long, John Hughes.
>
> [Charles McKenna made his mark.]

8.2 How to find a will

Prior to 1858 the Church of Ireland was responsible for administering all testamentary affairs. Ecclesiastical or Consistorial Courts in each diocese were responsible for granting probate and conferring on the executors the power to administer the estate. Each court was responsible for wills and administrations in its own diocese. However, when the estate included property worth more than £5 in another diocese, responsibility for the will or administration passed to the Prerogative Court under the authority of the Archbishop of Armagh. It must not be thought that just because the Church of Ireland was responsible for administering wills, only persons who belonged to that particular denomination left wills. Presbyterians and Roman Catholics also left wills; if they did not it was principally for economic rather than religious reasons.

Unfortunately, nearly all original wills probated before 1858 were destroyed in Dublin in 1922. However, indexes to these destroyed wills do exist and are available on the shelves of the Library at PRONI and in the National Archives in Dublin. These are useful, for although the will cannot now be produced, the index contains the name and residence of the testator and the date that the will was either made or probated. Occasionally the testator's occupation is given.

Because the Church of Ireland was responsible for administering wills, the indexes are arranged by diocese, not by county. A published index to the prerogative wills of Ireland covers the period 1536–1810. An index for pre-1858 surviving wills and will abstracts is available in the Public Search Room at PRONI. This is arranged alphabetically by the name of the testator, and provides the references to most of the wills or extracts from wills that are scattered throughout PRONI collections. Altogether PRONI has over 13,000 copies and abstracts of pre-1858 wills.

Of particular value with regard to prerogative wills are 'Burke's Pedigrees', which are available in PRONI under reference T/559. These are based on information extracted from the prerogative wills and the detail of each pedigree depends on the amount of information recorded in a particular will. Occasionally there is an attempt to link several generations of one family together through information extracted from two or more wills. In the Genealogical Office in Dublin are volumes of pedigrees extracted from the prerogative wills in the early nineteenth century by Sir William Betham, which include additions and amendments from other sources (see Chapter 13.2 for more information on the Genealogical Office).

In the absence of a will, letters of administration were sometimes granted. These were usually issued to close family members. The original administration bonds were also destroyed in Dublin in 1922, but index volumes for dioceses are available in the Library at PRONI and for prerogative administrations under T/490. Occasionally there will be an abstract of an administration bond; if so, it will be indexed along with surviving pre-1858 wills.

8.3 Surviving will and administration bond indexes

Diocese	Counties (all or part of)	Wills from	Administration bonds from
Armagh	Armagh, Londonderry, Louth, Tyrone	1666 (manuscript)	—
Clogher	Donegal, Fermanagh, Louth, Monaghan, Tyrone	1661 (manuscript)	1660
Connor	Antrim, Down, Londonderry	1636 (manuscript)	1636
Derry	Donegal, Londonderry, Tyrone	1612 (published)	1698
Down	Down	1646 (typescript)	1635
Dromore	Antrim, Armagh, Down	1678 (published)	1742
Kilmore	Cavan, Fermanagh, Leitrim	1682 (published)	1728
Newry and Mourne (exempt jurisdiction)	Armagh, Down	1727 (published)	post-1800
Raphoe	Donegal	1684 (published)	1684

9. Election records

9.1 Elections and the electorate

Until the latter part of the nineteenth century, the right to vote was closely linked to land tenure. Throughout the seventeenth and eighteenth centuries only adult males in possession of a 40-shilling freehold were entitled to vote. A 40-shilling freehold was property worth 40 shillings a year above the rent, and either owned outright or leased during the lives of named individuals. The possession of a lease for years, no matter how many years, did not entitle one to vote. Many important and indeed prominent people had no vote because they leased their property on the wrong terms. The franchise was further restricted between 1727 and 1793, when Catholics were forbidden to vote.

From 1728 onwards voters had to conform to an increasingly tight system of registration, designed to prevent electoral fraud. Registers of freeholders list the names and addresses of individuals entitled to vote at parliamentary elections. Only by being registered to vote could a freeholder exercise his electoral rights. Poll books list the names of voters and the candidates they voted for. Until the eighteenth century, elections were held infrequently. Before 1768 there was no law limiting the duration of Irish parliaments and nothing to compel the government to hold a general election except the death of the reigning monarch. The Octennial Act of 1768 provided that a general election should be held at least every eight years. Nevertheless, until the nineteenth century very few elections were contested, and parliamentary representation remained firmly in the hands of a small number of powerful landed families.

9.2 The information provided

In most of the freeholders registers and poll books the information provided is fairly basic – the name of the freeholder and his residence. The latter does not always include the name of the parish; further checking may be required to discover this. Occasionally, however, some additional information of interest is provided. In the list of Armagh freeholders, c.1710–37 the names of the lives in the lease are often recorded. For example, the entry for William Lyndsay reveals that he held his freehold of Cargans from Oliver St John by virtue of a lease of 10 June 1726 for the lives of himself and his sons John and Thomas. In the Armagh poll book of 1753 Robert Jones was objected to 'for being seen at Mass and giving offerings to the priest', while Silas Hamilton was objected to on the grounds that he was a 'rioter'.

The following extracts from the election book for County Antrim for 1776 (D/1364/L/1) reveal the nature of the information recorded in this document.

Robert Peerece, Aughnahough – 'Objected to for want of freehold – the last surviving life in the lease being a soldier & went to Africa about four years ago, since which there was no account from him, altho' he regularly wrote to his mother before that time & soe is dead so long – rejected.'

Robert Derham, Ballydonnelly – 'Registered in his father Israel Derham's name who is dead 12 years ago – acknowledges his father held more lands in the same townland than the lands the voter holds under his father's will – objected to for want of freehold & for undue influence.'

9.3 Surviving election records

The survival of election records for Ulster varies considerably from county to county. Coverage is best for Counties Armagh and Down. A list of the records is set out below.

County Antrim
Belfast voters, 1744 – R. M. Young (ed.), *The Town Book of the Corporation of Belfast* (Belfast, 1892), pp. 215–17.
Some County Antrim freeholders, 1768 – T/808/14900.
Deputy Court Cheque Book, 1776 – D/1364/L/1. An index was printed in the *Directory of Irish Family History Research*, no. 22 (1999), pp. 72–80.
Voters, 1790 (3,538 names plus townlands) – printed in *A collection of all the authenticated public addresses, resolutions, and advertisments, relative to the late election of Knights of the Shire for the County of Antrim: Together with a correct list of the poll, alphabeticallly arranged, shewing at one view how and when each elector voted*, by 'a member of the Independent Committee' (Belfast, 1790).

County Armagh
Freeholders list, *c.*1710–37 – D/1928/F/1A.
Freeholders list, 1738 – NLI, p. 206.
Armagh poll book giving the names and addresses of freeholders, 1753 – D/1928/F/1B; T/808/14936.
Objections to voters in poll book of 1753 – T/808/14949.
List of freeholders from the Portadown district, 1747–1802 – D/2394/3/5; T/281/5.
Memorial from freeholders and merchants of Oneilland West barony, 1763 – *Belfast Newsletter*, 2 August 1763.
Registered freeholders in the Portadown district, 1792–1802 – T/281/6.

County Cavan
Poll book, 1761 – T/1522. An index was printed in the *Directory of Irish Family History Research*, no. 23 (2000), pp. 93–101.

County Donegal
Poll book, 1761–75 – T/808/14999; MIC/353/1. An index was printed in the *Directory of Irish Family History Research*, no. 20 (1997), pp. 70–76.
Freeholders, 1775–81, 1789–90 – T/808/15006.

County Down

Election 'cheque book' for freeholders with surnames A–G arranged alphabetically, 1746–89 – D/654/A3/1/1A.

List of over 400 signatures of tenants on the Needham (Kilmorey) estates, Newry, election of 1768 – NLI Ms 8163.

Registers of freeholders, 1777, 1780–85 – DOW/5/3/1.

Registers of freeholders, 1790–95 – DOW/5/3/2.

Index book of electors for the borough of Downpatrick, c.1783 – D/2223/21/1.

'Deputy Court cheque book', 1789 – D/654/A3/1/1B.

Freeholders, Lecale barony, c.1790 – T/393/1.

Freeholders, Lecale barony, 1795–99 – T/808/15012.

Freeholders, Lecale barony, 1795–1800 – T/808/15018.

Lists of freeholders, Upper and Lower Iveagh baronies, 1796–1811 – D/654/A3/1C–X.

County Fermanagh

Poll book, 1747–68 – T/808/15063. An index was printed in the *Directory of Irish Family History Research*, no. 21 (1998), pp. 58–69.

Poll book, 1788 – T/543/1; T/808/15075.

Freeholders register, 1796–1802 – D/1096/92.

Lists of freeholders, no dates given [18th century] – John Rylands Library, Manchester, 3/26/1–145

County Londonderry

Names of those who voted at the County Londonderry by-election of 1697 – T/3161/1/4

Freeholders registers, Cumber parish only, 1761–81, 1791, 1796 – J. Rutherford, *Cumber Presbyterian Church and Parish* (Londonderry, 1939), pp. 117–25.

Freeholders from Tamlaght Finlagan parish, 1774 (136 names and addresses) – D/2094/46.

County Monaghan

Extracts from County Court of Monaghan giving lists of freeholders, 1692, c.70 names – MIC/170/5.

County Tyrone

Freeholders, Dungannon barony, 1763 – *Belfast Newsletter*, 30 August 1763.

Freeholders, Cookstown area, 1768–95 – T/808/15127.

Freeholders list, Dungannon barony only, 1795–8 – TYR/5/3/1.

The majority of eighteenth-century freeholders registers have been indexed by PRONI and are available on its website (www.proni.gov.uk).

10. Local government records

10.1 Grand jury records

From the early eighteenth century the grand jury was the most important local government body in Ireland. It had the power to raise money through the collection of rates, known as the 'county cess', and had responsibility for the repair of roads and bridges and the upkeep of local institutions such as hospitals and lunatic asylums. The grand jury was selected by the high sheriff from the leading property owners in the county. Its membership was almost exclusively Protestant and was often chosen from a limited group of well-connected families. Catholics were forbidden to serve until 1793.

10.1.1 Presentment books

The grand jury presentment books contain the names of those responsible for the repair of roads and bridges or maintaining prisons and session houses; the early manuscript volumes contain the signatures of many of these overseers, indicating that they had received payment for their work. Occasionally it is possible to weave together something of a story from various entries in a grand jury presentment book, as the following extracts from the presentment book for County Antrim, 1711–21, relating to Eneas or Neice O'Haghion, reveal.

> 21 July 1721 – £15 to Daniel Phillips of Ballymacscanlan and £5 to Mr John Hawkins 'for apprehending and bringing to justice Neice O'Haghion, a proclaimed Tory robber and rapparee'
> 7 April 1722 – £1 6s. 1d. paid to John McQuown for, *inter alia*, repairing 'some breaches made in the gaol by Eneas O'Haghian'
> 7 April 1722 – £1 paid to Francis Clements, High Sheriff of County Antrim, for transferring 'Neeice O'Haghian' from Belfast to Carrickfergus
> 17 July 1722 – £5 2s. 6d. paid to Francis Clements 'to reimburse him the like sume expended in procureing him a strong guard of sixty men when Eneas O'Haghion and six other men were executed and for fixing the said Haghion's head on the gaole'

Grand jury presentment books survive for most counties in Ulster, though coverage varies. A typescript volume of the County Antrim presentment book for 1711–21 (from which the above extracts were taken) is available on the open shelves in the Public Search Room at PRONI. For County Down there are also grand jury record books from 1780 onwards, which provide a detailed description of the roads being repaired. At this time the names of local individuals and the location of their properties were used to define a particular stretch of road.

10.1.2 Registers of trees planted
Concerns about deforestation in Ireland and the consequent shortage of timber led to a series of acts being passed from 1698 onwards to encourage tree-planting. One of these, an act of 1765, allowed a tenant to claim for the value of the trees he had planted on the expiration of his lease so long as he certified this and lodged the certificate with the clerk of the peace in his county. Very few of these registers of trees have survived from the eighteenth century for Ulster. For County Down the registers begin in 1769, while for County Londonderry they begin in 1773. For the latter county PRONI has published the register of trees planted.

10.1.3 Indictment books
Grand juries had an important judicial function in that members were to preside at the assizes and examine bills of indictment relating to criminal matters. For County Tyrone a grand jury indictment book survives for the period 1745–1809. This volume, sadly in a rather damaged state, gives the names of prosecutors, the names of the persons indicted, the offence and the finding of the grand jury. Extracts from a County Armagh indictment book, 1735–75, are also available and provide the same sort of information.

10.1.4 Surviving grand jury records

County Antrim
Presentment books, 1711–21, 1727–67, 1775–84, 1796–1804 – ANT/4/1/1–7
Grand warrant books: baronies of Upper and Lower Antrim, 1776–93, 1794–1804 – ANT/4/2/1/1–2
Grand warrant books: baronies of Upper and Lower Dunluce, 1776–92, 1792–1804 – ANT/4/2/2/1–2
Grand warrant books: baronies of Kilconway and Cary, 1776–92, 1793–1804 – ANT/4/2/3/1–2
Grand warrant books: baronies of Upper and Lower Massareene, 1776–92, 1792–1804 – ANT/4/2/4/1–2
Grand warrant books: baronies of Upper and Lower Belfast, 1775–92, 1792–1804 – ANT/4/2/5/1–2
Grand warrant books: baronies of Upper and Lower Glenarm, 1776–94, 1794–1816 – ANT/4/2/6/1–2
Grand warrant book: baronies of Upper and Lower Toome, 1791–1804 – ANT/4/2/7/1
Grand warrant book: Carrickfergus, 1766–1817 – ANT/4/2/8/1
Printed presentment book, 1778–1800 – ANT/4/4/1
Grand Jury resolution book with account, 1780–1824 – ANT/4/7/1

County Armagh
Assize indictment book, 1735–93 – Armagh Public Library
Grand Jury lists, 1735–97 – T/647

Extracts from Grand Jury records, 1735–75, providing names of prosecutors, persons
   indicted and reason; lists of jurors, 1735–98 – T/636/1, pp. 85–100
Presentment books, beginning in 1758 – ARM/4/1
Presentment book, 1790 – D/288/1

County Donegal
Grand Jury presentments, beginning in 1753 (with gaps) – Donegal County
   Archives Service
Grand Jury presentments, baronies of Boylagh and Banagh, 1772, 1784–98 –
   NLI Ms 12,910 (MIC/352/1)
Grand Jury queries, 1772–83, presentments, 1784–98 – NLI n.5374, p. 5505
Grand Jury book, Kilmacrenan barony, 1772–98 – NAI microfilm reels 22–3

County Down
Presentment books, beginning in 1778 – DOW/4/2
Grand Jury record books, beginning in 1780 – DOW/4/4
Register of trees planted, 1769–99 – DOW/7/3/2/1
Presentments at assizes, 1714–96 – T/808/15015

County Fermanagh
Presentment book for the county at large, 1792–1819 – FER/4/3/1
Criminal book, county assizes, 1792–1861 – FER/4/8/1

County Londonderry
Presentment books, beginning in 1788 – LOND/4/1
Register of trees planted, 1773–1894 – LOND/7/7/1

County Tyrone
Presentment books, beginning in 1799 – TYR/4/1
Grand Jury indictment book, 1745–1809 – TYR/4/2/1. This gives the names of prosecutors,
   the names of the persons indicted, the offence and the finding of the Grand Jury.
   The book is badly damaged.

10.2 Corporation records
Prior to 1841, local government in nearly thirty Ulster towns was controlled by a
corporation. With the exception of Carrickfergus and Downpatrick, which were medieval
boroughs, these corporations were seventeenth-century creations. Records relating to
about half of these corporations have survived. Often the minute books of the corporations
are fairly uninformative, usually being no more than a record of the fact that a meeting did
take place and listing only the names of those present. Occasionally, however, there will be
an entry of potential value. For example, on 5 October 1745 the corporation of
Hillsborough decided to appoint a town watch and issued it with the following
instructions: 'That once in each hour one half of the said Guard shall patrole from the
house of Patrick Jackson to the house of Moses Green in Hillsborough'. The watch was to
last from 10 p.m. to 6 a.m., and anyone found out after 11 p.m. was to be arrested. Of
particular interest from the Coleraine corporation minutes is the entry of the meeting of
2 October 1797, at which the Coleraine yeomanry were made freemen of the town. This
order is followed by a list of the officers and men of the yeomanry.

Armagh, County Armagh
Corporation records, 1731–1840 – Armagh Public Library
Miscellaneous papers about Armagh corporation, 1686–92, 1747–1824 – DIO/4/40/1/1/1–21;
   lists of burgesses of Armagh, 1747–96 – DIO/4/40/1/1/11–13
Extracts from Armagh corporation minute books, 1731–1818 – T/808/14932, 14983, 15318
Lists of Armagh City Grand Jurors, 1731–1833 – T/808/15319
Notes from Armagh city pipe water book giving personal names, 1796 – T/808/14983
Names of jurors extracted from corporation records, 1731–75, 1776–1815 – T/636/1,
   pp. 103–12, 114–21

Belfast, County Antrim
The corporation minutes of Belfast have been published as *The Town Book of the Corporation
of Belfast, 1613–1816*, edited by R. M. Young (Belfast, 1892), including the roll of freemen,
1635–1796 (pp. 246–300). See MIC/131/1 for a microfilm of the original.

Belturbet, County Cavan
Corporation minute books, 1660–64, undated (17th century), 1708–55, 1778–1840;
   corporation court book, 1740–95 – NAI M3571–3, M3606
Surveys of property belonging to the corporation (includes a map of lands belonging to the
   Reverend Samuel Madden listing names of occupiers), 1723, 1735, 1773 – NLI
   Ms 8105
Accounts relating to the Reverend Robert Robertson's charitable bequest, 1737–1821 –
   NAI M3607

Carrickfergus, County Antrim
Volume of *c.*90 pages containing information about Carrickfergus corporation, *c.*1568–
   *c.*1689 – D/162/1. It shows that in 1683 there were 105 freemen and 41 burgesses, of
   whom 17 were aldermen. Also included is a rental of Carrickfergus for the half year
   ending May 1674. Memoranda on elections of burgesses, 1672–1702 – D/162/5.
List of burgesses and freemen of the corporation, n.d. (pre-1706) – D/162/18.

Cavan, County Cavan
Minutes of meetings of the town council, together with lists of conformist freemen, 1697–
   1824, 1838–40 – NLI Mss 5832–3.
Freemen of the borough of Cavan, 1697–1838, printed in *Breifne*, vol. 1, no. 2 (1959),
   pp. 87–112.

Clogher, County Tyrone
Extracts from corporation book, 1783–98 – T/1566

Coleraine, County Londonderry
Minute books of the court of common council of the corporation of Coleraine, 1672–1707,
   1707–10, 1792–1840 (originals and copies) – LA/25/2AA/1A–2
Box of miscellaneous 18th-century papers relating to the corporation, including a list of
   members of the corporation in 1782 – D/668/O/1

Dungannon, County Tyrone
Corporation minute book, 1695–1840 – MIC/547/1

Hillsborough, County Down
Corporation books, 1740–74 and 1773–1841 – D/671/O/1

Lifford, County Donegal
Extract from the charter of Lifford, 1611 – D/1939/18/15/1
Petition of corporation to bishop of Derry, 1682 – printed in T. W. Moody and J. G.
    Simms, *The Bishopric of Derry and the Irish Society of London, 1602–1705* (2 vols,
    Dublin, 1968–83), ii, p. 51
Court and borough book, 1716–83 – D/1939/18/6/9
Extract from the 'Book containing the records of the Corporation of Lifford' giving details
    of tenures and rents, 172[?] – D/1939/18/14/5
Letter of 14 June 1748 giving the names of the warden and twelve burgesses of Lifford in
    1727 – D/1939/18/15/9

Limavady, County Londonderry (also known as Newtownlimavady)
Corporation minute books, 1659–1736, 1736–68, 1771–81, 1781–1808 – D/663/2–5.
    Published as *Records of the Town of Limavady, 1609 to 1808*, edited by E. M. F.–G.
    Boyle (Londonderry, 1912; reprinted Limavady, 1989).
Miscellaneous corporation records, 17th and 18th centuries – D/663 *passim*.

Londonderry, County Londonderry
Minute books of Londonderry corporation, 1673–1841 (with gaps) – LA/79/2AA/1–11B

Newtownards, County Down
Corporation minute book, 1741–75 – LA60/2AB/1
Borough act book, 1742–75 – T/433/1
Minute book of the grand jury of the corporation, 1756–1833 – LA/60/2AA/1

Strabane, County Tyrone
Corporation council minutes, 1755–1812; corporation minutes, accounts and borough
court proceedings, 1769–1850; jury book, 1773–1810 – MIC/159/1. The records include a
list of over 100 individuals upon whom quarterage was levied on 29 September 1773, and a
list of 66 townspeople fined 6¹/₂d. each for various misdemeanours on 9 November 1787.

10.3 Law and order
Records relating to the courts were largely lost in 1922 with the destruction of the Public
Record Office. Some material covering a few counties was transcribed by Tenison Groves
and other researchers prior to 1922; this is available in PRONI.

County Antrim
Fines in the Court of Wards, Lower Antrim, 1637, *c.*30 names – T/808/14884
Extracts from Assize and Quarter Session records, 1721–40 – T/808/14895
Summaries of cases at Assizes, 1717–30 – T/808/14896

County Armagh
Petitions and examinations relating to agrarian outrages, 1743 – T/808/14925
List of inditements at Lent assizes, 1771 – T/808/14951

County Tyrone
Extracts from early 17th-century Chancery and Exchequer Inquisitions etc., relating to
County Tyrone sessions and assizes – T/1365/1

Information about crime and punishment may also be found in the records of grand juries
(Chapter 10.1.3). The *Journals of the House of Commons of the Kingdom of Ireland*
also include information about trials and convictions (see Chapter 5.1 above for more
information). See also the entry on summonister rolls in Chapter 4.7.

10.3.1 Sheriffs and justices of the peace
The sheriff of the county was originally a lifetime appointee chosen by the King. By the
seventeenth century he was appointed annually. Justices of the peace and magistrates
played an important role in the administration of local justice. Some records relating to
these offices are set out below.

Lists of high sheriffs for every county in Ireland (with the exception of Londonderry),
     14th–19th centuries – D/302/1
County Antrim JPs in the seventeenth century – T/808/14893–4
County Antrim magistrates, 1773 (53 names) – D/4164/A/3
County Armagh JPs, 1655 – T/808/1495
County Donegal high sheriffs, 1607–1814 – T/808/14995
County Down high sheriffs, 1400–1874 – Alexander Knox, *A History of Down* (1875),
     pp. 91–8
County Monaghan JPs in 1758 – D/3053/8/4/1
County Tyrone high sheriffs, 1606–1895 – T/808/15116

11. Military records

For early seventeenth-century muster rolls see Chapter 4.8.

11.1 War Office records

Over the centuries many Ulstermen served in the British army. Any information that has survived about their military careers will generally be found in the War Office (WO) papers in The National Archives (TNA), Kew (formerly the Public Record Office). These records comprise commissions, muster rolls, pay rolls, pensions, regimental records, etc. The website of TNA (www.nationalarchives.gov.uk) has detailed guides on what is available and how it can be accessed. A useful published guide is *Army Records for Family Historians* by W. Spencer and S. Fowler (TNA, 1998). Of some interest for Irish researchers are the registers of in- and out-pensioners of the Royal Hospital Kilmainham, beginning in 1704 (WO 118).

11.2 Muster rolls from the 1640s

The 1640s was a period of warfare and devastation in Ireland following the outbreak of rebellion in October 1641. Several fighting forces were raised from among the settler population to defend their farms and families. In addition an army from Scotland was sent to Ulster in 1642 to assist the settlers. A large collection of muster rolls for the period 1642–5 is available in the Groves collection in PRONI (T/808/15166–15177). Researchers should look at the calendar list carefully. The following is a selection from this list.

Muster roll of Sir Robert Stewart's regiment at Raphoe, County Donegal, 1642 – T/808/15166

Muster roll of foot companies of Chichester, Clanaboy, Clotworthy and Montgomery, and of the horse company of Col. Arthur Hill, 1642, c.4,000 names – T/808/15172

Muster roll held at the city of Derry, 1642–3 – T/808/15176

Muster roll of Col. Audley Mervyn's company, 1643 – T/808/15175, 15177

Other muster rolls from this period include:

County Antrim muster roll, 1642 – T/3726/2

County Down muster roll, 1642–3 – T/563/1

Donaghadee muster roll, 1642 – T/3726/1

11.3 Military records, 1660–1800

The surviving military records for this period are varied. Before they are listed, some background notes on the three main military forces in Ireland at this time are provided below.

11.3.1 The militia

The militia was a local defence force usually raised when the country was under threat from foreign invasion. The force was almost exclusively recruited from the poorer classes, but commanded by members of the landed gentry. The militia was prone to poor discipline when sent to disturbed areas for policing duties. For example, on 12 July 1797 the Kerry Militia was involved in fight with Orangemen in Stewartstown, County Tyrone, with the result that six to eight of the militiamen were killed.

To raise a force of militia, local constables were empowered to draw up lists of all the able-bodied men in their area. A ballot was then held to decide which of these men were to be called upon to serve or else pay for a replacement. Peers, clergymen, articled clerks, apprentices, and those who had served previously were among those exempt from service. Any man selected by the ballot to serve could be excused if he could provide a suitable substitute. The availability of Volunteers frequently made the raising of men by compulsion unnecessary.

11.3.2 The Volunteers

The Volunteers was a part-time military force first raised in the late 1770s. Its original objective was to guard against French invasion and to preserve law and order. It was raised locally in companies and battalions. Shortly after its formation the Volunteers adopted a more overtly political role as radical politicians took leading positions in the force. The Volunteers played an important role in the campaign for free trade and then led the drive for legislative independence. The leadership of the Volunteer movement was by this time in the hands of a group of members of parliament, including Henry Grattan and Henry Flood, who had become known collectively as the Patriot Party.

In 1782 the Volunteers played a major role in forcing the British Government to concede the independence of the Irish parliament. They then campaigned for the reform of the legislature itself, and began to falter in 1784 as a result of the divisions caused by the question of Catholic emancipation. Although they lost their national importance, they continued to exist at a local level. Enthusiasm for Volunteering revived briefly after 1789 with the excitement caused by the French Revolution. In 1793, however, the Gunpowder Act, prohibiting the import of arms, and the Convention Act, which declared illegal all assemblies for the purpose of soliciting a change in the law that claimed the status of a representative body, effectively ended Volunteering.

11.3.3 The yeomanry

The yeomanry was formed in September 1796 under the threat of imminent invasion from France. Local gentry and magistrates throughout Ireland were empowered to raise infantry companies and cavalry troops in order to maintain a military presence in the absence of troops and militia called upon to intercept any invasion. The government paid, clothed and armed this volunteer force, whose main function was to free the regular army and militia from their local peacekeeping activities. Both cavalry and infantry corps were formed. For a detailed account of the yeomanry see Allan Blackstock, *Ascendancy Army: The Irish Yeomanry, 1796–1834* (Dublin, 1998).

11.3.4 Surviving military records, 1660–1800

County Antrim
Militia officers, 1691 – T/808/15185
Militia pay lists and muster rolls, 1799–1800 – T/1115/1A–B
Declaration of allegiance by officers of Carrickfergus Infantry, n.d. [*c.*1803] – D/162/103 (MIC/533/3)

County Armagh
Militia lists by parish in the barony of Oneilland West, 1793–5 – D/1928/Y/1
Muster rolls, Armagh Militia, 1793–7 – D/183
Ardress Yeomany Book, *c.*1796 – D/296
Churchill Yeomanry Book, *c.*1796 – D/321/1
Roll of the Armagh corps of Supplementary Yeomanry, 1798–1803 – T/808/15248
Militia pay lists and muster rolls, 1799–1800 – T/1115/2A–C
Miscellaneous notes on County Armagh Volunteers – D/3696/A
Roll of First Co. of Armagh Volunteers, n.d. – T/636/1, p. 339

County Donegal
Muster roll of the Abercorn estate, 1745 – printed in the *Directory of Irish Family History Research* 21 (1998)
Return of Yeomanry corps, naming captains, 1803 – D/623/A/161/12

County Down
Receipts for guns and bayonets to be used in Robert Maxwell's troop of militia, Inch parish, 1746 – D/1556/16/15/1–14
Minute book for the men of Mourne Volunteer Corps, 1778–92 – T/1317
Minute book of the 1st and 2nd Volunteer companies of Newtownards, 1787 – D/3030
Minute books of Newry 1st Volunteer company, 1778–93 – T/3202
Minute books of Newry [2nd] Volunteer company, 1778–87 – T/3202
Copy of Volunteer order, County Down, with extract of Volunteer muster roll, 1782 – T/441
Men in the parish of Inch who have subscribed towards finding substitutes for the Militia, 1793, *c.*150 names – T/1023/139
Signatures in relation to the formation of a yeomanry corps in Inch parish, 1797, around 200 names – T/1023/144–5
Oath and list of names of Ballyculter Supplementary Corps, 1798 – T/1023/153
Killyleagh yeomanry list, 1798 – D/303/3
Names of those proposing to form a cavalry unit to act with the Inch infantry and to be known as Inch Legion, *c.*1798, 18 names – T/1023/163
Miscellaneous notes on County Down Volunteers – D/3696/A

County Fermanagh

Various militia lists, 1689–1756 – printed in W. C. Trimble, *The History of Enniskillen* (3 vols, Enniskillen, 1919–21), iii, pp. 684–99

Papers about Enniskillen Light Horse commanded by Sir James Caldwell, 1759–61 – John Rylands Library, Manchester, 3/23/1–31

Militia pay lists and muster rolls, 1794–99 – T/1115/5A–C

Yeomanry muster rolls, 1797–1804 – T/808/15244

County Fermanagh military, yeomanry and volunteer infantry, 1797–1834 – T/808/15244

County Londonderry

Order from the Commissioners of the Army and Militia for the County of Londonderry to the constables of the parishes of Magilligan and Aghanloo that certain named individuals [*c.*70] appear 'with their best arms' at Limavady, 1666 – T/640/103

Names of men enlisted in the barony of Loughinsholin militia, 1745 – D/1449/11/1

Miscellaneous 18th-century papers about counties Londonderry and Tyrone militias, including lists of officers – D/1449/9

Coleraine Volunteers (1st Company), 1776–82 – D/4164/A/23, pp. 5597–8

Coleraine yeomanry, 1796 (116 names) – D/4164/A/12

Coleraine yeomanry, 1797 – LA/25/2AA/2

Yeomanry muster rolls, 1797–1804 – T/1021/3

County Tyrone

Miscellaneous 18th-century papers about Counties Londonderry and Tyrone militias, including lists of officers – D/1449/9

Muster roll of the Abercorn estate, 1745 – printed in the *Directory of Irish Family History Research* 21 (1998)

Notes on the Gortin Volunteers, 1782 – T/808/15114, 15121

Muster roll of Cookstown cavalry and Loughrey infantry, 1797 – T/808/15242

General

A list of militia officers for all counties, 1761 – T/808/15235

Extracts from the regular army muster rolls, 1741–80 – T/808/15196

The names of the men who commanded local militia and yeomanry regiments were published during the eighteenth and nineteenth centuries. These are available at major libraries such as the Linen Hall and Central Libraries in Belfast or the local Irish History Libraries supported by the Education and Library Boards.

12. Newspapers

Newspapers are excellent sources of information on family history. The main drawback to using them is usually the lack of a comprehensive index that would facilitate searching. The first edition of the *Belfast Newsletter* appeared in 1737, making it the longest continuously published newspaper in Ireland. Its readership extended far beyond Belfast to include much of Ulster. A volume listing subscribers to the *Belfast Newsletter, 1795–7,* is available in PRONI (T/2771/4). At first many news items related to national and international events; it was only later that local news began to feature prominently.

12.1 Eighteenth-century Ulster newspapers
Seven newspapers are known to have been published in Ulster in the eighteenth century; most of these were relatively shortlived. They were:

> *Belfast Evening Post* (also published under the title *Belfast Mercury or Freeman's Chronicle*), 1783–7
> *Belfast Newsletter*, 1737–present (now the *News Letter*)
> *Gordon's Newry Chronicle and General Advertiser*, 1777–*c.*1795
> *Londonderry Journal*, 1772–present (now the *Derry Journal*)
> *Newry Journal*, 1770–76
> *Northern Star*, 1792–7
> *Strabane Journal or the General Advertiser*, 1771–1801

For a full list of newspapers printed in Ireland with dates of publication and availability, visit the following website: www.nli.ie/ca_newsplan.htm.

12.2 Range of material
Material of genealogical value in newspapers comes in a number of forms. First of all, there are birth, marriage and death notices. In the eighteenth century few births were announced in newspapers, and those that did appear were generally for upper-class families and fairly uninformative, with the child's name and also that of the mother often omitted. Marriage notices usually provide a little more information, such as the residence of each party, though the bride's name will often be no more than 'Miss ...'. Death notices

occasionally provide a brief sketch of the life of the deceased. The following notice appeared in the *Londonderry Journal* on 1 January 1773.

> A few days since died in the parish of Ardstraw and County of Tyrone, Robert McCreary aged 106. He came over as a soldier with King William; he had three wives [and] a number of children and grandchildren; he was married to his third wife nine years ago by whom he has left three children, the youngest of which is but two years old. He was very healthy and retained his senses to the last.

Advertisements can also be of assistance to researchers, particularly if they provide details of local businesses. Notices of court cases provide details of convictions. Although most researchers do not want to find out that one of their ancestors was a criminal, many names do appear and may be relevant. When land was being sold the names of the sitting tenants were often published, along with a description of their holdings. Lengthy petitions often appear in eighteenth-century newspapers. In 1799–1800 petitions concerning the Act of Union were published in the *Belfast Newsletter* (see Chapter 5.12 above). Lists containing the names of those who had subscribed to something, such as a reward for information on a crime, also make regular appearances in newspapers.

Occasionally there will be information on emigrants from Ulster. Published in the *Belfast Newsletter* on 26 November 1771 is a letter from the passengers of the *Philadelphia* thanking their captain, James Malcom, for his conduct towards them on their voyage from Belfast to Philadelphia. In particular he 'distributed a greater variety of provisions than was promised; which, with his humane usage, helped much to the rendering the voyage unhurtful and agreeable. The signatories to the letter, which was penned at Delaware Bay on 4 July 1771, were as follows.

John McCollough	John McClughan	Hugh Ramsey
Thos Alexander	Samuel Irwin	Samuel Colvin
James McHenry	John Storry	Robert Bell
Michael Rankin	Richard McQuon	Wm Meek
Francis Lee	James Campbell	David Fairservise
James Boyd	John Hill	Wm Patterson
Adam Johnston	Thos Hill	David Parkinson
Wm Thompson	Samuel Long	Hans Woods
Daniel Young	James Duncan	John Cairns
John Gallaway	Samuel Duff	John Cooper
James Laird	David Leathin	John Clark
Wm Watson	Wm Hallyday	James Laird
Matthew McCauley	Robert Corry	Samuel Allan
Hugh O'Quin	Alex Boyse	George Willson
Joseph Wilson	Henry Hannah	
Hamilton Potts	Wm Stirling	

There are extensive extracts from the *Belfast Newsletter* in PRONI (MIC/19), from which the following lists of names have been taken as examples of what may be found.

Rent roll of part of the estate of Captain Ross of Portavoe, County Down: 34 names –
2 January 1749–50
List of free and independent inhabitants of Belfast: *c.*120 names – 26 February 1754
Offer of a reward in relation to the burning of a house on the lands of Connor, County
Antrim: 42 names of the principal inhabitants of Antrim, 74 names of inhabitants of
Kells and Connor – 16 January 1756
Petition from inhabitants of Ballywalter and Ballyhalbert in response to the threat of danger
from 'our most treacherous enemies the French': 78 names – 13 April 1756
Offer of reward from inhabitants of Ballymonistrogh and Tullynagee, Kilmood parish,
County Down: 29 names – 29 June 1756
List of registered linen lappers published by the Linen Board: 117 names from County
Antrim; 129 names from County Armagh; 31 names from County Cavan; 6 names from
County Donegal; 106 names from County Down; 4 names from County Dublin; 1
name from County Fermanagh; 28 names from County Londonderry; 4 names from
County Louth; 28 names from County Monaghan; 30 names from County Tyrone –
7 July 1758
List of subscribers from Antrim town offering reward: over 150 names – 27 January 1761
List of those willing to attend linen market at Portadown, County Armagh: 37 names plus
residences – 4 December 1761
List of those willing to attend linen market at Richhill, County Armagh: 122 names –
28 May 1762
Notice from distillers in Coleraine district, Kilrea Survey: 25 names – 9 December 1766

12.3 Newspaper indexes

A comprehensive index to the pre-1800 issues of the *Belfast Newsletter* is available on
microfiche at the Linen Hall Library and on the web: www.ucs.louisiana.edu/bnl. In
addition there is an index to the pre-1800 birth, marriage and death notices in the Linen
Hall Library and at PRONI (T/1584). The following indexes and extracts also relate to
pre-1800 newspapers.

Index to marriages and deaths in *Pue's Occurences* and the *Dublin Gazette* 1730–1740 –
NLI Ms 3197
Index to *Freeman's Journal*, 1763–71 – NLI
Index to the *Hibernian Chronicle*, 1769–1802 (compiled 1936)
Index to marriages, 1771–1812, in *Walker's Hibernian Magazine* (2 vols, London, 1897)
Irish Genealogical Abstracts from the Londonderry Journal, 1772–84 by Donald Schlegel
(Clearfield Publishing, 1990, reprinted 2001)
Extracts of births, marriages and deaths taken from *Gordon's Newry Chronicle*, 1778–9 –
T/699/6
A list of notices, 1785–7, extracted by Annette McKee from the Strabane Journal was
published in the *Directory of Irish Family History Research* 15 (1992), p. 65
Index to County Down and Lisburn items in the *Northern Star*, 1792–7, prepared by
J. McCoy and published by the South Eastern Education and Library Board in 1992.

13. Genealogical collections

PRONI has in its custody working papers of scholars and family historians that are of enormous interest to genealogists. Pedigrees for families from many different parts of Ireland are available. Most notable of these are pedigrees extracted from wills proved in the Prerogative Court of Ireland, 1536–1810, compiled by or for Sir Bernard Burke, Ulster King of Arms. This collection of 42 large volumes of pedigree charts is available at PRONI under T/559.

Another very important series for genealogists is the Blackwood Pedigrees held by the Linen Hall Library, Belfast, with microfilm copies at PRONI (MIC/315). Compiled by Reginald Walter Blackwood, the pedigrees consist of 94 volumes with a separate index. Genealogical material collected by F. C. Crosslé of Newry comprises 33 volumes of miscellaneous notes, newspaper cuttings, and monumental inscriptions relating to Newry and its neighbourhood (seventeenth–twentieth centuries), including transcripts of local Church of Ireland registers, 1784–1864 and of the Presbyterian Church, 1809–63 (NLI Mss 2202–34; PRONI T/618 and T/699). The antiquarian and genealogical papers of the Reverend David Stewart are also available in PRONI (D/1759 and MIC/637). Under D/3000 PRONI has gathered genealogical material deposited by those who have commissioned or carried out research into their ancestry. A large collection of notes of historical and genealogical interest relating to the Coleraine area may be found among the papers of Max Given (D/4164/A).

13.1 The Groves collection

The papers of Tenison Groves form the largest collection of genealogical notes in PRONI. Judging from the collection of over 9,000 items purchased by PRONI in 1939, Tenison Groves was a researcher of extraordinary prowess and industry. The value of his collection lies in the fact that it contains a vast amount of information derived from documents in the Public Record Office of Ireland prior to its destruction in 1922. The Groves collection is, for example, the best single source in PRONI for abstracts of pre-1858 wills. In addition to wills, the Groves collection includes muster rolls, militia lists, collectors' accounts, gravestone inscriptions, numerous abstracts from the Registry of Deeds, and extracts from court cases. The one drawback for the researcher is that Groves's handwriting is almost indecipherable in places. Fortunately, many of his notes were typed.

The genealogical material on families in the Groves Collection has been arranged roughly by surname starting with the same letter. The arrangement under each letter is not strictly alphabetical and material on one name can appear in several volumes. The family history collection is followed by material extracted on a county basis. This is arranged alphabetically by county, and within that some attempt has been made to order it chronologically. The sheer volume of information in the Groves Collection can be daunting for the researcher, and it is simply not possible here to provide a detailed listing of all the items of value to those researching the seventeenth and eighteenth centuries. Researchers are advised to consult the PRONI calendar for specific information on what is available.

13.2 The Genealogical Office

Founded as the Office of the Ulster King of Arms in 1552, the Office of the Chief Herald is the oldest Office of State in Ireland. The Chief Herald is the Heraldic Authority for Ireland, responsible for the regulation of heraldic matters and the granting and confirming of coats of arms. The Office passed to the control of the government of the then Irish Free State in 1943, since when it has been known as the Genealogical Office. It is now a department of the National Library of Ireland and, since 1995, the post of Chief Herald has been held by the Director of the National Library. Documents deriving from the functions of the Office include the Registers of the Chief Herald, armorials and ordinaries of arms, funeral entries, lords' entries and records of knights dubbed. Other collections may be considered equally important to the researcher, and certain information from now-lost sources previously held in the Public Record Office of Ireland is of particular value. Tabulated pedigrees contained in the abstracts of wills proved at the prerogative court of the Archbishop of Armagh can be consulted. Other collections have been acquired as sources of genealogical information include Ecclesiastical Visitations, a list of high sheriffs of counties, lists of freeholders, and a list of gentlemen attainted by King James. For an in-depth look at the Genealogical Office and its sources researchers should consult *Guide to the Genealogical Office, Dublin* (Dublin: Irish Manuscripts Commission, 1998). This includes a listing of the manuscripts (numbered 1 to 822) and an index to some 7,500 will abstracts in the Office.

14. Miscellaneous sources

14.1 Business records

Business records from this period are few and far between, and vary considerably in their usefulness for genealogical research. Some will contain detailed listings of customers and clients. A few of the more valuable surviving records are set out below.

Businessmen who issued tokens in Ireland, 1653–79; printed in *Irish Ancestor*, x, no. 1 (1978), pp. 51–60

Account book of a Ballycastle merchant, 1751–4; over 300 names listed in full in the calendar – T/1044

Thomas Greer's market book covering the purchase of cloth in the markets of Dungannon, Stewartstown, Caledon, Moneymore, Monaghan and Cootehill, 1758–9; over 700 names of sellers listed in PRONI calendar – T/1127/4

Cash book of William McCrea, salaried linen buyer, operating in the markets of Strabane, Newtownstewart, Omagh and Londonderry, 1765–80 – D/664/O/1

Account book of James Ferguson of Belfast, linen merchant, 1771–83 – D/468/1

Cash account book, recording, *inter alia*, wages paid, of the linen firm of the Richardsons of Bessbrook, County Armagh, 1784–9 – MIC/120/1

See also George Chambers, 'Divided loyalties in the business community of Belfast in 1798' in *Familia* no. 10 (1994), pp. 13–38, which includes brief pen pictures of 105 of the town's merchants.

14.2 Education records

A state-run system of education was not established in Ireland until 1831. Before that there were various schemes to provide education to children. The Church of Ireland in each parish was required to keep a school, but apart from the occasionally surviving name of the schoolmaster little is known about the way they were conducted. There were many instances where a Presbyterian minister conducted a school in his own home, but again records are lacking.

Of the very few school records surviving from the eighteenth century, the most interesting relate to Lurgan Free School, established by the Brownlows to provide education for the children of the poor in Shankill parish, County Armagh. Among the surviving records of this school is a book giving the names of the pupils who attended as well as the names of their parents, their religious denomination and age. The book covers the period 1786–95 and can be found among the Brownlow papers in PRONI (D/1928/S/1/1).

For the Vaughan Charity School there is a register of male pupils from 1787 (D/433/5). This records the name of the pupil, his age, religion, parish, county, date of certificate, by whom recommended, and a column titled 'Observations'. The last of these contains some interesting information about the fate of the boys. For example, John Finlay, who started the school in 1787, was apprenticed to Felix Magee, a shoemaker in Ardess, Magheraculmoney parish. Neal McCourt, who began his education there in 1788, was 'taken away by his mother rather than let him be ap[prentice]d to a Protestant master'. Other pupils at the school simply ran away. A list of the original pupils at the school and their addresses was published in *Clogher Record*, xii (1986), p. 178.

Other education records of potential interest are set out below.

Armagh Royal, County Armagh – *Register of the Royal School, Armagh*, compiled by Major M. L. Ferrar (Belfast, 1933).

Dungannon Royal, County Tyrone – alphabetical list of boys with notes on their careers, names of fathers, etc., *c.*1648–1920 – MIC/29/1.

Enniskillen (Portora) Royal School, County Fermanagh – pupils who matriculated at Trinity College, Dublin – printed in W. C. Trimble, *The History of Enniskillen* (3 vols, Enniskillen, 1919–21), iii, pp. 828–31.

Glasgow University – *The matriculation albums of the University of Glasgow from 1728 to 1858*, transcribed and annotated by W. Innes Addison (Glasgow, 1913).

King's Inns, Dublin – *King's Inns admission papers, 1607–1867*, edited by Edward Keane, P. Beryl Phair, and Thomas U. Sadleir (Dublin, 1982). This institution trained men for the legal profession in Ireland.

Trinity College, Dublin – *Alumni Dublinenses: a register of the students, graduates, professors and provosts of Trinity college, in the University of Dublin* edited by George Dames Burtchaell and Thomas Ulick Sadleir (London, 1924). A new edition with a supplement was published in 1935.

14.3 Emigration records

Records relating to emigration from Ulster prior to 1800 are sparse. Of the tens of thousands who left Ulster for Colonial America in the eighteenth century, information on their movements has survived for only a fraction. Some information may be gleaned from newspapers. For example, Chapter 12.2 above includes a letter printed in the *Belfast Newsletter* on 26 November 1771 from the passengers of the *Philadelphia* thanking their captain, James Malcom, for his conduct towards them on their voyage from Belfast to Philadelphia. Such items are, however, extremely rare. For 1791–2 there is a list of passengers sailing from Warrenpoint and Newry to New York and Philadelphia (T/711/1).

The best study of emigration from Ulster in the eighteenth century is R. J. Dickson, *Ulster Emigration to Colonial America, 1718–75* (London, 1966). A detailed study of one group of (mainly Reformed Presbyterian) migrants from Ulster is Jean Stephenson, *Scotch-Irish Migration to South Carolina, 1772 (Rev. William Martin and his five shiploads of settlers)* (privately published, 1971).

Located at the Ulster-American Folk Park near Omagh, County Tyrone, the Centre for Migration Studies has the best collection of material relating to migration from Ireland. Its Irish Emigration Database (IED) is a computerised collection of over 30,000 records drawn from a variety of eighteenth- and nineteenth-century sources, including emigrant letters, newspaper articles, shipping advertisements, and passenger lists. The IED can currently be accessed in the Research Library of the Centre for Migration Studies, at PRONI, and in the Local Studies Departments of the Education and Library Boards in Armagh, Ballymena, Ballynahinch, Belfast, Enniskillen, Londonderry and Omagh.

14.4 Secret societies

The Grand Lodge of Freemasons of Ireland was founded in 1725. For anyone who thinks their ancestor may have been a member of this institution, the best place to find out more is the archive in Freemasons' Hall in Dublin. Membership registers are available here from 1760, but in general pre-1800 material is limited as far as genealogical information is concerned. Minutes of the Grand Lodge survive from 1780 and those of the Committee of Charity from 1795. For more information see C. G. Horton, 'The records of the Freemasons of Ireland' in *Familia* vol. 2 no. 2 (1986), pp. 65–9, which also includes a map showing the location of Masonic lodges in Ireland in 1770. The Orange Order was formed in 1795, but there is as yet no centralised record of members. Material of interest in PRONI includes an account book of Masonic Lodge no. 138, 1756–73 [Coleraine area?] and a list of members of Orange Lodge no. 316, Coleraine, 1797–9 (D/668/O/1). Extracts from the records of Ballymoney Masonic Lodge no. 240 for the period 1761–1849 are also available at PRONI (T/1177/19/3–8). These include lists of members of the lodge and names of members expelled for their involvement in the 1798 rebellion.

14.5 Tithe records

The tithe system earmarked one-tenth of the produce of the land for the maintenance of the clergy of the Church of Ireland. Until 1823 tithes could be paid in money or in kind (the Tithe Composition Act of that year stipulated that henceforth all tithes were to be paid in money). The payment of tithes was deeply resented by non-conformist Protestant denominations and by Catholics, and was a major source of contention. Disputes over the payments of tithes were common. In Donagheady parish, County Tyrone, in the 1730s, for example, when two farmers were unable to agree the value of their tithe with the rector, the latter came with a posse of sixty horsemen and rode through their farm, tearing up the fields and destroying the crop. Early tithe records are extremely rare and may be no more than a list of names by townland with perhaps the value of the tithe indicated. They will only record the names of tenant farmers, not urban-dwellers or landless labourers. Those tithe records that have survived are listed under the respective parishes in Appendix 3.

APPENDIX 1

Pre-1800 church records for Ulster

Unless otherwise indicated all references are to sources in PRONI. For Church of Ireland records in local custody, consult the most recent *Church of Ireland Directory* or visit www.ireland.anglican.org/dioceses/index.html for contact details of ministers. For Presbyterian records in local custody, consult the most recent *Directory of the Presbyterian Church in Ireland.*

Acton CI *see under* BALLYMORE

AGHADERG, COUNTY DOWN

CI Aghaderg (Dromore diocese)
Vestry minutes, 1747–   Local custody

P Glascar
Baptisms, 1780– ; marriages, 1781–   MIC/1/63

AGHADOWEY, COUNTY LONDONDERRY

CI Aghadowey (Derry diocese)
Vestry minutes, 1774–   Local custody

P Aghadowey
Session minutes, 1702–61   PHS

P Killaig
Communicants roll, 1749–   PHS

AGHALOO, COUNTY TYRONE

CI Aghaloo or Caledon (Armagh diocese)
Baptisms, 1791–5; marriages, 1792–5; burials,   T/679/286, 290
1792–5; vestry minutes, 1691–   (MIC/583/25);
                                                         MIC/1/326A/1; D/2602/1

The vestry records of the Church of St John parish
of Aghalow, Caledon, Co. Tyrone, 1691–1807
edited by J. J. Marshall (Dungannon, 1935)

AGHALURCHER, COUNTIES FERMANAGH AND TYRONE

CI Aghalurcher (Clogher diocese)
Baptisms, 1788–   T/679/25 (MIC/583/3)

Vestry minutes, 1747–   Local custody

AGHANUNSHIN, COUNTY DONEGAL
CI Aghanunshin (Raphoe diocese)
Vestry minutes, 1788–   MIC/1/214

AGHAVEA, COUNTY FERMANAGH
CI Aghavea (Clogher diocese)
Vestry minutes, 1762– , including poor list, 1774   MIC/1/229D/1–2
(name and address of poor person plus name of
person making recommendation), names of
persons appointed to sit on a committee to
decide on the poor, 1774

AHOGHILL, COUNTY ANTRIM
MOR Gracehill
Diaries that record baptisms, marriages and deaths   MIC/1F/3
as well as the movement of members, 1750– ; baptisms,
1749– ; marriages, 1758– ; burials, 1766– ; elders'
conference minutes, 1755– ; congregational committee
minutes, 1788– ; congregational council minutes,
1790–95; lot conference minutes, 1755–91;
register of members with an index, 1755–91

ALL SAINTS, COUNTY DONEGAL
CI All Saints (Raphoe diocese)
Vestry minutes, 1773–   MIC/1/176

P Crossroads
Church history, c.1780–1885   MIC/1P/259

Annageliffe CI *see under* URNEY

ANNAHILT, COUNTY DOWN
CI Annahilt (Dromore diocese)
Baptisms, 1784–91; marriages, 1777; burials,   MIC/1/101/1
1784; vestry minutes, 1777–

Annahilt P *see under* HILLSBOROUGH

ANTRIM, COUNTY ANTRIM
CI Antrim (Connor diocese)
Baptisms, 1700–55, 1785– ; marriages,   T/679/133, 134
1700–56, 1788– ; burials, 1700–54; 1786–   (MIC/583/11, 12);
                                                         MIC/1/328A/1–2

P 1st Antrim (Millrow)
Baptisms, 1677–1733 (including index), 1753–85,   MIC/1P/3, CR/3/2A/1
1791–2; marriages, 1675–1736 (including index);
family records for the 18th and 19th centuries

Antrim or Grange RSF *see under* **GRANGE OF BALLYSCULLION**

ARBOE, COUNTIES LONDONDERRY AND TYRONE
CI Arboe (Armagh diocese)
Baptisms, 1775– (including index); marriages,   T/679/111
1773– (including index); burials, 1776– ; vestry minutes,   (MIC/583/10); D/1278/1
1773– ; lists of the poor, 1789, 1794; census,
1775; confirmation list, 1775

ARDKEEN, COUNTY DOWN
CI Ardkeen (Down diocese)
Baptisms, 1745– ; marriages, 1748– ; burials,   T/679/121
1746– (all with gaps); confirmations, 1745–   (MIC/583/10);
                                                       T/1065/28/1

ARMAGH, COUNTY ARMAGH
CI Armagh (Armagh diocese)
Baptisms, 1750–58, 1775– ; marriages,   T/679/140 (MIC/583/12)
1750–58, 1776– ; burials, 1750–58, 1770–75
Vestry minutes, 1791–   Local custody

P 1st Armagh
Baptisms, 1707–28, 1796– (including index); marriages,   MIC/1P/4, D/1759/1B/1
1707–28, 1796– (including index); copies of session   (MIC/637/1); T/636/1,
accounts, 1707–32, with a list of session members, 1707   pp. 277–337

Session accounts, 1707–32   PHS

RC Armagh (Armagh diocese)
Baptisms, 1796–   MIC/1D/41

ARMOY, COUNTY ANTRIM
CI Armoy (Connor diocese)
Vestry minutes, 1758–   MIC/1/334D/1

ARTREA, COUNTIES LONDONDERRY AND TYRONE
CI Artrea (Armagh diocese)
Vestry minutes, 1723–   MIC/1/319D/1

Copy of vestry minutes, September 1730   T/500/3

CI Woods Chapel (Armagh diocese)
Vestry minutes, 1792–   MIC/1/97

MOR Gracefield
Diaries, 1759– (with gaps); baptisms, 1750– ; burials, 1765– ;   MIC/1F/3
register of members with an index, 1759– (with gaps)

AUGHNISH, COUNTY DONEGAL

**CI Aughnish or Tullyaughnish, including
Tullyfern (Raphoe diocese)**
Baptisms, 1798– ; marriages, 1788– ; burials, 1798–   MIC/1/167A/1

BALLEE, COUNTY DOWN

CI Ballee (Down diocese)
Baptisms, 1792–   T/679/157 (MIC/583/14)

RC Ballee and Saul
Baptisms, 1785– ; marriages, 1785–   UHF

BALLINDERRY, COUNTY ANTRIM

CI Ballinderry (Connor diocese)
Vestry minutes, 1790–   T/679/167 (MIC/583/14)

MOR Ballinderry
Baptisms, 1754– ; marriages, 1784– ;   MIC/1F/1
register of members, 1755– ; ministers' diary, 1768

BALLINDERRY, COUNTIES LONDONDERRY AND TYRONE

CI Ballinderry (Armagh diocese)
Vestry minutes, 1773–   Local custody

BALLINTOY, COUNTY ANTRIM
[This parish was created out of Billy *c.*1670]

CI Ballintoy (Connor diocese)
Vestry minutes, 1712– ; poor list, 1790, census, 1803   T/679/68, 69
                                                               (MIC/583/6, 7);
                                                               MIC/1/111

Ballyalbany P *see under* TEDAVNET

BALLYBAY, COUNTY MONAGHAN

P 1st Ballybay
Baptisms, 1799–   PHS

Ballycarry NSP *see under* TEMPLECORRAN

Ballycopeland P *see under* DONAGHADEE

BALLYCULTER, COUNTY DOWN
CI Ballyculter (Down diocese)
Baptisms, 1777–   D/2319, T/679

Ballyhagen RSF *see under* KILMORE, COUNTY ARMAGH

BALLYHALBERT ALIAS ST ANDREW'S, COUNTY DOWN
P Glastry
Baptisms, 1728– ; marriages, 1750–   MIC/1P/111

Ballykelly P *see under* TAMLAGHT FINLAGAN

BALLYMONEY, COUNTY ANTRIM
P 1st Ballymoney
Baptisms, 1751–71 (with gaps); session minutes,   MIC/1P/373; CR/3/1
*c.*1733–4; poor accounts, 1751–9

See also the call to Rev. Benjamin Mitchell,
1800, available as as online database at
www.ballymoneyancestry.com

BALLYMORE, COUNTY ARMAGH
CI Acton (Armagh diocese)
Vestry minutes, 1793–   Local custody

CI Ballymore (Armagh diocese)
Baptisms, 1783– ; marriages, 1783– ; burials,   T/679/52, 271
1783– ; vestry minutes, 1771–   (MIC/583/5, 24);
                                                       MIC/1/324A/1

Extracts from vestry minutes, 1771–1810   T/2706/6, pp. 125–42

P Tyrone's Ditches
Baptisms, 1793– ; marriages, 1794– ; stipend collected,   MIC/1P/457
1790– (the foregoing are all loose–leaf bundles of pages)

Ballynahinch P *see under* MAGHERADROOL

BALLYPHILIP, COUNTY DOWN

CI Ballyphilip (Down diocese)

Baptisms, 1745– ; marriages, 1746– ; burials, 1745–   T/679/218, 219
                                                          (MIC/583/17, 18)

Vestry minutes, 1751–   Local custody

P Portaferry
Baptisms, 1699–1786; marriages, 1750–84   MIC/1P/137/1

BALLYWILLIN, COUNTIES ANTRIM AND LONDONDERRY

CI Ballywillin (Connor diocese)
Vestry minutes, 1710–55   MIC/1/287D/1

Banbridge 1st NSP *see under* SEAPATRICK

BANGOR, COUNTY DOWN

CI Bangor (Down diocese)
Vestry minutes, 1788–   CR/1/87/D/1

BELFAST *see under* SHANKILL, COUNTY ANTRIM

BLARIS, COUNTIES ANTRIM AND DOWN

CI Lisburn (Christ Church cathedral) (Connor diocese)
Baptisms, 1637, 1639–41, 1643–6, 1655– ; baptisms of   T/679/112
Huguenot children, 1707–36; marriages, 1639–41,   (MIC/583/10);
1643–6, 1664– ; burials, 1639–41, 1661– ; burials in   MIC/1/3–5; CR/1/35
Lisburn Cathedral churchyard, 1670– ; vestry minutes,
1675– ; confirmations, 1667, 1675, 1678; cess book,
c.1800; notebook of the Reverend Thomas Haslam, c.1675–95

Register of the Church of St Thomas, Lisnagarvey,
Co. Antrim, 1637–1646 (Dublin, 1996)

P 1st Lisburn
Baptisms, 1692–1732, 1736–64, 1779– ; marriages,   MIC/1P/159; CR/3/11
1688–96, 1711–19, 1782– ; session minutes, 1688–1709,
1711–63; subscription list for the new meeting house,
1764–5; seat lists and pew rents, 1764– ; accounts, 1775–

RSF Lisburn
Men's monthly meeting minutes, 1675– ;   MIC/16/7–23
women's monthly meeting minutes, 1793–1800;
minsters' and elders' minutes, 1791– ; births,
1781– ; marriages, 1731–86 ; removal certificates,

1766– ; register of members, 1794– ; disownment records,
1703– ; account book, 1789– ; register of tithe sufferings, 1706–11

Boardmills 1st P *see under* **KILLANEY**

BOVEVAGH, COUNTY LONDONDERRY
CI Bovevagh (Derry diocese)
Vestry minutes, 1777–   Local custody

BRIGHT, COUNTY DOWN
CI Bright (Down diocese)
Vestry minutes, 1770– , with poor lists, 1791–   MIC/1/115/1

BURT, COUNTY DONEGAL
Burt P
Session minutes, 1676–1719   Union Theological College

Cahans P *see under* **TULLYCORBET**

CAPPAGH, COUNTY TYRONE
CI Cappagh (Derry diocese)
Baptisms, 1753– ; marriages, 1752– ; burials,   T/679/4, 303, 328
1758– ; vestry minutes, 1755–   (MIC/583/1, 27, 30)

Carland P *see under* **DONAGHMORE, COUNTY TYRONE**

CARNMONEY, COUNTY ANTRIM
CI Carnmoney (Connor diocese)
Baptisms, 1788– ; marriages, 1791–   T/679/332 (MIC/583/29)

P Carnmoney
Baptisms, 1708– ; marriages, 1708– ; session minutes,   MIC/1P/37/4–9; T/1013/1
1686–1748, 1767– ; poor lists, 1716–84; names of those
who transferred from other congregations, 1708–25

Notebook giving marriages, births and deaths of   T/1013/2A–B
various families with an index, 1708–1917

See also Robert H. Bonar, *Nigh on three and a half centuries.
A history of Carnmoney Presbyterian Church* (2004), including
a call to Rev. John Thomson sen., 1730 (pp. 328–9) and
a call to Rev. John Thomson jun. (pp. 330–31)

CARNTEEL, COUNTY TYRONE
CI Carnteel (Armagh diocese)
Vestry minutes, 1712–   T/679/355 (MIC/583/31)

CARRICKFERGUS, COUNTY ANTRIM
CI Carrickfergus (Connor diocese)
Baptisms, 1740–99; marriages, 1740; burials, 1740–1800   T/679/323 (MIC/583/28)

Accounts of building church spire, 1778   CR/1/25

Carrickmacross CI *see under* **MAGHEROSS**

CASTLERAHAN, COUNTY CAVAN
RC Castlerahan and Munterconnaught (Kilmore diocese)
Baptisms, 1752–71, 1773–6; marriages, 1751–71, 1773–5;   MIC/1D/81
deaths, 1751–8, 1761–9, 1773–5

CASTLETARA, COUNTY CAVAN
RC Castletara (Kilmore)
Baptisms, 1763– ; marriages, 1763–93   MIC/1D/83–4

Clogh CI *see under* **CLONES**

CLOGHER, COUNTY TYRONE
CI Clogher (Clogher diocese)
Baptisms, 1763– ; marriages, 1777–8, 1796– ;   MIC/1/22, 23
burials, 1783, 1798– ; list of churchwardens,
1713– ; vestry minutes, 1713–95

'Some christenings, marriages and burials in the parish
church of Clogher, Co. Tyrone in 1666 with some notes'
by Jack Johnston in *Clogher Record* xiv (1992), pp. 63–5

CLONCA, COUNTY DONEGAL
CI Cloncha (now Raphoe diocese, formerly Derry)
Vestry minutes, 1693–1707   D/803/1

CLONDAVADDOG, COUNTY DONEGAL
CI Clondevaddock (Raphoe diocese)
Baptisms, 1794– ; marriages, 1794– ; burials, 1794– ;   MIC/1/164A/1
census, 1796

CLONDUFF, COUNTY DOWN

CI Clonduff (Dromore diocese)
Baptisms, 1782– ; marriages, 1786– ; burials, 1787–   T/679/17 (MIC/583/2)

RC Clonduff (Dromore diocese)
Printed history of Clonduff parish from the   CR/2/4
17th century to 1940

CLONES, COUNTIES FERMANAGH AND MONAGHAN

CI Clogh (Clogher diocese)
Marriages, 1792–   MIC/1/288

CI Clones (Clogher diocese)
Baptisms, 1682– ; marriages, 1682–1788, 1792– ;   MIC/1/147; CR/1/58/1, 2
burials, 1682–1704, 1709, 1722–5, 1733–34;
vestry minutes, 1688– , which include lists of
seatholders, 1735–83; poor list, c.1741

CLONFEACLE, COUNTIES ARMAGH AND TYRONE

CI Clonfeacle (Armagh diocese)
Extracts from vestry minutes, 1763–   T/679/43 (MIC/583/4)

RSF Grange ('near Charlemont')
Men's monthly meeting minutes, 1726–70, 1776–9,   MIC/16/34–8
1787–95; record book of testimonies against Quakers,
1686–1784; family record books, 1653–1814, 1725–1805;
testimonies of disownment, 1755–84; accounts, 1733–40

CLONLEIGH, COUNTY DONEGAL

CI Clonleigh (Raphoe diocese, formerly Derry)
Vestry minutes, 1788–   MIC/1/179

RC Clonleigh and Camus (Derry diocese)
Baptisms, 1773–95; marriages, 1778–81   MIC/1D/61

CLONOE, COUNTY TYRONE

CI Clonoe (Armagh diocese)
Vestry minutes, 1783–   MIC/1/11

CLONTIBRET, COUNTY MONAGHAN

CI Clontibret (Clogher diocese)
Vestry minutes, 1711, 1749–   MIC/1/149

Clough NSP *see under* LOUGHINISLAND

Clough P *see under* LOUGHINISLAND

COLERAINE, COUNTY LONDONDERRY
CI Coleraine (Connor diocese)
Baptisms, 1769– ; marriages, 1769– ; burials, 1769– ;   MIC/1/7A
vestry minutes, 1769–

Extracts from vestry minutes, 1769–1816   D/4164/A/28

P 2nd Coleraine (New Row)
Extracts from treasurers' book, 1774–1834   T/1069/9–11

COMBER, COUNTY DOWN
CI Comber (Down diocese)
Baptisms, 1683– ; marriages, 1683– ; burials, 1683– ;   T/679/411–13, 415B
vestry minutes, 1700– , which include a list of   (MIC/583/36, 37)
churchwardens, 1797– , and poor lists, c.1799

Extracts from registers, 1712–   T/921/1

CONNOR, COUNTY ANTRIM
RP Kellswater
Session minutes of Antrim meeting   CR/5/9
(Kellswater and Cullybackey), c.1789–

Coronary P *see under* KNOCKBRIDE

CRAIGS, COUNTY ANTRIM
[This parish was created out of Ahoghill c.1840]
P Cullybackey (Cunningham Memorial)
Baptisms, 1726– ; marriages, 1727–92   PHS

CREGGAN, COUNTIES ARMAGH AND LOUTH
CI Creggan (Armagh diocese)
Vestry minutes, c.1730–   MIC/1/112/1

RC Upper Creggan (Crossmaglen) (Armagh diocese)
Baptisms and marriages, 1796–   MIC/1D/43

Croghan P *see* Killeshandra P *under* KILDALLON

Crossroads P see under ALL SAINTS

CULDAFF, COUNTY DONEGAL
CI Culdaff (Raphoe diocese, formerly Derry)
Baptisms, 1668–c.1790 (with gaps); marriages, 1713–21,   D/803/1
1770–82; burials, 1714–18; vestry minutes, 1693–1803

Cullybackey P *see under* **CRAIGS**

Cullybackey RP *see under* **CONNOR**

DERRYAGHY, COUNTY ANTRIM
CI Derriaghy (Connor diocese)
Baptisms, 1696–1763, 1771– ; marriages, 1696–1746,   MIC/1/32, 33; T/679/35
1772; burials, 1696–1738, 1772–3; vestry minutes,   (MIC/583/4)
1709–58, 1794– , including confirmation list, 1705

DERRYLORAN, COUNTIES LONDONDERRY AND TYRONE
CI Derryloran (Armagh diocese)
Baptisms, 1795– ; marriages, 1797– ; burials, 1797–   MIC/1/15/1

DERRYNOOSE, COUNTY ARMAGH
CI Derrynoose (Armagh diocese)
Baptisms, 1710–46 (with gaps); marriages,   MIC/1/14; T/679/10
1712–43; vestry minutes, 1709–   (MIC/583/2)

DESERTCREAT, COUNTY TYRONE
CI Desertcreat (Armagh diocese)
Burial (1 entry), 1791; vestry minutes, 1740– ,   MIC/1/9/1
including a poor list of 1784

DESERTLYNN, COUNTY LONDONDERRY
CI Desertlynn (Armagh diocese)
Baptisms, 1797– ; marriages, 1797– ; burials, 1798–   MIC/1/10A

DESERTMARTIN, COUNTY LONDONDERRY
CI Desertmartin (Derry diocese)
Baptisms, 1785– ; marriages, 1784– ; burials, 1783, 1788;   MIC/1/16; T/679/6
vestry minutes, 1751– , with some baptisms for 1752   (MIC/583/1)

List of tithes, 1794   Local custody

DEVENISH, COUNTY FERMANAGH

CI Devenish (Clogher diocese)
Vestry minutes, 1739–   MIC/1/31

DONACAVEY, COUNTY TYRONE

CI Donacavey or Fintona (Clogher diocese)
Vestry minutes, 1779– , including poor lists, 1783–   MIC/1/45/2

Notes on the vestry book, 1778–1802   D/1048/4

Donacloney P *see under* **DONAGHCLONEY**

DONAGH, COUNTY DONEGAL

CI Donagh (Raphoe diocese, formerly Derry)
Vestry minutes, 1782–   Local custody

DONAGH, COUNTY MONAGHAN

CI Donagh (Clogher diocese)
Baptisms, 1736, 1796– ; marriages, 1736, 1797– ; burials,   MIC/1/127
1736, 1797– ; vestry minutes, 1731– ; poor list, 1775

DONAGHADEE, COUNTY DOWN

CI Donaghadee (Down diocese)
Baptisms, 1771– ; marriages, 1772– ; burials, 1771– ;   MIC/1/17; T/679/44
vestry minutes, 1779– ; list of parishioners, 1797   (MIC/583/5)

Indexes to baptisms, marriages and burials, 1771–   PSR

Cess applotment, 1779–   Local custody

P Ballycopeland
Baptisms, 1773–   PHS

P 1st Donaghadee
Baptisms, 1793– ; session and committee minutes, 1783–   MIC/1P/167

P Millisle
Baptisms, 1773– ; list of elders and members, 1777   MIC/1P/230/7;
                                                         MIC/1P/382A/1

See also T. Kilpatrick, *Millisle and Ballycopeland Presbyterian
Church. A short history* (Newtownards, 1934) for a list of
subscriptions to Millisle meeting house, 1773 (pp. 2–7),
a list of seats let to members, 1776 (pp. 9–13), and names
subscribed to a call to the Rev. Andrew Greer, 1777 (pp. 17–18).

DONAGHCLONEY, COUNTY DOWN

CI Donaghcloney (Dromore diocese)
Baptisms, 1697– ; marriages, 1697– ; burials, 1697– ;   MIC/1/92, 93
vestry minutes, 1772– ; parish accounts, 1745–8

P Donacloney
Baptisms, 1798–   MIC/1P/342

DONAGHEDY, COUNTY TYRONE

CI Donagheady (Derry diocese)
Baptisms, 1697–1723, 1753–65; marriages,   MIC/1/35–6
1697–1726, 1754–64; burials, 1698–1726, 1754–7;
vestry minutes, 1697–1723, 1754– ; confirmation list,
1701; poor lists, 1726–38

Churchwardens' account book, 1793   Local custody

DONAGHENRY, COUNTY TYRONE

CI Donaghenry or Donaghendry (Armagh diocese)
Baptisms, 1733–4, 1754–68; marriages, 1733–5, 1754–68,   T/679/331 (MIC/583/29)
1763– ; burials, 1735, 1754–68; vestry minutes, 1738–

DONAGHMORE, COUNTY DOWN

CI Donaghmore (Dromore diocese)
Baptisms, 1783– (including index); marriages, 1795   MIC/1/54/2
(including index); burials, 1784– (including index)

DONAGHMORE, COUNTY TYRONE

CI Donaghmore (Armagh diocese)
Baptisms, 1748– ; marriages, 1741– ; burials, 1741–;   T/679/19 (MIC/583/2);
vestry minutes, 1781–2   MIC/1/106/1–2

Typescript copy of baptisms, 1748– ;   MIC/1/106/3
marriages, 1741– ; burials, 1741– (with indexes);
vestry minutes, 1778, 1781–2

Vestry minutes, 1783–   Local custody

P Carland
Baptisms, 1759–99; marriages, 1770–1802   MIC/1P/28

DOWN, COUNTY DOWN

CI Down or Downpatrick (Down diocese)

Baptisms, 1733–4, 1750– ; marriages, 1701– ; burials, 1718–36, 1752– ; vestry minutes, 1704– ; briefs read out in the church after which money was collected, 1716–35; list of poor widows and others exempted from paying hearth money tax, 1733; vestry accounts, 1753–69	MIC/1/38, 39; CR/1/33
Copy of baptisms, marriages and burials, 1752–	T/684/1
Copy of baptisms, 1733– , marriages, 1701– , and burials, 1719–	D/1759/1D/3 (MIC/637/2)

Memoirs of seatholders in 1735, printed in R. E. Parkinson (ed.), *The City of Downe* (London, 1927), pp. 62–76

NSP Downpatrick

Memoranda and account books, *c.*1740–	T/1268/1/1–6

DROMARA, COUNTY DOWN

P 1st Dromara

Baptisms, 1762– ; marriages, 1799–1802; session minutes, 1763– ; accounts, 1762–99	MIC/1P/89, T/1447
History of the church, 1713–1913	D/2453/85

DROMORE, COUNTY DOWN

CI Dromore (Dromore diocese)

Baptisms, 1784– ; marriages, 1784– ; burials, 1784–	T/679/395 (MIC/583/35)

DROMORE, COUNTY TYRONE

CI Dromore (Clogher diocese)

Vestry minutes, 1762–	Local custody

DRUMACHOSE, COUNTY LONDONDERRY

CI Drumachose (Derry diocese)

Baptisms, 1730–52; marriages, 1728–53; burials, 1730–36; vestry minutes, 1729–77, 1787, 1794– , which include a list of those who attended church on Easter Day, 1754	T/679/3, 394 (MIC/583/1, 35)

DRUMBEG, COUNTIES ANTRIM AND DOWN

NSP Dunmurry

Notes about the history of the church, *c.*1686–1820	CR/4/1
Burials in the churchyard, 1781–1954	T/1602

DRUMBO, COUNTY DOWN
CI Drumbo (Down diocese)
Baptisms, 1791– ; marriages, 1791– ;   MIC/1/41
burials, 1792– ; vestry minutes, 1788–

P Drumbo
Baptisms, 1699–1723, 1764–73, 1781–92; marriages,   MIC/1P/291;
1706–21, 1772, 1782–83, 1786–91   D/1759/1D/1
                                                           (MIC/637/2)

Printed history of the congregation from the early 17th century   CR/3/54

DRUMCREE, COUNTY ARMAGH
CI Drumcree (Armagh diocese)
Baptisms, 1788–   MIC/1/21

Vestry minutes, 1767– ; cess applotment book, 1767   Local custody

DRUMGATH, COUNTY DOWN
P 1st Rathfriland
Marriages, 1782–   MIC/1P/131;
                                                           D/1759/1D/14
                                                           (MIC/637/4)

DRUMGLASS, COUNTY TYRONE
CI Drumglass (Armagh)
Baptisms, 1665–1767, 1774–1802; marriages,   MIC/1/18; MIC/1/36
1677–1766, 1791–2, 1799–1804; burials, 1672–1767;
vestry minutes, 1693–

P 1st Dungannon
Baptisms, 1790– ; marriages and notices of marriages   MIC/1P/3A
with rebukes for irregular marriages, 1789–

DRUMGOOLAND, COUNTY DOWN
CI Drumgooland (Dromore diocese)
Baptisms, 1779–92; marriages, 1779–91   MIC/1/40A/1

DRUMGOON, COUNTY CAVAN
RSF Cootehill
Men's monthly meeting minutes, 1766–96   MIC/16/45

DRUMHOME, COUNTY DONEGAL

CI Drumhome (Raphoe diocese)
Baptisms, 1719–20, 1739–48, 1764, 1783– ; marriages,   MIC/1/148
1691–1718, 1764, 1783– ; burials, 1696–1715, 1764, 1783–

Vestry minutes, 1783–   Local custody

DRUMKEERAN, COUNTY FERMANAGH
[This parish was created out of Magheraculmoney c.1774]

CI Drumkeeran (Clogher diocese)
Vestry minutes, 1794–   Local custody

DRUMRAGH, COUNTY TYRONE

CI Drumragh (Derry diocese)
Vestry minutes, 1792–   MIC/1/40C/1

RC Drumragh
Printed history of the parish from the 17th century to c.1900   CR/2/9/1

DRUNG, COUNTY CAVAN

CI Drung (Kilmore diocese)
Baptisms, 1759– ; marriages, 1785– ; burials, 1774–   MIC/1/300

DUNAGHY, COUNTY ANTRIM

CI Dunaghy (Connor diocese)
Notebook of the Rev. Andrew Rowan, 1672–80   T/796/1

DUNBOE, COUNTY LONDONDERRY

CI Dunboe (Derry diocese)
Vestry minutes, 1783– , including some baptisms,   MIC/1/135D/1
1790–91, 1795 and accounts, 1796

DUNDONALD, COUNTY DOWN

P Dundonald
Session book, including baptisms and marriages, 1678–1716   PHS

For extracts, see 'The Old Session Book of the Presbyterian
Congregation at Dundonald' in *Ulster Journal of Archaeology*,
2nd series 3 (1893).

Dungannon 1st P *see under* DRUMGLASS

DUNGIVEN, COUNTY LONDONDERRY
CI Dungiven (Derry diocese)
Baptisms, 1795– ; marriages, 1795– ; vestry minutes, 1778–   T/679/70 (MIC/583/7)

Baptisms, 1778–94; marriages, 1778–94   Local custody

DUNLUCE, COUNTY ANTRIM
CI Dunluce (Connor diocese)
Vestry minutes, 1778–   MIC/1/90/1

Dunmurry NSP *see under* DRUMBEG

EMATRIS, COUNTY MONAGHAN
CI Ematris (Clogher diocese)
Vestry minutes, 1767– , with baptisms, 1753–91,   MIC/1/132
and marriages, 1753–75

ENNISKILLEN, COUNTY FERMANAGH
CI St Macartin's Cathedral, Enniskillen (Clogher diocese)
Vestry minutes, 1731–

Extracts of baptisms, 1667–1789, marriages, 1668–1794,   MIC/1/110/1; D/2296/1
and burials, 1667–1781   CR/1/21A/1

Extracts from baptism, marriage and burial registers,   T/3548/1
1666–1826

Printed copy of *Old Enniskillen Vestry Book*,   D/3007/T/578
with extracts of births, marriages and deaths, 1666–c.1797

Extracts from vestry minutes, 1666–1912, which   D/1588/6
include some baptisms, marriages and burials

ERRIGAL, COUNTY LONDONDERRY
P 1st Garvagh
Baptisms, 1795– ; marriages, 1795– ; census of   MIC/1P/257
congregation, 1796

ERRIGAL KEEROGUE, COUNTY TYRONE
CI Errigal Keerogue (Armagh diocese)
Vestry minutes, 1757   MIC/1/2/1

ERRIGAL TROUGH, COUNTIES MONAGHAN AND TYRONE

CI Errigal Trough (Clogher diocese)
Baptisms, marriages and burials, 1671–2;   MIC/1/125A/1
1719–20, 1722–3, 1728–9

FAHAN UPPER, COUNTY DONEGAL

CI Fahan Upper (Derry diocese)
Baptisms, 1762– ; vestry minutes, 1792– ;   MIC/1/180D/1
cess applotment, 1793–

FAUGHANVALE, COUNTY LONDONDERRY

CI Faughanvale (Derry diocese)
Census, 1803   MIC/1/7B

Fintona CI see under DONACAVEY

FINVOY, COUNTY ANTRIM

CI Finvoy (Connor diocese)
Vestry minutes, 1791–   Local custody

GALLOON, COUNTY FERMANAGH

CI Galloon (Clogher diocese)
Baptisms, 1798– ; marriages, 1798– ;   MIC/1/51/1
burials, 1798– ; vestry minutes, 1779–

Garvagh 1st P *see under* ERRIGAL

Gilnahirk P *see under* KNOCKBREDA

Glascar P *see under* AGHADERG

Glastry P *see under* BALLYHALBERT

GLENAVY, COUNTY ANTRIM

CI Glenavy (including Camlin and Tullyrusk) (Connor diocese)
Baptisms, 1707– ; marriages, 1707– ; burials,   T/679/1 (MIC/583/1);
1707– ; vestry minutes, 1707–   MIC/1/43, 44

Gracefield MOR *see under* ARTREA

Gracehill MOR *see under* AHOGHILL

GRANGE, COUNTY ARMAGH

CI Grange (Armagh diocese)
Baptisms, 1780– ; marriages, 1780– ; burials, 1783–   MIC/1/65/1

GRANGE OF BALLYSCULLION, COUNTY ANTRIM

RSF Antrim or Grange (Grange, Ballynacree, Toberhead, Coleraine and Antrim)
Men's monthly meeting minutes, 1740– ; women's   MIC/16/43
monthly meeting minutes, 1794–1800; volume containing
testimonies of disownment etc., 1758–1800; marriages,
1768–77; births, 1751–1800; deaths, 1741–97

Grange ('near Charlemont') RSF *see under* **CLONFEACLE**

GREYABBEY, COUNTY DOWN

CI Greyabbey (Down diocese)
Vestry minutes, 1789–   MIC/1/49/1

HILLSBOROUGH, COUNTY DOWN

CI Hillsborough (Down diocese)
Baptisms, 1686–95, 1763–9, 1772– ; marriages, 1688–95,   MIC/1/62A, B
1772–4, 1782– ; burials, 1688–1735, 1772–3, 1784;
vestry minutes, 1709–

Register of marriages by licence, 1796–   D/1944/8/1

P Annahilt
Baptisms, 1780–   MIC/1/360A/1

INCH, COUNTY DOWN

CI Inch (Down diocese)
Baptisms, 1767– ; marriages, 1764, 1791– ;   MIC/1/49;
burials, 1788– ; vestry minutes, 1757–   MIC/1/311/1, 7

Manuscript copy of baptisms, marriages and   D/1759/1D/4
burials, 1796–1933   (MIC/637/3)

INISHARGY, COUNTY DOWN

CI Inishargy (Down diocese)
Baptisms, 1783– ; marriages, 1783; burials, 1783– ;   T/679/278 (MIC/583/24);
vestry minutes, 1706–84, which include baptisms,   MIC/1/96/1
1728–69, marriages, 1728–69 and burials, 1769–71;
vestry minutes, 1783–

P Kircubbin
Baptisms, 1778– ; marriages, 1781– ;
collections and accounts, 1777–87

MIC/1P/396;
D/1759/1D/12
(MIC/637/4)

INISHKEEL, COUNTY DONEGAL
CI Inishkeel (Raphoe diocese)
Baptisms, 1699–1700, marriages, 1699; burials,
1699–1700; confirmations, 1715, 1723

CR/1/51/1–3

INISHMACSAINT, COUNTIES DONEGAL AND FERMANAGH
CI Inishmacsaint (Clogher diocese)
Vestry minutes, 1765–

MIC/1/50/1

Extracts from baptisms, 1660–72, marriages,
1663–72, and burials, 1662–72

T/808/15274–6

Extracts from baptisms, marriages and burials,
1660–1814

T/3548/2

Extracts from baptisms, marriages and burials,
1660–1866 with gaps

CR/1/7

INVER, COUNTY ANTRIM
CI Inver (Connor)
Vestry minutes, 1763– , including poor lists, 1769,
1800 and a list of cess payers in Raloo parish, 1769–70

T/679/59 (MIC/583/6);
MIC/1/49/1

INVER, COUNTY DONEGAL
CI Inver (Raphoe diocese)
Vestry minutes, 1782–

MIC/1/159C/1

JONESBOROUGH, COUNTY ARMAGH
CI Jonesborough (Armagh diocese)
Vestry minutes, 1799–

Local custody

KEADY, COUNTY ARMAGH
CI Keady (Armagh diocese)
Baptisms, 1780– ; marriages, 1780–

T/679/8A (MIC/583/1);
MIC/1/51/1

Kellswater RP see under CONNOR

KILBARRON, COUNTY DONEGAL
CI Kilbarron (Raphoe diocese)
Baptisms, 1785–93; marriages, 1785– ; burials, 1785–   MIC/1/156A/1

Vestry minutes, 1691–1781   Local custody

KILBRONEY, COUNTY DOWN
CI Kilbroney (Dromore diocese)
Vestry minutes, 1798–   MIC/1/87/1

Parish registers, 1784–1867   DIO/1/14/1

KILCOO, COUNTY DOWN
CI Kilcoo (Dromore diocese, formerly Down)
Baptisms, 1786–   T/679/57 (MIC/583/5);
                         MIC/1/55/1

KILCRONAGHAN, COUNTY LONDONDERRY
CI Kilcronaghan (Derry diocese)
Baptisms, 1790– ; marriages, 1748–   MIC/1/52/1

Vestry minutes, 1749–   Local custody

KILDALLON, COUNTY CAVAN
P Killeshandra (formerly known as Croghan)
Baptisms, 1743–81, 1799; marriages, 1741–76; register   MIC/1P/164/1–3
of members, c.1835, with dates of birth of children in
each family, the earliest being in 1790; accounts, 1743–80

KILDRESS, COUNTY TYRONE
CI Kildress (Armagh diocese)
Baptisms, 1794– ; marriages, 1794– ; vestry minutes, 1709–   MIC/1/107/1

KILDRUMSHERDAN OR KILLERSHERDONY, COUNTY CAVAN
CI Killersherdoney (Kilmore diocese)
Baptisms, 1796– ; marriages, 1796– ; burials, 1797–   MIC/1/281A/1

KILLAGHTEE, COUNTY DONEGAL
CI Killaghtee (Raphoe diocese)
Vestry minutes, 1748–   DIO/3/40

Killaig P *see under* AGHADOWEY

KILLANEY, COUNTY DOWN

P 1st Boardmills

Baptisms, 1782– ; marriages, 1782– ; session minutes, 1784– ; private censures, 1784–	MIC/1P/72
Copy of baptisms and marriages, 1724–54, 1782–	D/1759/1D/1–2 (MIC/637/2)

KILLEA, COUNTY DONEGAL [Formerly part of Templemore parish]

CI Killea (Raphoe diocese, formerly Derry)

Vestry minutes, 1788–	Local custody

KILLESHANDRA, COUNTY CAVAN

CI Killeshandra (Kilmore diocese)

Baptisms, 1735; marriages, 1735– ; burials, 1735–	MIC/1/220

Killeshandra P *see under* **KILDALLON**

KILLESHER, COUNTY FERMANAGH

CI Killesher (Kilmore diocese)

Baptisms, 1798– ; marriages, 1798–	T/679/48 (MIC/583/5); MIC/1/56/1

KILLINCHY, COUNTY DOWN

CI Killinchy (Down diocese)

Vestry minutes, 1716–57, 1779; accounts, 1778–90, 1794	T/679/109, 109a (MIC/583/10)

NSP Killinchy

[Includes records of Killinchy Presbyterian
Church prior to the setting up of Killinchy NSP
Church in 1835]

Pew rent book, c.1785; accounts, 1781–	CR/4/17; D/1759/1D/9 (MIC/637/3)

KILLINKERE, COUNTY CAVAN

RC Killinkere (Kilmore diocese)

Baptisms, 1766–90; marriages, 1766–89	MIC/1D/82

KILLOWEN, COUNTY LONDONDERRY

CI Killowen (Derry diocese)

Vestry minutes, 1747–	Local custody
Extracts from vestry minutes, 1747–1872	D/4164/A/23

KILLYBEGS UPPER, COUNTY DONEGAL

CI Killybegs (Raphoe diocese)
Baptisms, 1787–96; vestry minutes, 1788–   Local custody

KILLYGARVAN, COUNTY DONEGAL

CI Killygarvan (Raphoe diocese)
Vestry minutes, 1706– (including some baptisms, 1706–8,   MIC/1/166D/1
1725–7, 1737–8, 1785, 1788, 1790, 1792–3; marriages,
1706–8, 1725–6, 1737; burials, 1706–8, 1727–8, 1786–7,
1793, 1796, 1799)

Typescript list of 18th-century baptisms, marriages   MIC/1/166A/1
and burials extracted from vestry minutes

KILLYLEAGH, COUNTY DOWN

P Killyleagh
Baptisms, 1693–1757; marriages, 1692–1757;   MIC/1P/53;
minute books, 1725–32   D/1759/1D/11
    (MIC/637/4)

KILLYMAN, COUNTIES ARMAGH AND TYRONE

CI Killyman (Armagh diocese)
Baptisms, 1745– ; marriages, 1741– ; burials, 1745– ;   T/679/383–5
vestry minutes, 1756–   (MIC/583/33, 34)

KILMOOD, COUNTY DOWN

CI Kilmood (Down diocese)
Burials, 1793–   MIC/1/59A

KILMORE, COUNTY ARMAGH

CI Kilmore (Armagh diocese)
Baptisms, 1789–95, 1799– ; marriages, 1799– ;   MIC/1/8/1
vestry minutes, 1733–79

Extracts from vestry minutes, 1732–79   T/476/1; T/636/1,
    pp. 73–80

P Vinecash
History of the church, 1697–1923   MIC/1P/348

RSF Ballyhagen (includes Richhill)
Family lists with details of births and burials, *c.*1680–1814   MIC/16/39
(Ballyhagen and Richhill); marriage certificates, 1692–1789
(Ballyhagen); testimonies of disunity, 1708–1813

(Ballyhagen and Richhill); wills and inventories, 1685–1740
(Ballyhagen); account book of Ballyhagen monthly
meetings, 1714–66; minutes of men's meetings, 1705–43

RSF Richhill and Grange
Men's minutes, 1793–   MIC/16/42

KILMORE, COUNTY CAVAN
CI Kilmore (Kilmore diocese)
Baptisms, 1702– ; marriages, 1702– ; burials, 1702–   MIC/1/255A/1

KILREA, COUNTY LONDONDERRY
CI Kilrea (Derry diocese)
Vestry minutes, 1736– ; notes on the parish of Kilrea,   MIC/1/55/1
1607–1947

KILSKEERY, COUNTY TYRONE
CI Kilskeery (Clogher diocese)
Baptisms, 1767– ; marriages, 1778– ; burials, 1796–   MIC/1/6/1

Indexes to baptisms, 1767–1844, marriages, 1778–1841,   PSR
and burials, 1796–1841

Kilwaughter NSP *see* **Larne and Kilwaughter NSP** *under* **LARNE**

KINAWLEY, COUNTIES CAVAN AND FERMANAGH
CI Kinawley (Kilmore diocese)
Baptisms, 1761–3, 1768–83, 1794– ;   MIC/1/76; CR/1/62A/1
marriages, 1761–3, 1768– ; burials, 1768– ;
vestry minutes with accounts, 1775–

CI Swanlinbar (Kilmore diocese)   MIC/212
Baptisms, 1798– ; marriages, 1798– ; burials, 1799–

Kircubbin P *see under* **INISHARGY**

KIRKINRIOLA, COUNTY ANTRIM
CI Kirkinriola (Connor diocese)
Baptisms, 1789– ; burials, 1780, 1792; vestry minutes, 1777–   T/679/192 (MIC/583/16);
                                                                MIC/1/327A/1;
                                                                CR/1/78A/1

KNOCKBREDA, COUNTY DOWN
CI Knockbreda (Down diocese)
Baptisms, 1785– ; marriages, 1784– ; burials,   MIC/1/57/1
1787– ; vestry minutes, 1791–

P Gilnahirk
Baptisms, 1797–   MIC/1P/432

KNOCKBRIDE, COUNTY CAVAN
P Coronary
Baptisms, 1764– ; marriages, 1768–87; session minutes,   MIC/1P/179
1764–87; history of the congregation and details of
Sunday collections, 1769–89

LARNE, COUNTY ANTRIM
NSP Larne and Kilwaughter
Baptisms, 1720–69, 1796; marriages, 1721–69;   MIC/1B/6
session minutes, 1720–48; discipline cases, 1721–49;
poor accounts, 1720–57

Lisburn CI *see under* **BLARIS**

Lisburn 1st P *see under* **BLARIS**

Lisburn RSF *see under* **BLARIS**

LISSAN, COUNTIES LONDONDERRY AND TYRONE
CI Lissan (Armagh diocese)
Baptisms, 1753–95; marriages, 1744–94; burials,   T/679/9a (MIC/583/1)
1753–95; vestry minutes, 1734–

LOUGHGALL, COUNTY ARMAGH
CI Loughgall (Armagh diocese)
Baptisms, 1706–29, 1779– ; marriages, 1706–29, 1779– ;   MIC/1/59C
burials, 1706–29, 1779–94; vestry minutes, 1774–

Vestry minute book, 1774–1809, including a list of the   D/54/1
proprietors of seats, 1775; a detailed list of those charged
with responsibility for repairing roads, 1778 (over 50 names);
and several poor lists

Extracts from the registers, 1709–1841   T/636/1, p. 101

LOUGHGILLY, COUNTY ARMAGH

CI Loughgilly (Armagh diocese)
Vestry minutes, 1797–   Local custody

P Tullyallen
Baptisms, 1792–1834   Local custody

LOUGHGUILE, COUNTY ANTRIM

CI Loughguile (Connor diocese)
Extracts from vestry minutes, *c.*1701–*c.*1730   DIO/1/24/3/1–13

LOUGHINISLAND, COUNTY DOWN

CI Loughinisland (Down diocese)
Baptisms, 1760– , with index; marriages, 1760– , with   D/1407; T/1
index; burials, 1760–93, with index; vestry minutes, 1773–

NSP Clough
Baptisms, 1792– ; marriages, 1791–   T/1701/1

P Clough
Baptisms, 1791– ; marriages, 1791–   MIC/1P/308

LURGAN, COUNTY CAVAN

RC Lurgan (Virginia) (Kilmore diocese)
Baptisms, 1755–95 (with gaps, 1778–9 and 1785–6);   MIC/1D/80–81
marriages, 1755–70, 1773–80

Lurgan 1st P *see under* SHANKILL, COUNTIES ARMAGH AND DOWN

Lurgan RSF *see under* SHANKILL, COUNTIES ARMAGH AND DOWN

Lylehill P *see under* TEMPLEPATRICK

MAGHERA, COUNTY LONDONDERRY

CI Maghera (Derry diocese)
Baptisms, 1785– ; marriages, 1798–   MIC/1/20, 77

MAGHERACULMONEY, COUNTY FERMANAGH

CI Magheraculmoney (Clogher diocese)
Baptisms, 1767– ; marriages, 1767– ; burials, 1767– ;   MIC/1/67, 68
vestry minutes, 1763– , including poor lists, 1769–

MAGHERADROOL, COUNTY DOWN

P Ballynahinch
Baptisms, 1696–1735; marriages, 1696–1733; collections
and disbursements, 1704–24; testimonials and certificates,
1715–34†

MAGHERAFELT, COUNTY LONDONDERRY

CI Magherafelt (Armagh diocese)
Baptisms, 1718–93, 1799– ; marriages, 1720– ; burials,   MIC/1/1A
1716–71, 1799; vestry minutes, 1718–95, 1798–

P 1st Magherafelt
Baptisms, 1703–6, 1771–80; marriages, 1769–82   PHS

MAGHERAGALL, COUNTY ANTRIM

CI Magheragall (Connor diocese)
Baptisms, 1776– ; marriages, 1772– ; burials,   MIC/1/75/1
1772–81; vestry minutes, 1771–

Miscellaneous papers, 1641–1930   T/1398/12

MAGHERALIN, COUNTIES ARMAGH AND DOWN

CI Magheralin (Dromore diocese)
Baptisms, 1692– ; marriages, 1692–82, 1785– ; burials,   T/679/365, 368, 376,
1692– ; vestry minutes, 1692–   380 (MIC/583/32, 33);
                                                             MIC/1/18/1

Churchwardens' accounts, 1766–94   Local custody

Extracts from parish registers, 1784–1853   DIO/1/14/6

MAGHERALLY, COUNTY DOWN

CI Magherally (Dromore diocese)
Extracts from parish registers, 1784–91   DIO/1/14/7

P Magherally
Account books relating to stipends, collections   MIC/1P/211D/1
and expenses, 1788–

MAGHEROSS, COUNTY MONAGHAN

CI Magheross or Carrickmacross (Clogher diocese)
Baptisms, 1796– ; marriages, 1798– ; burials, 1798–   MIC/1/173A/1

---

† Available on the internet at the following address:
http://freepages.genealogy.rootsweb.com/~rosdavies/WORDS/BallynahinchPresbyterianIndex.htm.

MAGILLIGAN OR TAMLAGHTARD, COUNTY LONDONDERRY
CI Tamlaghtard (Derry diocese)
Baptisms, 1747–68; marriages, 1747–53; burials,   MIC/1/86/1
1768–75; vestry minutes, 1747– ; list of the poor, 1773

Millisle P *see under* DONAGHADEE

MOIRA, COUNTY DOWN
CI Moira (Dromore diocese)
Baptisms, 1725–56; marriages, 1725–56; burials,   MIC/1/79, 80
1725–56; vestry minutes, 1725–55, 1758– ;
accounts, 1745–8

Extracts from parish registers, 1784–1860   DIO/1/14/8

MOVILLE LOWER, COUNTY DONEGAL
CI Moville Lower (Raphoe diocese, formerly Derry)
Vestry minutes, 1783–   MIC/1/138

MULLAGH, COUNTY CAVAN
RC Mullagh (Kilmore diocese)
Baptisms, 1760– ; marriages, 1766–   MIC/1D/82

MULLAGHBRACK, COUNTY ARMAGH
CI Mullabrack (Armagh diocese)
Baptisms, 1764–83, 1799– ; marriages, 1767–83, 1798– ;   MIC/1/83/1
vestry minutes, 1764–89

Typescript copy of marriages, 1767–83, 1798–1811,   CR/1/72B/1
plus 5 entries of death, 1732–1762, and birth dates of
the children of Squire Barker and Sara Bury, 1730–50

NEWRY, COUNTIES ARMAGH AND DOWN
CI Newry (Dromore diocese)
Marriages, 1784– ; vestry minutes, 1775–   MIC/1/47A/1;
          D/2034/2/1–2, /4/1

Index to marriages, 1784   D/2034/1/1

NSP Newry
Baptisms, 1779–97; marriages, 1781–95   T/699/7

Portaferry P *see under* BALLYPHILIP

RAPHOE, COUNTY DONEGAL
CI St Eunan's Cathedral, Raphoe (Raphoe diocese)
Baptisms, 1771–83; marriages, 1771– ; burials,   MIC/1/95/1
1771–83; vestry minutes, 1673–

RATHLIN, COUNTY ANTRIM
CI Rathlin (Connor diocese)
Vestry minutes, 1769–95   MIC/1/115/1

Rathfriland 1st P *see under* DRUMGATH

Richhill RSF *see under* KILMORE, COUNTY ARMAGH

ROSSORY, COUNTY FERMANAGH
CI Rossory (Clogher diocese)
Baptisms, 1796–7, 1799– ; marriages, 1799– ;   MIC/1/22/1
burials, 1799– ; vestry minutes, 1763–

ST ANDREW'S *see* BALLYHALBERT

Saul RC *see under* BALLEE

SAINTFIELD, COUNTY DOWN
CI Saintfield (Down diocese)
Baptisms, 1724–57, 1793– ; marriages, 1724–57,   MIC/1/69/1
1798; vestry minutes, 1730–

SEAGOE, COUNTY ARMAGH
CI Seagoe (Dromore)
Baptisms, 1672–1731, 1735– ; marriages, 1672–1731,   MIC/1/73, 74A, 75
1735– ; burials, 1672–1731, 1735– ; vestry minutes, 1683– ,
including over 130 names arranged by townland of those
required to plant trees, 1709, and a series of poor lists
beginning in 1691

Indexes to baptisms, marriages and burials, 1672–1919   PSR, UHF

Analysis of registers of baptisms, marriages and burials,   T/2588
1672–1904

SEAPATRICK, COUNTY DOWN
NSP 1st Banbridge
Baptisms, 1754–94; marriages, 1756–94   T/2995/1

SHANKILL, COUNTY ANTRIM
CI St Anne's, Shankill (Connor diocese)
Baptisms, 1745– ; marriages, 1745; burials, 1745–69,   T/679/224, 225, 237, 238,
1784– ; indexes to baptisms, marriages and burials, 1745–   256 (MIC/583/18, 22, 23);
                                                              MIC/178A/12–18

Typed copy of marriages, 1745–99   D/1759/1C/2 (MIC/637/2)

Typed transcript of burial registers, 1745–71   MIC/583/19, 22

NSP All Souls, Belfast
Baptisms, 1782–92; marriages, 1771–87;   CR/4/9/A/1
poor accounts, 1792–

NSP Rosemary Street, Belfast
Baptisms, 1757– ; marriages, 1790– ; burials,   CR/4/5/1/1–3
1712–36, with funeral accounts, lists of members,
1760, 1775, 1781, 1783, 1790

P Rosemary Street, Belfast
Baptisms, c.1723– (including index); marriages,   MIC/1P/7/1–2;
c.1741– (including index); pew rent books, 1726–73,   T/654/1–3, 6–7
1788–96; lists of communicants, 1728–42; lists of
catechisable persons, 1725–6; committee minutes,
1774– ; accounts, 1721–70; stipend book, 1789–

Typed copy of marriages, 1741–61, with index   D/1759/1C/1 (MIC/637/2)

RC St Patrick's, Belfast
Baptisms, 1798–; marriages, 1798–   MIC/ID/66-67

SHANKILL, COUNTIES ARMAGH AND DOWN
CI Shankill (Dromore diocese)
Baptisms, 1681– ; marriages, 1676– ; burials, 1675– ;   MIC/1/18, 24, 25
vestry minutes, 1672–

Churchwardens' accounts, 1790– ; list of churchwardens,   Local custody
1760–

P 1st Lurgan
Baptisms, 1746– (including index); marriages,   MIC/1P/71
1746, 1754, 1759

RSF Lurgan
Births, 1632– ; marriages, 1632– ; burials, 1632– ;   MIC/16/24–33

minutes of men's meetings, 1675– ; minutes of women's
meetings, 1794– ; removal certificates, 1796– ; testimonies of
disownment, 1688–96; testimonies against Quakers, 1673–1700

Swanlinbar CI *see under* **KINAWLEY**

TAMLAGHT FINLAGAN, COUNTY LONDONDERRY
CI Tamlaght Finlagan (Derry diocese)
Baptisms, 1796– ; marriages, 1796– ; burials, 1796– ;   MIC/1/38/1
vestry minutes, 1748–

Index to the registers, 1796–1861   CR/1/8/1

P Ballykelly
Baptisms, 1699–1709 (including index); marriages,   MIC/1P/208
1699–1740 (including index)

Tamlaghtard CI *see under* **MAGILLIGAN**

TAUGHBOYNE, COUNTY DONEGAL
CI Taughboyne (Raphoe diocese)
Vestry minutes, 1796   MIC/1/174D/1

TEDAVNET, COUNTY MONAGHAN
P Ballyalbany
List of over 160 names of individuals who subscribed to
a call for a minister for Ballyalbany Presbyterian Church
in 1751 and a list of seatholders in the church in 1804, in
S. Lyle Orr and Alex Haslett, *Historical Sketch of Ballyalbany
Presbyterian Church* (Belfast, 1940), pp. 10–12, 64–9

TEHALLEN, COUNTY MONAGHAN
CI Tyholland (Clogher diocese)
Vestry minutes, 1712–   Local custody

TEMPLECARN, COUNTIES DONEGAL AND FERMANAGH
CI Templecarn (Clogher diocese)
Vestry minutes, 1777–   Local custody

TEMPLECORRAN, COUNTY ANTRIM
NSP Ballycarry
[Part of this church seceded from the Synod of Ulster in 1829]
Session minutes, 1704–80   CR/3/31/1–2, CR/4/18/1

TEMPLECRONE, COUNTY DONEGAL

CI Templecrone (Raphoe diocese)
Vestry minutes, 1776–   Local custody

TEMPLEMORE, COUNTY LONDONDERRY

[This parish formerly included the parishes of Burt, Killea and Muff.]

CI St Columb's cathedral, Templemore
Baptisms, 1642– ; marriages, 1649– ; burials, 1642–1775;   MIC/1/18, 19, 20, 26,
vestry minutes, 1741–93; acts of vestry, 1741–4, 1750–60;   27, 28
lists of cess payers, 1743–9, 1756–60, 1772–93;
tithe applotment book, 1772–84, 1786–93

Transcript of baptisms, marriages and deaths, 1703–32,   CR/1/6/1–3
with an index

Registers of Derry Cathedral, 1642–1703 (Dublin, 1910)

Register of the Cathedral Church of St Columb, Derry,
1703–32 (Dublin, 1997)

Register of the Cathedral Church of St Columb, Derry,
1732–75 (Dublin, 1999)

Parish cess applotments and lists, 1751–6   T/1020/1

Extracts from vestry book, 1772–84   T/945/1; T/946/1

TEMPLEPATRICK, COUNTY ANTRIM

NSP Templepatrick
[Prior to 1830 the records relate to Templepatrick
Presbyterian church]
Baptisms, 1796– ; marriages, 1797– ; accounts, 1799– ;   MIC/1B/11/1;
session minutes, 1646–1743; farm accounts, 1799–1812   CR/4/12B/1

P Lylehill
Stipend books, 1768–92   PHS

P Templepatrick
Baptisms, 1758– ; marriages, 1797–   PHS

The old session-book of Templepatrick Presbyterian Church,
ed. W. T. Latimer (Dublin, 1901)

TERMONMAGUIRK, COUNTY TYRONE

CI Termonmaguirk (Armagh diocese)
Vestry book, 1786–   MIC/1/340D/1;
                                                      CR/1/46/1

TICKMACREVAN, COUNTY ANTRIM

CI Tickmacrevan or Glenarm (Connor diocese)
Baptisms, 1719–23, 1727, 1788– ; indexes to baptisms,   MIC/1/72/1; T/3054
1788– ; marriages, 1719, 1723, 1727–8, 1789– ; index to
marriages, 1719–28 and 1788– ; vestry minutes, 1718–

Transcript of vestry minutes, 1718– ; with marriages,   T/3054
1719, 1723, 1727–8, and baptisms, 1719–23

TOMREGAN, COUNTIES CAVAN AND FERMANAGH

CI Tomregan (Kilmore diocese)
Baptisms, 1797–   MIC/1/218A/1

TRORY, COUNTY FERMANAGH

CI Trory (Clogher diocese)
Baptisms, 1779, 1784, 1796– ; marriages, 1779, 1799;   MIC/1/94/1; CR/1/19D/1
vestry minutes, 1778–

Tullyallen P *see under* **LOUGHGILLY**

TULLYAUGHNISH *see* **AUGHNISH**

TULLYCORBET, COUNTY MONAGHAN

CI Tullycorbet (Clogher diocese)
Baptisms, 1796–   MIC/1/44

Index to baptisms, 1796–   CR/1/44

P Cahans
Baptisms, 1751–9, 1767– ; session minutes with   CR/3/25A/1, 2, 4
discipline cases, 1751– ; indexes to baptisms, and
session minutes, 1751–

TULLYLISH, COUNTY DOWN

CI Tullylish (Dromore diocese)
Vestry minutes and accounts, 1792–   MIC/1/71/1

TULLYNISKAN, COUNTY TYRONE

CI Tullaniskan (Armagh diocese)
Baptisms, 1794– ; marriages, 1794– ; vestry minutes, 1791–   MIC/1/10A, 11

TYNAN, COUNTY ARMAGH

CI Tynan (Armagh diocese)

Baptisms, 1686–1725; marriages, 1683–1723; burials,   MIC/1/12, 13, 18
1683–1723; vestry minutes, 1699–

Baptisms, 1686–95; marriages, 1683–1723;   T/808/15294
burials, 1683–1723

Tyrone's Ditches P *see under* BALLYMORE

Upper Creggan RC *see under* CREGGAN

URNEY, COUNTY CAVAN

CI Urney (including the parish of Annageliffe) (Kilmore diocese)

Vestry minutes, 1737, 1741, 1753–99, including a list   MIC/1/239
(purpose unknown) of *c.*100 names, n.d. [*c.*1753],
poor lists, 1760–84 (that for 1775 has nearly 100 names)

Vinecash P *see under* KILMORE, COUNTY ARMAGH

Woods Chapel CI *see under* ARTREA

APPENDIX 2

Estate collections with records pre-dating 1800

This appendix lists by county some 250 estate collections with records pre-dating 1800. While it has not been possible to list in detail every pre-1800 estate record for Ulster, considerable lengths have been gone to present the surviving material in as accessible a format as possible. Particular attention has been given to rentals (or rent rolls, rent books, etc.), as generally these provide the easiest way of identifying a tenant farmer by townland. Collections of leases, particularly if these have been expertly calendared by staff at PRONI, are also listed. Maps are usually only included if they have extensive coverage of a particular estate or are perhaps the only relevant item from an estate archive.

In many instances a landowner may have held lands in more than one county. The way of dealing with such estates varies in the following list. If the nature of the estate archive allows it, the records will be listed under the appropriate county. For example, the nature of the Belmore archive means that it is possible to list separately the records pertaining to County Fermanagh and County Tyrone. On the other hand, the organisation of the Donegall estate archive means that it is not possible to divide the records properly between Counties Antrim and Donegal. In this instance all Donegall estate material for the pre-1800 period has been grouped together under County Antrim. Cross-referencing is used to indicate if an estate archive with relevance to one county is listed under another county. Depending on the volume of estate material, categories have been introduced to simplify matters.

COUNTY ANTRIM

Adair estate, Ballymena
Map of the estate, 1747, naming tenants – T/1333/3
Map of estate, 1789, naming tenants – T/1310/1–3
Leases for Ballymena estate, 17th-18th century, calendared in full, particularly good for 1680–1750 – D/929 *passim*
Rent roll of the Ballymena estate, 1794 – D/929/HA12/F3/2

Agnew estate, Kilwaughter and Larne
List of tenants and their stock, *c.*1645 – Scottish Record Office GD/154/514 (printed in R. G. Gillespie, *Colonial Ulster: the settlement of east Ulster, 1600–1641* (Cork, 1985), p. 228)
Leases etc., 18th century onwards – T/502 *passim*
Volume of maps by James Williamson, 1788, naming tenants: 18 townlands in Kilwaughter parish, 10 in Kilraghts, 9 in Carncastle, 2 in Larne and one each in the parishes of Kilbride, Tickmacrevan and the Grange of Doagh – T/2309/1

Antrim estate, Ballycastle, Ballymoney, Glenarm, Larne, etc.
Leases
A vast collection of leases starting in the early seventeenth century – D/2977/3A. These are arranged alphabetically by townland within barony. Leases covering more than one townland and those covering more than one barony are listed separately.

See also Ian Montgomery, 'Tenants on the estates of the Earls of Antrim in the seventeenth century' in *Directory of Irish Family History Research* no. 23 (2000), pp. 80–92, which lists some 340 leases alphabetically by lessee.

Lease books
Lease book of Glenarm barony, 1736 – D/2977/3B/1
General return of leases and tenures, 1737–1821 – D/2977/3B/2
Details of leases for Glenarm, Ballymoney and Larne, *c*.1743 – D/2977/3B/3
Counterpart lease register for Dunluce barony, Ballymoney and Coleraine Liberties, 1783, also used as a rent roll for Glenarm barony, 1795 – D/2977/3B/4
Notebook containing lease extracts relating to Glenarm town, *c*.1736–*c*.1881 – D/2977/3B/10
Notebook containing lease extracts relating to Larne town, 1736–1892 – D/2977/3B/11
Notebook and copy containing extracts from rent ledger, *c*.1685, 1720–58 – D/2977/3B/12–13
Notebook and copy containing details of fee farm and renewable leases for lives, *c*.1637–1781 – D/2977/3B/17–18
Notebooks and copies providing details of how land was held and rent and fees payable for the following baronies: Cary, Upper and Lower Dunluce, Upper and Lower Glenarm, Kilconway and the North East Liberties of Coleraine, *c*.1623–1785 – D/2977/3B/19–27
Extracts of early grants, 1637–1737 – D/2977/3B/29

Rentals
Rent roll, 1641 – T/694/1
Rent ledgers of the 'North' estate beginning in 1751 – D/2977/9/1–4
Rent ledger of the 'South' estate beginning in 1791 – D/2977/9/5

Maps and surveys
Survey and valuation of Antrim estate, 1734 – D/2977/25/1A
Reference to map of the barony of Glenarm, 1734 – D/2977/25/1B
Volumes of maps of holdings in the baronies of Cary, Dunluce, Glenarm and Kilconway, 1734, naming tenants – D/2977/35/1–4
Volumes of maps of holdings in the baronies of Cary, Glenarm and Kilconway, 1782, naming tenants – D/2977/35/5–7
Map of 'Old Town of Lairn alias Gardenmore', 1735, naming tenants – D/2977/36/2/1
Map of Glenarm with a list of tenants, 1779 – D/2977/36/3/1–2

Manor court records
COURT LEET
J. B. Hamilton (ed.), *Records of the Court Leet for the Manor of Dunluce in the County of Antrim held in the town of Ballymoney, 1798–1847* (Ballymoney, 1934) (originals destroyed)
Court leet book, manor of Glenarm, 1765–1812 – D/2977/23/2/1
Bundle of loose papers relating to the court leet of Glenarm, 1786–1845 – D/2977/23/2/3
Court leet book for the manor of Oldstone or Kilconway, 1773–1819 – D/2977/23/4/1
Several pages of an account and receipts book concerning the treasurers of the manor of Oldstone, 1776–80 – D/2977/23/4/2

MANOR COURT/COURT OF RECORD
Unbound section of a court book, manor of Dunluce, 1742–3 – D/2977/23/3/1
Court book, manor of Glenarm, 1755–96 – D/2977/23/1/1
Court book, manor of Glenarm, 1797–1814 – D/2977/23/1/2
Unbound section of a court book, including records of courts for the manor of Oldstone, held in Ballymoney, 1742–3 – D/2977/23/3/1
See also Ian Montgomery, 'The manorial courts of the Earls of Antrim' in *Familia* no. 16 (2000), pp. 1–23

Miscellaneous
Bundle of documents, including wages accounts of Antrim's servants, *c.*1763; list of tenants of Duneykiltar (Dunmakelter), *c.*1760 – D/2977/25/2

See also **McGildowney estate**

Boyd estate, Ballycastle
Rent roll of Boyd property in and around Ballycastle, 1799 – D/1375/7/12

Brytt estate, Carrickfergus
Map of William Brytt's estate in the Liberties of Carrickfergus, 1780, naming tenants – D/2121/5/3

Caledon estate, Ballycastle
Letters, rentals and accounts, 1788–96 – D/2433/A/2/6/1–57 (/1 is a rent roll of 1788)
Rent roll of Lord Caledon's estate, 1793 – D/1375/3/59/3

Conway estate, Lisburn
Rental of the manor of Killyleagh, London, Lisburn, Lambeg, Derryaghy, Magheragall, Magheramesk, Aghalee, Aghagallon, Ballinderry and Glenavy, 1719–23 – D/427/1
Rent roll, 1728–30 – D/427/2
Maps of the estate in the parishes of Blaris, Derryaghy, Lambeg and Magheragall, 1726, naming tenants – D/427/3
Maps of the estate in the parishes of Tullyrusk, Camlin, Glenavy, Ballinderry, Aghagallon, Aghalee and Magheramesk, 1729, naming tenants – D/427/4

Davy estate, Cullybackey
Map of Charles Davy's estate at Cullybackey, 1760, naming tenants – D/2121/5/1. Townlands of Carndonaghy, Corbally, Dreen and Lisnafillan.

Donegall estate, Belfast, Antrim, Inishowen etc.
Leases
Leases, early 17th century onwards, covering Belfast, Carnmoney, Carrickfergus, Donegore, Inishowen, etc. – D/509 *passim*
Leases, 1671 onwards (over 500 items prior to 1800) – D/652 *passim*

Maps
Maps of the estate in Inishowen, County Donegal, and in County Antrim, 1767–70, naming
    tenants – D/835/1/1–3

Rentals
Rental for Belfast, Moylinny, Ballylinny, Island Magee and Carrickfergus, 1719 – D/2249/61
Rent ledgers, Antrim estate, 1783–6, 1787–97, 1798–1806 – D/835/2/1–3
Rentals, 1775–82, 1798 (including a rental for Inishowen, County Donegal for 1741) –
    D/835/3/1–2
Cash rent book, Antrim estate, 1796–1800 – D/835/4/1

Other
Typescript volume of Donegall estate material, including accounts of payments and receipts,
    1706–15 – T/455/1
Donegall estate letter book, 1771–4 – T/1893/1

See also Peter Roebuck, 'The making of an Ulster Great Estate: the Chichesters, Barons of
Belfast and Viscounts of Carrickfergus, 1599–1648' in *Proceedings of the Royal Irish Academy*,
vol. 79C (1979); C. E. B. Brett, *Georgian Belfast, 1750–1850: Maps, Buildings and Trades*
(Dublin, 2004).

Downshire estate, Carrickfergus etc. – see under COUNTY DOWN

Dungannon estate, Island Magee, Raloo
Collection of leases, many from 18th century, for townlands including Allyvallagh, Ballyryland,
    Ballyrickard, Ballywillin, Carneal, Altilevelly, Ballygowan and Tureagh – D/1954/4 *passim*
List of lands and tenants of Lord Dungannon on Island Magee – *Belfast Newsletter*, 13 February
    1770

Edmonstone estate, Red Hall, Carrickfergus
Rent roll for the half year, 1777 – D/233/7
Ledger of Sir Archibald Edmonstone's estate (purchased by the Ker family c.1780), 1780–83 –
    MIC/261

Edwards estate, Glendun
Rentals and agents' accounts of the Edwards estate, including lands in County Antrim, 1777,
    1792 – MIC/343/1

Gage estate, Rathlin Island
Estate books, c.1789–1821 – D/463/1

Hamilton estate, Clogh Mills
Rent roll of the estate of William Hamilton, 1744 – T/2408/16
Rent roll of part of same to be sold, c.1760 – T/2408/20

Hutchinson estate, Portglenone
Account and notebooks of Bishop Francis Hutchinson, 1721–39 – DIO/1/22/1–3.

An additional volume, including rentals of the Portglenone estate from the 1730s, is in the process of being accessioned by PRONI.

Kirk estate, Ballyclare and Carrickfergus
Correspondence, c.1718–35 – T/2524
Leases, 1629 onwards (53 pre–1800, not all relating to the Kirk family) – D/2121/4 *passim*
Map of William Kirk's estate in Carrickfergus, 1786, naming tenants – D/2121/5/4

Langford and Langford-Rowley estate *see* Pakenham estate

Legg(e) estate, Malone etc.
Maps of the estate of Alexander Legg in the barony of Dunluce and in Shankill parish, 1774, 1782, 1796, and Lacken near Ballyroney in the parish of Drumballyroney, 1781, 1791 – D/915/18/1
Leases, 1777 onwards – D/915/7/3
Map of Legg estate in the parish of Derrykeighan, 1790 – D/915/18/3

McGildowney estate, Ballycastle
(Some of the material in this collection relates to the earl of Antrim's estate)
Rental of Glenarm, 1742 – D/1375/5/2
Memorandum book of Edmund McGildowney recording receipts and expenditure in connection with estate and business concerns (other than the earl of Antrim's estate), 1790–94 – D/1375/7/1
Volume containing accounts of rents received by Edmund McGildowney in payment of Marchioness of Antrim's jointure, 1800–1 – D/1375/5/3/1

Macartney estate, Carrickfergus, Lissanoure, Loughguile
Leases
Abstracts of leases for lands near Carrickfergus, 1607–1683, compiled c.1770 – T/2408/8A
17th- and 18th-century deeds and leases – D/1062/2/1

Maps
Volume of estate maps, c.1760–c.1800, naming tenants – T/1064/7/1–24
Volume of estate maps, c.1760–c.1800, naming tenants – D/1062/2/4/1
Map of 'Loughgeel', c.1770 – T/1064/2/1
Map of lands in Dunluce and Kilconway baronies, 1790 – D/588/1
Map of Loughguile estate, 1790 – T/1064/6/1
Map of Dervock, 1802, naming tenants – D/662/1

Miscellaneous
Memorandum books, 1790 – D/557/1
Survey and valuation of estate, 1767 – D/572/21/96 (MIC/438/7)

Rentals
Printed rental of the Loughguile estate, 1759 – D/1375/5/2
Rent rolls of Loughguile estate, 1768, 1789 – D/426/3, 5

Rent roll of Loughguile, Dervock, Carrickfergus and Killinchy estates, 1790 – D/2225/7/47 (MIC/530/2)

Variations in rent rolls, 1793–6 – D/2225/7/55 (MIC/530/2)

Rent roll, 1796 – D/572/21/98 (MIC/438/7)

Rent roll of estates in counties Antrim and Down, 1801 – D/572/21/101 (MIC/438/7)

Magenis estate, Derrykeighan etc. *see* **Magenis estate, Dromara etc.** *under* **COUNTY DOWN**

Massereene estate, Antrim

Rental of '16 Townes of Antrim', 1668, tenants listed alphabetically – D/207/16/6

Rental of the manor of Muckamore, 1685 – D/4084/1/4/1

Rent roll of Killylough estate, 1700–2 (125 tenants) – D/562/216

Rent roll of Connor parish, 1705 (c.50 tenants) – D/562/210

Roster of duty days for Muckamore, 1709 (30 tenants) – D/562/58

Rent roll and statements of debt for Muckamore, Ardmore, Ballynageeragh and The Grange, 1712–13 – D/562/834

Rent roll of Muckamore etc., 1715 (88 tenants) – D/562/57

Duty book for Antrim etc., 1733–4 – D/562/99

Leases for Antrim parish and town, 1698 onwards – D/4084/1/3/1

Leases for lands in other parts of County Antrim, 1670 onwards – D/4084/1/3/2

Account of wages paid to 38 labourers, 1754 – D/4084/1/5/2/1

Montgomery estate, Benvarden

Volume of maps of estate, 1788, naming tenants – T/1638/31/1

Moore estate, Ballydivity and Clogh

Over 110 unsorted leases relating to the Ballydivity estate of James Moore, 1725–1848, and a volume containing a schedule of leases for the estate, c.1764–c.1839 – D/915/7/1

Map of part of the estate of James Stewart Moore, 1793, naming tenants – D/915/18/4A. Townlands of Drumnagroagh, Glenleslie and Tullykittochs.

Mountcashell estate, Glenwhirry

Money received from Glenwhirry for Mr Harrison, n.d. [pre-1775], naming tenants – D/1494/3/6 (MIC/506/1)

Copy rent account, 1777–93, naming tenants, but not townlands – D/1494/3/44 (MIC/506/1)

Copy receiver's account for rents received to 1791 in Glenwhirry – D/1494/3/42 (MIC/506/1)

Accounts of rents received from Glenwhirry, 1795–1804, naming tenants by townland – D/1494/4/16 (MIC/506/1)

Leases for lives, Racavan parish, 1788 – D/1835/15

Mussenden estate, Carnmoney

Rent roll, c.1750 – D/354/285A (MIC/510/2). Townlands of Whitehouse, Jordanstown, Carnmoney, Ballycraigy, Ballyhenry, Cloughfern, Dunany and Ballyveally.

Neale estate, Magheramorne
Map of the manor of Magheramorne, property of John Neale, 1747, naming tenants –
D/1602/1. Calendar names townlands covered.

O'Hara estate, Crebilly
Leases, c.1740–c.1800 – D/1911/2
Maps of the estate in the parishes of Ballyclug, Connor and Dunaghy, 1783–4, naming tenants
– T/2971/1. Calendar names townlands.

O'Neill estate, Shane's Castle
Lands to be let with names of sitting tenants – *Belfast Newsletter*, 9 November 1750, 16
November 1756, 16 August 1757, 3 February 1758, 13 February 1759, 26 March 1761, 17
December 1762, 4 January 1763, 31 May 1768

Owens estate, Killead
Survey of farms in Lisnataylor townland, naming tenants, 1762 – D/1824/B/1/1/6/12

Pakenham estate, Crumlin, Templepatrick (formerly Langford and Langford-Rowley)
PRONI calendar provides names of townlands covered.
Miscellaneous leases, including many from 17th and 18th centuries – D/971/1/E
Vouchers, 1686–94 – MIC/537/3
Rentals, surveys and valuations of the manor of 'Killelaugh', 1699–1700 – MIC/537/3
Rent roll of estate of Sir Arthur Langford in Templepatrick and Carnmoney areas, 1700 –
D/2624/2
Rental of Killelagh and Ederowen, 1727 – MIC/537/3
Rent rolls of Langford estate in Templepatrick and Crumlin areas, 1743, 1774, 1777, 1778,
1780 – D/2634/4A–B, 6, 7, 8, 9
Accounts and arrears, 1750–52 – MIC/537/3
Rental, survey and lease book, 1750–76 – MIC/537/3

Rawdon estate, Brookhill *see under* COUNTY DOWN

Rowan estate, Clogh etc.
Document, seemingly a recovery of debts, relating to the estate of the late Rev. Robert Rowan
of Mullans, 1761, naming over 140 tenants – D/1835/15B
Leases, 1784 – D/1835/15

Saunders estate, Belfast, Carrickfergus, Newtownards and Comber
Rent roll, 1771–8 – D/1759/3B/7 (MIC/637/10)

Stewart estate, Ballintoy
34 expired leases for Ballintoy etc., 1788–90 – D/2007/1

Stewart estate, Finvoy
Printed rent roll (incorporating a survey and valuation) of the 13 quarters near Ballymoney, part
of the unsettled estate of Alexander Stewart, late of Acton (County Armagh), c.1750 –

D/642/G/7 (MIC/593/9). Lands of Enogh, Unshenogh, Drumskea, Ballynamonie, Claghie, Knockan, Derra, Upper Derrra otherwise Drumock, Lower Derra, Long Mullans, Broad Mullans, Cultifaghan otherwise Craigs called Slavebey, Scotch Craigs, Irish Craigs, Tulloghans, all in the parish of Finvoy.

Upton estate, Templepatrick
Deed of feoffment, 1625, naming tenants on estate – T/712/1
Lands to be let with names of sitting tenants – *Belfast Newsletter*, 26 July 1768, 15 November 1768, 28 March 1769

Vesey estate, Carrickfergus
Map of part of the Vesey estate in Carrickfergus, 1722, naming a few tenants – T/2524/26

Wallace estate, Lisburn
Leases, 1741–1813 – T/457/1–113

Wray estate, Dunseverick
23 leases for lives from Jackson Wray, 1766–72 – D/915/7/2

COUNTY ARMAGH

Armagh (archbishopric of) estate, Armagh
This was an enormous estate and comprised lands in counties Armagh, Down, Londonderry, Louth and Tyrone. The material relating to this estate is extensive and may be summarised as follows.

Leases
Small folio volume providing details about leases to lands in the archbishopric, 1628–1722 – DIO/4/34/1/1
Abstracts from the Primate's leases – DIO/4/34/2/2/1–8. Includes a folio volume entitled 'Of the Primacy or Archbishopric of Armagh, a rent roll from the 1st of May 1703, per Thomas Ashe, containing details of leases', 1685–1703. Also an alphabetical list of tenants holding leases under the see with dates of granting, 1749.
Leases granted by the dean and chapter – DIO/4/34/3/1–15. Includes a volume of lease abstracts, 1768–1802.
Leases granted by the Vicars Choral, 1703–64 – DIO/4/34/4/1
Abstracts of leases granted by the Governors and Guardians of Primate Robinson's library, 1790–94 – DIO/4/34/5/1

Rentals and surveys
Volume of bound-in documents, 1524–1628 – DIO/4/5/2A–B. Includes: no. 10, rent roll of 1615; no. 11, survey of holdings in Armagh city; no. 12, rent roll of all lands and houses owned by the Primate, *c*.1620; no. 16, rent roll of the see of Armagh, n.d. [early 17th century]; no. 17, rent roll of the rents payable quarterly to the Primate, n.d. [early 17th century]; no. 18, names of tenants bound by their leases to provide light horses to the

Primate during time of war, n.d. [early 17th century]; no. 19, rent roll of lands and houses of the Primate, 1628; no. 20, arrears of rent in Counties Armagh and Tyrone, 1628.

Volume of bound-in rentals for the lands of the archbishopric and houses in Armagh, 1628–1726 – DIO/4/35/1. Includes rentals etc. for 1628, 1629, 1631, 1636, 1639, 1640, 1660, 1661, 1663, 1664, 1686, 1709, 1726.

Extracts from rent rolls of see of Armagh, 1615–24 – T/625/1

Rent rolls of archbishopric, n.d. [1676], 1724, 1742 – DIO/4/35/2, 6, 8

'A view or an account taken by Thomas Ashe Esq. in anno 1703 ... of the archbishopric of Armagh' – DIO/4/35/3. Photostat copy available at T/848/1 (see Chapter 5.2 above).

Same as above, described as 'Walter Dawson's rental', 1713 – DIO/4/35/4

Rent rolls of the 'Cavan estate', 1779, 1782 – DIO/4/35/13

An old rent roll called 'Captain Chambers' rent roll', n.d. [?17th century] – DIO/4/22/1/1

Rent rolls of the Primate's mensal lands near Armagh, 1725, 1728, 1743 – DIO/22/3/1–2

Rent rolls of the see of Armagh, 1615–1746, including a list of the names of tenants returned at a manor court held by the archbishop of Armagh, 1714 – T/729/1A–3B

Maps

A large collection of maps relating to lands in the archbishopric, some with names of tenants, 1662 onwards – DIO/4/22/4–5. Calendared in full in PRONI.

Manor court records

Volume of bound documents, of which no. 2 is a return of tenants' names of Armagh returned to a manor court held by the archbishop of Armagh in 1714, and a list of the chief undertenants in the manor of Armagh – DIO/4/22/1/1

List of the manors annexed to the archdiocese of Armagh with the names of seneschals, *c.*1775 – DIO/4/22/2/1

Atkinson and Hoope estate, Crowhill, Loughgall

Cash book for rents, 1778–85 [Atkinson family?] – D/1815/2/1

Map of the 'lower half townland of Toigy [Teagy]', Tartaraghan parish, naming tenants, 1731 – D/1815/4/1

Map of Drumanphy, naming tenants, 1732 – D/1815/4/2

Map of Clonakle, naming tenants, 1780 – D/1815/4/3

Ball estate, Cullyhanna

Box of expired leases, including some from late 18th century – D/3012/2/1/1

Barton estate *see* **Jackson estate**

Brownlow estate, Lurgan

Leases and lease books

Lease books, 18th century – D/1928/L/1

Leases for townlands in the estate and tenements in Lurgan, arranged alphabetically, 17th and 18th centuries – D/1928/L/2–177

A lease book of 1667–1711 was printed in full in Raymond Gillespie (ed.), *Settlement and Survival on an Ulster Estate* (Belfast, 1988)

Rentals
Rent rolls for the 17th and 18th centuries, including a rental of Sir William Brownlow's estate, 1636–77 (listed as missing) – D/1928/R/5
Rent books, 1755–1804 – D/1928/R/1/1–65
Large rent day book for Lord Lurgan's estate, 1796–9 – D/1928/R/3/1

Maps
Volume of maps for manor of Brownlowsderry, 1751 (see calendar for details) – D/1928/P/1A–B
Maps, 1751–94 – T/2485/2
Map of Lurgan, 1794 – D/1928/P/2

Miscellaneous
Names of William Brownlow's tenants in or near Lurgan, 1622 – MIC/171/1
Accounts, some relating to the estate, 18th century – D/1928/A/1
Estate court book for manor of Brownlowsderry, 1776–1847 – D/1928/J/1
Wages books, 1748–83 – D/1928/W/1–4

See also W. H. Crawford, 'Tenants' occupations on the manor of Brownlow's-Derry, Lurgan estate, County Armagh, *c.*1670–1799' in *Familia* no. 16 (2000), pp. 51–60.

Burges estate *see under* **COUNTY TYRONE**

Caledon estate *see under* **COUNTY TYRONE**

Charlemont estate, Charlemont
Leases and lease books
Schedule of leases, *c.*1750–1817 – T/1176/1–6
Expired leases, 1782–1904, arranged in bundles by townland – D/1644/1–30
Leases, 1788–1804 – D/2394/1
Lease book of Charlemont estate, 1818–30, including a schedule of leases, some of which date back to the 18th century – D/266/260A

Maps
Map of Moy and part of Drumgranon, 1771, naming tenants – D/291/3
Map of Blackwatertown, 1782, naming tenants – T/1208/1
Map of Cladybeg and Cladymore, 1786, naming tenants – D/266/378/2

Rentals
Rental, mainly in the Charlemont, Blackwatertown and Loughgall areas, 1752–65 – T/1175/2
Rent roll, 1774 – T/387/1
Rentals, 1798–1802 – NLI Ms 3784

Miscellaneous
Copy statement of account, 1759–61 – D/2644/1

Cope estate, Drumilly and Loughgall
Leases from 18th century – D/1345 *passim*

Dawson (later Dartrey/Cremorne) estate, Armagh, Blackwatertown
Collection of 18th-century leases – D/266 *passim*. Includes 85 leases dated 9 January 1794 from Viscount Cremorne for farms in Anacleary, Blackwatertown, Crockenrow, Drumcullen, Englishtown, Killmore, Mullinary and Mullylegan.
Collection of leases, 1757 onwards – D/526/2E *passim*
List of tenements in Armagh city owned by Thomas Dawson, 1779 – D/526/2E/22
List of leases in Blackwatertown delivered to Richard Olpherts, 1781 – D/526/2E/23
Survey and valuation of estate of Thomas Dawson, 1st Baron Cremorne, *c.*1800 – D/526/2F/2
Rent roll of Lord Dartrey's church lands in County Armagh, 1781 – D/2394/3/2. Townlands (in addition to those listed above): Drumash & Drumarm and Tullyhevin, plus Armagh city.
Rent agreement, 1751, naming tenants (67 names) – D/2394/3/1
Rent rolls, 1787, 1797 – NLI Mss 3183, 3283, 3185

De Salis estate, Tanderagee
List of tenants holding leases with observations on the state of lives in the manor of Clare 1733–87 – D/763/2
List of tenants in possession of farms without leases, n.d. – D/763/3
Leases for lives, 1764 onwards – D/1393/1
List of tenants holding farms in jointure whose leases expired on death of Rt Hon. Lady Viscountess Fane, 1792 – D/763/4
Observations and extracts of leases of part of northern estate, 1793 – D/763/5
Memorandum on rentals, 1794 – D/763/6

Dillon estate *see* Molyneux estate

Gosford Estate, Markethill
Map of the manor of Lower Coolmillish, 1693, naming tenants – D/384/2
Survey and rent roll of Hamilton's Bawn demesne, 1739 – D/1606/6B/3
Map of Hamiltonsbawn estate, 1785 – D/1606/6B/8
Rent rolls of the original Armagh estate, including notes on leases, 1787–99 – D/1606/7A/1–5
Leases arranged by townland, including many from the 18th century – D/1606/3
Volume containing an abstract of leases for the manors of Baleek and Coolmalish, 1801 – D/1606/3/48/1

Hall estate, Mullaghglass *see* Hall estate, Narrow Water *under* COUNTY DOWN

Hamilton estate, Ballynaleck
Rent roll of estate of James Hamilton of Ballynaleck, 1790 – D/476/37

Hamilton estate, Hamilton's Bawn
Tenants on the estate of John Hamilton, 1617 – printed in *Familia*, no. 11 (1995), p. 92

Houston estate, Eglish and Tynan
Map of Turry and Lower Ballymacully, 1777, naming tenants – D/2433/A/13/3

Report of commissioners appointed to value and prepare a scheme for the partition of the
Houston estate, 1801, townlands of Delay, Killylin, Ballymacullow Lower and Upper,
Anagharap, Drumgolva, Clonticarty – D/2433/A/1/21/11

Irwin estate, Carnagh, Keady

Maps
Map of part of the estate of Arthur Irwin in Derrynoose parish, naming tenants, 1758 –
D/2523/M/1
Map of Carnagh, naming tenants, 1766 – D/2523/M/2
Map of Carrickduff owned by William Irwin, naming tenants, 1799 – D/2523/M/3
Map of Kilcarn owned by William Irwin, naming tenants, 1799 – D/2523/M/4

Rentals
Rental of Tievenamara, Kilcarn, Carrickduff and Crossnenagh, *c.*1750–1800, including a list of
writs and judgements, *c.*1749–50 – D/2523/1/1
Rental of same area, 1768–86 – D/2523/1/2
Rental of Tievenamara, 1785–1834 – D/2523/1/3

Jackson estate, Forkhill

Leases for the Forkhill estate, 17th and 18th centuries (70 from 1789–96) – D/294 *passim*
Return of lands set on 1 November 1788 by Mrs Susanna Barton, Forkhill estate, lately in
possession of Richard Jackson deceased – D/294/10

Jenny estate, Derryanvil

Map of Derryanvil [Drumcree parish] belonging to Henry Jenny, 1757, naming tenants –
D/243/5

Johnston estate, Drumbanagher

Map of estate, 1784, naming tenants – T/1175/3/1

Johnston estate, Eglish

Rent rolls, 1785–1805 – T/933/1–5
Rentals annually for the period 1791–1802 – NAI M 3502

Ker estate, Navan

Leases in bundles arranged by townland of the estate of Mrs Hannah Ker of Dublin, 1791 –
D/1747/1/1–4

Kilmorey estate, Newry *see under* COUNTY DOWN

McCombe estate, Altamoyan

Large collection of 18th-century leases, many of them for lives – D/462 *passim*

McGeough-Bond estate, Drumsill

Leases, 1759 onwards – D/288 *passim*
Box of miscellaneous 18th- and 19th-century rent material, including 'Mr Pooler's rent book',

which appears to relate to Bondville, 1770–82; rentals of Eglish and Glengavelin, 1779–81; Joshua McGeough's rent receipt and general cash book, 1778–1803; rental of Glenall leased by Joshua McGeough from the see of Armagh, 1788–9 – D/288/G/1

Rent roll for year ending November 1803 – D/3012/2/2/13

Valuation of Umrecam with information on tenants, houses, etc., 1804 – D/3012/2/2/12

Manchester (Duke of) estate, Portadown and Tandragee

Leases, 1669 onwards (listed individually, c.1,000 pre-1800) – D/1248/L

Rentals etc. of Kernan and Ballymore, 1715–92 (mainly for the 1760s and 1780s) – D/1948/R/79–105

See also St John estate

Maxwell estate, Fellows Hall

Rental of the manor of Balteagh, 1770–71 – T/1307/1

Molyneux (formerly Dillon) estate, Castledillon

Names and freeholders and leaseholders on the estate of Sir John Dillon, 1622 – MIC/171/1

Survey of the estate, 1696 – MIC/215

Lease book of the manor of Castledillon with observations by William Molyneux and details on tenants' dwellings and land usage, c.1700 – MIC/80/3

Lists of tenants on the estate, 1617, 1696 – T/636/1, pp. 247–52

Rentals of the estate, 1721–2, 1722–3, 1723–4 – T/636/1, pp. 252–4

Rental of 1828 giving details from 18th-century leases – T/636/1, pp. 157–87

Nicholson estate, Cranagill, Loughgall

Maps of Killdaraghin (1753) and Cranagill (1768) – T/2167/1–2

Obins estate, Portadown

Rent rolls, 1753, 1770 – NLI Ms 4736

Richardson estate, Moyallen

Rental of Bocombra [Seagoe parish], 1756, and two surveys of same, 1757, 1775 – D/1252/7/1

Sachervell estate, Richhill

Map of part of the manor of Mullalellish owned by Henry 'Schacheverle', 1695, naming tenants – D/384/3

St John estate, Tanderagee

Map and survey of Ballymore (1750), map of Tanderagee demesne (1791) and map of the manor of Clare (copied in 1806 from a survey of 1795) – D/720/1–2

Maps of the manor of Ballymore and manor of Kernan, 1701 onwards – D/727 *passim*

See also Manchester estate

Sandwich estate, Clare

Printed sale particulars of the estate of the earl of Sandwich, n.d. [pre-16 February 1807], giving details of tenancies from 18th century – T/3059/1

Stewart estate, Acton
Leases and maps, 1786 onwards – D/1166 *passim*

Trinity College, Dublin estate *see under* COUNTY DONEGAL

Verner estate *see under* COUNTY TYRONE

Whaley estate, Armagh
Survey of estate of Thomas Whaley (a minor), 1769 – T/636/1, pp. 143–51

COUNTY CAVAN

Annesley estate, Cavan etc.
Rough rent roll of the Cavan estate, 1780 – D/1503/4/2

Butler estate *see* Lanesborough estate

Clements estate, Ashfield
Volume of maps of the manor of Ashfield, barony of Tullygarvey, 1775–1844 – NLI 15 B 24
House account book, 1797–1800 – NLI Ms 9818

Coote estate, Cootehill
Leases and renewals of premises in Cootehill, 1766 onwards – NLI D 6791–6863

Coyne estate, Drumlumman parish etc.
Volume of maps of the estate in counties Cavan and Westmeath, *c*.1760, limited information on tenants – D/2784/2/1. Lands in County Cavan: Big Clonuse, Callanagh, Drumcorr, Garrysallagh Beresford, Kilgola, Killeboy, Killekeen, Knockanore, Lisnafea, Lisnatinne, Little Clonuse, Loghdovan, Muckram, Mullaghoran and Tideeghan.

Craige estate, Kildallan and Killeshandra
Names of tenants on the estate, 1703–4, printed in *Irish Ancestor*, viii, no. 2 (1976), pp. 86–7.

Crofton estate, Kinawley
Rentals and accounts, 1769, 1783–1814 – NLI Ms 20,783
Rent roll of the estate of Hugh Crofton, 1792 – NLI Ms 4530

Farnham estate *see* Maxwell estate

Fingall estate *see* Plunkett estate

Fitzherbert estate, Shercock
Deeds etc. relating to Shercock etc., 1656–1754 – NLI D 6956–62

Gosford estate, Arvagh
Leases from 1703 – D/1606/3/44–5
Volumes of maps and surveys of estate, c.1800 and 1801 – D/1606/6D/2–3

Farnham estate, Cavan etc.
Rent rolls, 1718–90 – NLI Ms 11,491
Farm and household accounts, 1734–1862 – NLI Ms 11,492
c.250 maps, some with names of tenants – NLI 21 F 115–20

Lanesborough (Butler) estate, Belturbet
Deeds, 17th-19th centuries – NLI D 8896–8926
Correspondence relating to estate management, 1780 – D/1908 *passim*

Plunkett (Earls of Fingall) estate, Virginia etc.
Leases, conveyances, rentals, maps, surveys, plans, etc., 16th-19th centuries – NLI Mss
      8024–8028, 8030
Rent roll, 1750 – NLI Ms 8024

Pratt estate, Kingscourt and Cabra
Surveys, accounts etc., 18th-19th centuries – NLI Mss 13,314–13,327
Unsorted material, 17th-20th centuries – NLI D 22,134–22,403
Map of property in Enniskeen parish, 1735 – NAI M5746

Saunderson estate, Castle Saunderson
Rent roll, 1779 – NLI Ms 13,340

Stanford estate, Kildallan
Deeds, leases, will etc., 1641–1823, including a map of the estate of Daniel Stanford in
      Kildallan parish, 1787 – NLI n. 526, p. 799

Storey estate, Kilmore
Rent ledger of Joseph Storey, bishop of Kilmore, 1738–57; household account book of same,
      1742–50 – NLI n. 3624, p. 3242

COUNTY DONEGAL

Abercorn estate *see under* **COUNTY TYRONE**

Abraham estate, Raphoe
Bundle of c.15 expired leases, c.1780–1800 – D/1550/103/1

Alexander estate, Moville
Collection of 18th-century leases of the churchlands in the parish of Moville leased from the
      bishop of Derry, 1737, 1784–9, calendared in full – D/2433/A/1/24

Clements estate, Kilmacrenan, Mevagh
Lord Boyne's rent roll, 1743 [year in which estate was purchased by Nathaniel Clements] –
printed in L. W. Lucas, *Mevagh Down the Years* (Portlaw, Waterford, 1972), pp. 81–3
Maps of the estate, Kilmacrenan barony, 1779 – NLI 14 A 17 (names from maps printed in
Lucas, *Mevagh*, pp. 91–2)

Conolly estate, Ballyshannon, Castlefinn
Rentals
Rent roll of the manor of Ballyshannon, n.d. [early 18th century] and a survey and valuation
of same, 1718, with details on tenants – D/2094/24A–C
Rentals of the manor of Tirhugh (leased from Trinity College, Dublin), 1686, 1692–4, 1706,
1709 – T/2825/C/24
Rental of Castlefinn, 1707 – T/2825/C/44/1
Rentals of the manor of Ballyshannon, including the Collegelands of Tirhugh and Bundrews,
1718, 1722, 1724–6 – T/2825/C/26
Rent accounts for the manor of Ballyshannon, 1729 – D/2094/33, 34
Rent roll of the Castlefinn estate, 1731–4 – D/2094/23
Rent rolls, 1724–1831 – NLI Ms 17302
Rent rolls, 1772–93 – NAI M 6917/1–19
Rentals of the Ballyshannon estate, 1774, 1782–6, 1800 – T/2825/C/36

Other
Correspondence relating to estate matters, 1718–29, 1731 – T/2825/C/27
A list of the lives in each lease on the Ballyshannon estate, 1748 – NLI Ms 5751
Survey of property in Drumhome, 1770, naming tenants – MIC/435/20

See also J. B. Cunningham, 'William Conolly's Ballyshannon estate' in *Donegal Annual*, no. 33
(1981).

Derry (bishopric of) estate – *see under* COUNTY LONDONDERRY

Donegall estate – *see under* COUNTY ANTRIM

Ferguson estate, Donagh
Maps with names, 1790 – NLI Ms 5,023

Folliott estate, Ballyshannon
(This estate was purchased by William Conolly in 1718, *see* **Conolly estate**)
Rent book of the manor of Ballyshannon, 1680–87 – T/2825/23/1

Forward estate, Newtowncunningham
Valuation of the Forward estate by Archibald Stewart, 1727 – NLI Ms 4,247
Rental, *c.*1790 – NLI Ms 9,582

Gage estate, Castlefinn
Survey of part of the Castlefinn estate, April 1780, naming tenants – D/673/61

Hamilton estate, Castlefinn
Volume containing an 'Inventory of leases made by the late Councellor Hamilton' in the manor of Castlefinn, 1763–77 – D/1449/7/1

Hart estate, Kilderry
Rent and cash accounts, 1757–67, 1796–1803 – NLI Ms 7885

Leslie estate, Pettigo
Rentals, 1777–1800 – NLI Mss 5810–12
Box of leases, almost all for 1786–7 – Castle Leslie, B/4
Box of rentals, including 1800 – Castle Leslie, D/2
See **Leslie estate, Glaslough** *under* **COUNTY MONAGHAN** for more information.

McClintock estate, Glenmaquin
Map of Lower Glenmaqueen, Raphoe parish, property of William McClintock, 1782, naming tenants – D/642/G/9

Mansfield estate, Killygordon
Leases relating to estate, 1706–15, 1737–96, 1766–1822 – D/1550/78/1–3

Murray of Broughton estate, Boylagh and Banagh
Rentals
'A Rentall of Rentts of the landes newely lett at this August 1638 ...' – Muniment Room, Scone Palace, Perth (printed in *Donegal Annual*, 54 (2002), pp. 61–5)
Rent roll of proportions of Balliweell, Duncanally, Killkar and Monorgan in possession of Richard Murray, 1673 – D/2860/24/1
Rental, n.d. [late 17th century] – D/2860/25/11
Rent roll of Alexander Murray's estate, 1719 – D/2860/4/25
'Rent roll of the estate ... as the several tenants now propose', 1727 – D/2860/25/10
Remarks on arrears in the manors of Castlemurray and Ballyboyle for the year ending 1 May 1732 – D/2860/12/28
Rent arrears, 1749 – D/2860/24/11
Rent arrears, 1751 – D/2860/12/54–6
Rent roll of Killybegs estate, n.d. [*c.*1755] – D/2860/16/2

Leases
'A particular of the leases of the Manor of [Castle Murray deleted] Ballyweele that are out and were out', 1638 – Muniment Room, Scone Palace, Perth (printed in *Donegal Annual*, 54 (2002), pp. 61–5)
Counterpart and expired leases, 1680–1728, 1751, 1789 – D/2860/36/1–64
Accounts of rents and duties fixed on for leases, n.d. [*c.*1730] – D/2860/25/2
List of the leases signed by the trustees of Alexander Murray since 24 May 1731 – Scottish Record Office, GD/10/944

Surveys

Surveys of the estate, one by Thomas Addi of Donaghadee from 1730, the other by John Hood of Moyle, County Donegal from 1755, plus associated papers – D/2860/25/1–11. The survey by Addi is particularly detailed and has been printed in full in the PRONI calendar.

Survey and book of maps of Alexander Murray's estate in the baronies of Boylagh and Bannagh, 1749 – NLI 21 F 66

Miscellaneous

Memoranda about estate matters, *c.*1740–80, including one of 1780 listing undertenants – D/2860/26/1–13

See also Graeme Kirkham, "'No more to be got off the cat but the skin'": Management, landholding and economic change on the Murray of Broughton estate, 1670–1755' in William Nolan, Liam Ronayne and Mairead Dunlevy (eds), *Donegal: History and Society* (Dublin, 1995).

Raphoe, bishopric of, estate
Rent book of the bishopric of Raphoe, 1674–85 – NLI Ms 9987

Stewart estate, Ards etc.
Account book, 1781–90, relating to the estate and personal affairs of Alexander Stewart of Ards, which records expenses and rent accounts in connection with the Mercers' Proportion at Kilrea, Co. Londonderry, Ards and Killygordon, Co. Donegal, 'Drummatticonnor', Co. Down – D/2784/19

Stewart estate, Fortstewart, Ramelton
Leases, 1699 onwards – D/2358/2
Rent roll of Country Farm on Ramelton and Fanet estate, 1714 – D/2358/3/1
Valuation of Ramelton estate, including a rental of 1727 – D/2358/5/1
Account book, 1758–74, including a rent roll of Ramelton and Fannet from 1769, and a rental of Aughnish from 1767 – D/2358/4/1
Surveys and valuations, 1770–*c.*1800 – D/2358/5/3–11
Rental of Ramelton estate, 1785–90 – D/2358/3/2
Rent and fees for 'new leting' of part of estate, 1787 – D/2358/3/3
Rental, 1789 – D/2358/3/4

Stewart estate, Mount Stewart
Survey of part of the manor of Mount Stewart, Raphoe barony, belonging to Mrs Alice Stewart, 1717, including a terrier of 1726 – NLI 15 B 16 (8)

Styles estate, Kilteevogue
Valuation and survey of estate, 1773 – NLI Ms 402

Trinity College, Dublin estate, Tirhugh, Kilmacrenan, etc.
A large collection of documents, including rentals, leases, maps and petitions, relating to the College's estates in Counties Armagh, Donegal and Fermanagh is available in the

Manuscript Department of Trinity College, Dublin. Unfortunately it was not possible to examine this material in any detail. It is, however, well catalogued under reference MUN/P/24, and easy to use.

COUNTY DOWN

Anglesey Estate, Newry, Mourne
General estate matters, 17th-19th centuries, including lease records from 1700 – D/619/14
Rent rolls, 1688–1714, 1750–59, 1764–77, 1783–8 – D/619/7/1/1–72
Agents' accounts, rent and disbursements, 1707–1834 – D/619/8/1–81
Agents' correspondence, 1714–1855 (over 1,600 letters) – D/619/21, 22
Rent arrears, 1715–1844 – D/619/10/1–66
Tenants' proposals for farms, 1734–1841 (particularly centring on the major re-lettings of the estate in 1735 and 1765) – D/619/6/1–110
Estate/household bills and receipts, 1735–95 – D/619/12
Tenants' petitions, 1766–1851 (generally for financial assistance or rent reductions, but some of them seeking help in disputes with neighbours) – D/619/11/1–121
Rent arrears, 1744–1853 – D/619/9/1–14
Survey of the whole estate made in 1783–4 – D/619/3/1–56
See also **Bagenal estate** *and* **Kilmorey estate**

Annesley estate, Castlewellan, Newcastle, Dunlady and Bannfield
Leases
Leases beginning in the 18th century relating to the County Down estate, arranged by townland, but not calendared individually – D/1503/1
Leases beginning in the 18th century relating to the Annesley estate at Ballynahinch, including 30 leases issued on 30 November 1782 by Arthur Annesley for Cargacreevy, Burren and Ballycreen – D/500 *passim*

Map
Map of the manor of Castlewellan owned by William Annesley Esq., 1742, naming tenants in townlands of Backaderry, Ballymaginaghy, Ballymegrechan, Benra[w], Castlewillian, Clarkhill, Legananny, Leitrim, Lurgan, Maghrymayo and Sleavenaboley – T/1025/1

Rentals
Rentals, 1788–9 – D/1503/6/1A–B
Annotated almanac including payments to labourers and rent accounts for Slevenaboley and part of Bannfield estate, 1765 – D/1854/8/2

Other
Annotated almanac including payments to labourers, 1768–9 – D/1854/8/3
Copy out-letter books relating to estate administration, c.1774–86 – D/2309
Cash account book, 1775–93, 1825–35 – D/1503/8/37
Timber account book, including notes on wages paid, 1792–1802 – D/1503/8/38

Ardglass estate, Downpatrick
Rental of estate of Thomas, earl of Ardglass, 1669 – T/724/2 (typescript copy avilable in PRONI calendar)

Bagenal estate, Newry
Rent roll of Newry, 1575 – MIC/322
See also **Anglesey estate** *and* **Kilmorey estate**

Blackwood (Dufferin) estate, Clandeboye
Map and survey of the estate of Sir John Blackwood, *c.*1720, naming tenants – T/3666/1
Transcript of an Exchequer Bill of 28 April 1741 involving Robert Blackwood, naming 274 tenants – T/808/15009. Lands named: Cherryvalley, Ringrevy, Littleballyhenry, Barnymackry, Troopersfield, Raffrey, Maghernycrosse alias Magherycoyle, Ballykile, Lislee, Monerea, Monlough, Ballybeen, Tullyhubbert, Adnislate, Tullygirvan, Ballycloghan and Ballygowan.
Rent account books, 1739–82 – D/1071/A/B/1/1–4
Cash books, 1720–39 (includes rent accounts, 1735–9) and 1752–74 – D/1071/A/B/2/1–2
Vouchers, 1708–18, *c.*1720–*c.*1770 – D/1071/A/C/1/39, 40
Survey of Ballygrott and Ballyskelly, 1743 – D/1071/A/F/1
Leases, pre-1800 – D/1071/A/J/1 (for other 18th–century leases see D/1071/A/H *passim*)

Clanbrassil estate, Ballywalter, Bangor, Dundonald, Holywood, Killyleagh
Maps of the estate by Thomas Raven, 1625, naming tenants – T/870
Entry book of tenancies, 1615–78 – T/761/3
Letter book relating to estate, 1632–1715 – T/761/7
Rent roll, *c.*1670, with early 18th-century annotations – T/2253/1
Rental of 1681 of the lands of the Ards, Holywood and Bangor – printed in T. K. Lowry (ed.), *The Hamilton Manuscripts* (Belfast, 1867), pp. 108–11
Rent roll of the jointure lands of Ann, late Countess of Clanbrassil, 1688–92, parishes of Killyleagh, Killinchy and Tonochneive (Saintfield) – printed in Lowry, *Hamilton Manuscripts*, pp. 125–32

Clanwilliam estates, Montalto and Ballynahinch
Rent roll of Kinelarty (Montalto) estate, 1791–7 – D/3044/A/5/1
Leases arranged by townland and calendared individually, 1684 onwards – D/3044/A/4

De Clifford estate, Downpatrick etc.
Leases issued for the following townlands: Killinchy in the Woods (1738–), Conlig Quarter, Annacloy (1792–), Ran Quarter, Annacloy (1792–), Sufficial Quarter, Annacloy (1770–), Ballynoe (1790–), Ballyvange (1792), Carnagrane [Cargebane] (1790–), Downpatrick (1790–), Erenagh (1790–), Legamaddy (1790–), Part of Lisboy and Island of Lisbane (1790–), Listooder (1749–), Marshallstown (1790–), Saul (1790–), Castle Quarter, Quoile (1790–), Ferry Quarter, Quoile (1792–), Quarter Cormick (1777), Old Sound (1790) – D/1167/1 *passim*
Lease book containing extracts of leases for the Moira (Rawdon) estate at Ballynahinch and also the Townparks of Downpatrick, 1760–1847 – D/1167/1/391

Rental of Downpatrick and surrounding townlands, 1789–92 – D/3696/C/6

Maps of Ballycreen (1776), Ballykine (1786) and Clough (1787), naming tenants – D/1167/3/1–3

Delacherois estate, Donaghadee

Rent roll of Donaghadee parish and 'Killmore' (the churchlands in Kilmore parish), 1729 – D/2223/9/6

Court leet books of the manor of Donaghadee, c.1770–91, 1792–9; volume recording the business done at the Three Weeks Court of Record in and for the manor of Donaghadee, 1771–83 – MIC/321/1–3

Downshire estate, Banbridge, Castlereagh, Dundrum, Hilltown, Kilwarlin and Newry

Rentals, rent rolls, rent ledgers

Rent roll of 'Killwarling', 1698 – T/201/1

Rent roll of Banbridge estate, 1725 – D/671/R1/1A

Dundrum rental, 1734 – D/671/V/948 (transferred to D/607/A)

Rent rolls of Kilwarlin and Carrickfergus estates, 1744–5, 1745–6 – D/2784/23/1/1–2

Rent roll of Lurganville and Ballygowan (Kilwarlin estate), 1763–4 – D/671/R8/161

Dundrum rent roll, 1801 – D/671/V939

Rentals for Banbridge, Castlereagh, Hilltown, Kilwarlin and Newry starting in 1801 which provide details of leases issued in the 18th century – D/671/R1/2, R4/1, R7/1, R8/1, R9/1

Large collection of 18th-century ledgers – D/671/A1. These contain information on leases, lives in leases, etc. They are not usually arranged by estate.

Leases and lease books

Vast collection of 18th-century leases – D/671/L, LE, mainly arranged in bundles by townland within estate. For the Kilwarlin estate alone there are over 250 pre-1750 leases.

Lease books beginning in 1794, but recording details of leases from c.1700, arranged by estate – D/671/A4

Lease agreements, Dundrum estate, 1795–7 – D/671/A40/1

Miscellaneous

18th-century cash books, recording rent payments – D/671/A2

18th-century specie books, recording rent payments – D/671/A3

Alphabetical list of tenants in the Kilwarlin estate, c.1800 – D/671/A26/1

Moss book (for Kilwarlin estate?), 1757–77, recording names of tenants permitted to cut turf in the mosses – D/671/A14/1

Dufferin estate *see* Blackwood estate

Dungannon estate, Breda

Collection of leases, many from 18th century, for townlands including Ballynahatty, Moneyreagh, Ballynavally, Galwally, Crossgar and Deehommed – D/1954/4

Rental, 1766 – D/162/85

Fitzgerald (Kildare) estate, Ardglass and Strangford
Lecale estate title deeds and leases, 1514–1715 – D/3078/1/29/1–8

Small folio volume containing copies of letters to 16th earl of Kildare, 1628–37, including material on the Lecale estate – D/3078/3/1/5

Transcripts of deeds etc., some of which are leases for the Lecale estate from the early 17th century – D/3078/1/1/1–3

Map of the manor of Ardglass, 1734, naming tenants – D/642/G/2 (MIC/593/9)

Map of the Strangford estate, 1734, naming tenants – D/642/G/3 (MIC/593/9)

Names of 82 tenants of the Rt Hon. Charles Fitzgerald offering to assist HM service with cars and horses, c.1798 – D/272/18

Forde estate, Seaforde
Leases starting in 1714 (158 pre-1800) – D/566 *passim*

Rental commencing in 1801 – D/566/B/1/1

Hall estate, Ballyhornan etc.
Map and survey of the estate of Rowley Hall, n.d. [c.1730–40] – D/424/89

Leases, 1731 onwards – D/424 *passim*

Hall estate, Narrow Water
Survey of the manor of Mullaghglass, County Armagh, 1730, naming tenants – D/1540/1/8

Servants account book, 1783–1802 – D/1540/1/48. This provides information on servants' wages, their character and length of service. Currently listed as missing.

Volume of maps of the manor of Mullaghglass and the Narrow Water estate, 1800, naming tenants – T/2821/1A

Hamilton estate, Tollymore
Rent rolls of Tollymore, 1743, 1768–9 – MIC/147/2

Letters, including correspondence about estate matters, 1679–96 – MIC/147/8

Abstracts of accounts, Tollymore, c.1790 – MIC/147/9

Hutcheson estate, Drumalig, Saintfield
Account of lives in leases of Mr Hans Hutcheson of Drumalig, 1768 – D/971/34/B/8

Innis estate (formerly Magenis), Manor of Glen Drumantine
Leases from the 18th century – T/1514 *passim*

Rent roll, 1750–51 – T/1514/58. Townlands of Ballyblough, Ballylough, Carrickrovaddy, Corgory, Dromantine, Dromiller, Lisnaterny and Lurganare.

Ker estate, Ballynahinch
Valuation of Ballynahinch, n.d. [c.1802] – D/500/96

Kilmorey estate, Newry and Mourne
Leases, including many from the 18th century, calendared by townland or street in Newry – D/2638/B *passim*

Rent ledgers covering estates in Counties Armagh, Down and Louth, 1810–11, providing details of leases, 1731–1811 – D/2638/G/3/1–2
See also **Anglesey estate** *and* **Bagenal estate**

Johnston estate, Gilford etc.
Rental of estate, 1725 – T/1054/1
Rent roll of Richard Johnston's estate, 1731 – T/1007/38 (another copy at T/1175/1). Townlands of Loughans, Drumaran, Emdall, Glaskermore, Glaskerbeg, Moybrick, Finnis, Derryneill, Garvegery, Clunmaghery, Clanvaraghan, Slievenisky, County Down; Carricklais and Sheetrim, County Armagh; and Cloughnart, Dunmadigan, Kingory, Carrachan, Mullaghboy, Killyleg, Clossdaur and Kinnkelly, County Monaghan
Rent roll of lands to be sold in Counties Armagh, Down and Monaghan, c.1748 – D/1835/34
Map and survey of Drumaran and Loughans, 1769 – T/1007/90
Rental, 1795 – T/1007/194

Lascelles estate, Killough
Volume including rent accounts, 1796–7 – D/1944/8/1

Lawrence estate, Lawrencetown, Tullylish
Rental of estate of Thomas Dawson Lawrence, covering townlands of Knocknagor, Coose, Lisnafiffy and Kiernon, 1796 – T/426/1, pp. 25–30

Legg estate *see under* **COUNTY ANTRIM**

Leslie estate, Lecale
These were the Leslies of Ballybay, County Monaghan.
Leases arranged by townland of the County Down estate in the barony of Lecale, 1793 onwards – D/3406/D/8

Londonderry estate, Newtownards, Comber
Leases and lease books
Pre-1750 leases arranged by townland and calendared in full – D/654/LE
Post-1750 leases arranged in bundles by townland – D/654/L
Lease book for the town of Newtownards, 1726–1825 – D/654/LB/1
Lease book for the towns of Newtownards and Comber, 17th century–1859 – D/654/LB/2
Lease book of Newtown and Comber estates, 17th century–1802 – D/654/LB/3
Lease reciting names of tenants in manor of Newtown, 1744 – D/859/83

Rent rolls and rent ledgers
Rent rolls for the Comber estate, 1684 (transcribed in full and available in PRONI calendar), 1767, 1768, 1769 – D/654/R2/1–6
Rent rolls of the Newtown and Greyabbey estates, 1740, 1744, 1767, 1768, 1769 – D/654/R1/1A–7
Rent rolls of the Newtown, Greyabbey and Comber estates, virtually every year from 1769 – D/654/R3/1
Rent ledgers for Newtown and Comber, 1791–8, 1797–1800 – D/654/H3/1–3

Rent roll of the manor of Newtone, 1712–17 – Cambridge University Library, Ms Add. 4349
(copy in NLI under n. 5328, p. 5437)

Maps
Collection of 18th-century maps calendared in full – D/654/M

Macartney estate, Killinchy *see* Macartney estate *under* COUNTY ANTRIM

Magenis estate, Castlewellan, Dromantine
Volume of maps of Arthur Magenis' estates at Castlewellan and Dromantine, 1727 – T/2215/1
For other Magenis estate material *see* Innis estate

Magenis estate, Dromara etc.
Rent rolls of the estate of Richard Magenis in Counties Antrim, Armagh and Down, 1754
(Antrim lands only), 1765, 1770 – D/1835/34
Rental, 1761–89 (Finnis, Sheeplandmore, etc.) – D/1835/34
Account of lands out of leases, Finnis and Moybrick, c.1762 – D/1834/34
Leases for Sheeplandmore etc., c.1789–99 – D/1835/34
Surveys and maps of various farms, late 18th century – D/1835/34

Mathews estate, Newcastle, Mourne
Volume of maps, incorporating a survey and valuation of the Newcastle estate of Edward
Mathews, 1737 – T/2215/2
Rent roll (printed) of part of the Newcastle estate, 1748, naming tenants and lives named in
leases (together with current ages and annotated to indicate if an individual had died), with
interesting observations – D/1835/34
Rental of Edward Mathews' property in Ballinran and Ballaghanery, Lordship of Mourne,
c.1752 – D/207/19/104

Maxwell estate, Saintfield etc.
Assignment with rental attached, Robert Maxwell to James Maxwell of Drum [?Drumbeg],
1674–5 – T/640/120. Lands of Drumcha, Criviargan, Glumteneglare, Lisdalgan, Oughly,
Lisdawnen, Killmure, Bresagh, Killinchie, Ballimullen, Ballialligan, Tolleveery, Ballimillin.

Meade Estate, Rathfriland
Rent account book for Rathfriland estate, 1740 – D/1629/1
Renewable lease book, 1677–1831 – D/875/4
Day book of renewable fines on leases, 1771–1841 – D/875/3
Maps of the Rathfriland estate, 1776, naming tenants – T/855/1

Moira estate *see* Rawdon estate

Montgomery estate, Rosemount, Greyabbey
Rent roll of Rosemount estate, 1725, including the townlands of Ballynester/Ballymurphy,
Bogleboe, Grangee/Flushinhill, Gordenall and Greyabbey – T/1030/21
Map of part of Ballynester and Ballymurphy, 1789, naming tenants – T/1030/1

Map of Kirkistown and Ratallagh, 1791, naming tenants (owned by Robert Johnston, but leased by Montgomery family) – T/1031/2

Moor estate, Bangor
Rent roll of Rathgill and Ballow, part of the estate of John Moor Esq., 1773 – D/1494/3/25 (MIC/506/1)

Mount Ross estate, Portaferry
Rent roll of Mount Ross estate, Portaferry, post-1770 – T/656/1, no. 74

Perceval-Maxwell Estate, Bangor, Lecale, Groomsport
Estate accounts, c.1700, naming tenants but not townlands, and a rent roll of 1702–3 for the Bangor estate – D/1494/3/4 (MIC/506/1)
Leases, 17th century onwards – D/2480/2
Map of Groomsport, 1763, naming tenants – D/3244/J/2
Survey of Groomsport, 1763, naming tenants – D/3244/J/2 (copy at T/1023/70)
Rent rolls for estates in the barony of Lecale and in the parish of Bangor, 1743–1800 – T/1023 *passim*
Rent roll, 1742–3 – T/518/1
List of arrears of rent, Lecale and Bangor estates, 1745 – T/1023/32

Pollock estate, Ballymacreely
Rent roll, accounts etc., 1792–1803, relating to Ballymacreely and Carrickruskey, acquired, via a mortgage, by John Pollock in trust for Lord Downshire – MIC/619/1

Price, later Perceval Price, estate, Saintfield
Miscellaneous deeds, including 18th-century leases – D/650 *passim*
Rent rolls, Saintfield estate, 1751 – D/240/1
Rent book, Saintfield estate, 1767 – D/650/62A
Rental for the manor of Saintfield, 1788–1802 – T/2101/3–4
Rent arrears, 1751–2 – D/993

Rawdon (later earls of Moira) estate, Moira, Ballynahinch
Voluminous 17th- and 18th-century material relating to estates at Brookhill, County Antrim and Moira (Clare) and Ballynahinch (Kinelarty), County Down – T/3765/L. See calendar for more details.

Rentals
Arrears of the Kinelarty estate, 1703 – T/3765/L/14/1
May rental for Moira estate with a list of lives dropped, 1704 – T/3765/L/2/15/1–2
Rentals of all the Rawdon estates in Ireland and England, 1717, 1723–5 – T/3765/L/2/19/1–6
Rent rolls of Brookhill, Kinelarty and Clare estates, 1717 – T/3765/L/14/7

Surveys
Survey of Madam Dorety Rawdon's part of the manor of Kinelarty, n.d. (early 18th century) – T/3765/L/14/9

Survey of Sir John Rawdon's lands in the manor of Kinelarty, n.d. (early 18th century) – T/3765/L/14/10

Survey by Sir John Rawdon to determine how many Protestants and Catholics lived in each townland in his estate, 1716 – Huntington Library, San Marino, California, Hastings Mss, Box 75

Other

Letters, tenants' petitions etc. for Ballynahinch, 1681–1704 – T/3765/L/2/12/1–8

Leet rolls for the manor of Kinelarty, 1705, 1706, 1707, 1708 – T/3765/L/14/2, 3, 4, 5

Maps of Earl of Moira's estate in Kinelarty, 1782 – T/1451/4

Leases beginning in 1692 for estate at Ballynahinch – D/500 *passim*

See also De Clifford estate *and* Ker estate

Ross estate, Portavoe, Holywood, Dundonald

Maps of estate of Captain James Ross, 1732, naming tenants – T/1451/1

Rent roll of part of the estate of Captain Ross of Portavoe – *Belfast Newsletter*, 2 January 1750

Ross estate, Rostrevor

Bundle of 18th-century documents, including a rental of Rostrevor of *c.*1770 – D/2223/15/32

Saunders estate, Newtownards, Comber *see under* County Antrim

Savage estate, Ardkeen

*c.*100 leases for lives issued by Francis Savage, relating to Ballycran, Lisbane etc. *c.*1792-3 – D/2223/40/6

Miscellaneous bundle of documents including writs to appear at the manor of Ardkeen, 18th century; small volume comprising the Grand Jury book for the manor of Ardkeen, *c.*1779–84, including two lists of inhabitants of the manor arranged by townland, 1779 and 1783 – D/2223/15/10

Savage-Nugent estate, Portaferry

Accounts, receipts from 1630 – D/552/B/3/1

Correspondence, including letters on 18th-century estate business – D/552/A/2, 4

Title deeds and leases to the Savages from 1568 – D/552/B/1/1

Leases from the Savages from 1615 (277 pre-1800) – D/552/B/1/2

Rentals, 1641, 1644–6, 1718 and then fairly regularly for the rest of the 18th century – D/552/B/3/2

Printed rent roll of part of the estate, 1746 – D/552/B/2/1/157

Rent rolls of lands to be sold, n.d. [post-1746] – D/552/B/2/1/159–60, 162

Southwell estate, Downpatrick

Rentals

Rent roll, 1700 – T/518/1

Rental of the manor of Down, *c.*1705 (typed version) – T/793/1

Rent roll, 1742-3 – T/518/1

Rent roll, 1742–4 – D/3300/19/1
Rent roll, 1743–4 – D/1759/3B/2
Rent roll, with rent arrears, 1751–2 – D/2961 (see also T/943/1)

Surveys
Survey of estate, *c.*1700, mainly concerned with infrastructure, but naming some tenants –
  D/477B
Survey of Downpatrick, 1708, including an index of tenants and comments on houses –
  D/477/A

Map
Map of Downpatrick, 1729, naming tenants – D/3300/19/1

Ward estate, Castleward and Bangor
Leases
Five boxes of expired leases, including many from 18th century, arranged in bundles by
  townland and not calendared individually – D/2092/4
Leases from the 17th and 18th centuries, calendared in full – D/2092/5 (see also T/1878 for
  more leases or duplicates)

Rentals
Rent rolls of Ward estate at Bangor, 1746–7 – D/5, D/6
Rent rolls 'in and near Killough', 1748, 1750 – D/2092/1/7, pp. 92, 110
Rentals of the Ward estate, 1752, 1756 – D/2092/6/1–2
Rental of Edward Ward's portion of the estate in Lecale, 1799 – printed in *Lecale Review*,
  1 (2003), pp. 44–7

Other
Exceptionally detailed 18th-century estate correspondence – D/2092/1
Accounts beginning in 1743, including lists of arrrears, 1743 and 1753 – D/2092/6/10
Estate maps, earliest 1778 – D/2092/3

Waring estate, Ballynafern
Rent roll of Ballynafern, barony of Upper Iveagh [Annaclone parish], property of Richard
  Waring, *c.*1750 – T/1023/40

Waring estate, Garvaghy
Maps, surveys and leases etc., 1662–1731 – T/3425/1/1–35
Map and survey of the estate of John Waring of London, 1725, naming tenants in the
  townlands of Garvaghie, Feddeny and Carnew – T/1922/2

Waring estate, Waringstown
157 original and copy letters mainly relating to Clanconnell lands, 1641–*c.*1700; letters and
  accounts, *c.*1667–*c.*1700 – D/695
Valuation of Waringstown, 1696 – printed in E. D. Atkinson, *An Ulster Parish: Being a History
  of Donaghcloney (Waringstown)* (Dublin, 1898), pp. 156–8

Whyte estate, Loughbrickland
Leases, 1738 onwards – D/2918/1/1
Rentals, 1738, 1740, 1746–7, 1749–50, 1762, 1765–80, 1783, 1788 – D/2918/2/1–21
Rent accounts, 1792–1803 – D/2918/2/22–43
Maps, some from 18th century – D/2918/6

COUNTY FERMANAGH

Archdale estate, Castle Archdale, Devenish
Map of the estate in the barony of Lurg, 1733 – T/1174/1
Map of Aghinver, 1734 – T/1174/2
Rent roll of estate in Devenish parish, 1753 – printed in W. B. Steele, *The Parish of Devenish, County Fermanagh: Materials for Its History* (Enniskillen, 1937), p. 108
Rent roll of estate in Devenish parish, 1799 – printed in Steele, *The Parish of Devenish*, p. 108

Balfour estate, Lisnaskea *see* Erne estate

Barton estate, Clonelly
Map of Kilmore, 1769 – D/1016/4

Belmore estate, Castle Coole
Leases, arranged by townland, 1708 onwards – D/3007/A/23
Rentals of the County Fermanagh estate, beginning in 1759 – D/3007/B/4
Maps, surveys and valuations, beginning in 1718 – D/3007/D/1
Vouchers of the County Fermanagh estate, beginning in 1780 – D/3007/C/3
Workmen's account books, 1794–6 – D/3007/B/5
See also Earl of Belmore, *The History of Two Ulster Manors* (London and Dublin, 1903)

Brooke estate, Colebrook
Maps and surveys of townlands in the estate, many from 18th century – D/998/1 *passim*
Leases beginning in 1713, calendared in full (186 pre-1800) – D/998/26 *passim*
Lease book recording leases from *c.*1735, but mainly 1750–1818, information on lives given in detail; 'Observations' column includes many references to emigration to America – D/998/19/1 (currently listed as missing)
Leases for various townlands, beginning in the 18th century – D/3004/A/3–4
Leases in the manor of Brookeborough, beginning in the 18th century, listed alphabetically by townland, but not calendared individually – D/3004/B/2/1
Rent receipt book, 1799–1815 – D/3004/B/2/1

Caldwell estate, Castlecaldwell
Rental of the estate, 1770 – John Rylands Library, Manchester, B 3/28/5
Estate accounts, 1784–5, 1789–91 – John Rylands Library, Manchester, B 3/44/1, 3
Rental, 1786 – John Rylands Library, Manchester, B 3/44/2
Day accounts of work at Castle Caldwell, 1796–7 – John Rylands Library, Manchester, B 3/44/6–7

See also J. B. Cunningham, *Castle Caldwell and Its Families* (Enniskillen, n.d.), pp. 181–92 ('Leases and miscellania')

Cooper estate, Rossfad, Boho, etc.

'Rent roll ... for arrears due November 1757, and three years rent due and ending November, 1760', including observations – D/4031/C/6/1

Rental rolls, 1770, 1774, 1796 – D/4031/C/6/2, 3, 9

Rents received, Rossfad and Tyrone lands, *c*.1783 – D/4031/C/6/10

Survey of Tyrone and Rossfad lands, 1793 – D/4031/C/6/7

Rentals, including a rental of the Boho churchlands, 1803 – D/4031/C/19/1–20

Bundle of miscellaneous documents, including rentals, 1769–1805 – D/4031/C/14/1–82

Lease and renewal of premises in Enniskillen, 1769, 1800, with receipts for rent paid for same, 1785–9 – D/4031/C/11/1–13

Lists and abstracts of deeds and leases, 1771–92 – D/4031/12/1–5

Surveys of Drumshane (1779) and Rossfad, Drumconny and Drumshane (1791) – D/4031/C/15/1–2

Clogher (bishopric of) estate *see under* COUNTY TYRONE

Conolly estate, Ballinamallard

Letters and accounts relating to the manor of Newporten, 1718–19, 1726–9 – T/2825/C/20

Survey and valuation of the manor of Newporten, 1718, with information on tenants – D/2094/24A–C

Rent account for Newporten estate, 1774 – D/2094/47

Dawson estate, Clones

Rent roll, *c*.1745 – D/3053/4/6/1 (currently listed as missing). This estate was purchased from Hugh Willoughby Montgomery by the Dawsons of Dartrey, County Monaghan, and sold by them before the end of the 18th century.

Ely estate, Castle Hume

Rent roll, 1742 – D/535/1

Rental of part of the estate, 1793 – printed in W. B. Steele, *The Parish of Devenish, County Fermanagh: Materials for Its History* (Enniskillen, 1937), p. 109

Over 300 expired leases and *c*.60 maps of townlands and tenements in the manors of Ardgart, Drumcose, Tully and Moyglass, 1724 onwards (mainly 1769–1778) – D/580 *passim*

Enniskillen estate, Florence Court

Map of Enniskillen and adjoining townlands, 1772 – D/53/1

Lease book, 1613–1879, including notes on leases for the Glenawley, Knockninny, Magheraboy, Montagh, Tirkennedy and Enniskillen Town estates – D/1702/5/1

Miscellaneous leases etc. from the 17th and 18th centuries – D/1702/1 *passim*

Erne estate, Crom

Leases

Leases relating to the Crom, Aghalane and other estates, from 1616 – D/1939/11

Leases relating to the Callowhill and Eyles Irwin estates, from 1725 – D/1939/13

Leases relating to the Cole-Hamilton estate in and north of Enniskillen and the Crawford estate at Drumgamph etc., from 1746 – D/1939/14
Leases relating to the Balfour estate at Lisnaskea, from 1616 – D/1939/15
Leases relating to the Knockballymore estate – D/1939/22

Rentals
Rental of Dresternan, *c.*1630 – D/1939/21/3
Rent rolls of the Balfour estate, Lisnaskea, 1632, 1636 – D/1939/15/2/1–2
Rentals and other papers relating to the Lisnaskea estate, 1695–1770 – D/1939/17/J
Rent roll of the manors of Liggin and Dresternan, 1714–15 – D/1939/21/2
Rentals of the Balfour estate, 1735–89 – NLI Ms 10259
Rental of Mr Montgomery's estate in Counties Monaghan and Fermanagh, 1739 – D/1939/19/6/2
Rentals of the Crom estate and manor of Highgate, 1747, 1749 – D/1939/19/6/3
Rental and survey of the bishop's lease held under the see of Clogher, *c.*1800 – D/1939/22/3/4

Maps
Volume of maps of part of the manor of Aghalane, 1775 – D/1939/2/4

See also A. P. W. Malcomson, 'The Erne estate, family and archive', in Eileen Murphy and William Roulston (eds), *Fermanagh: History and Society* (Dublin, 2004).

Hassard estate, Skea
Collection of 18th-century leases for estate – D/2469 *passim*
Rent roll of estate, 1732 – D/2469/16

Huntington estate *see under* COUNTY TYRONE

Lanesborough estate *see under* COUNTY CAVAN

Lendrum Estate, Ballinamallard
Leases, 1773 onwards – D/1834/1 *passim*
Maps of the estate, 1788 – T/2735/1

Lenox estate, Boa Island
Printed sale particulars of the estate of William Lennox [sic], including lands in County Fermanagh, 1778 – T/3161/1/26

Madden estate *see under* COUNTY MONAGHAN

Maguire estate, Tempo *see* Tennent estate

Montgomery estate *see under* COUNTY TYRONE

O'Brien estate, Monea
Abstracts of leases for the manor of Castletown beginning in 1790 – printed in W. B. Steele, *The Parish of Devenish, County Fermanagh: Materials for Its History* (Enniskillen, 1937), p. 108

Tennent (formerly Maguire) estate, Tempo
Leases, 1737–8, 1773, 1785, 1790, 1793, 1795 – D/2922/E–H *passim*
Survey of estate, 1799 – D/2922/H/1

Trinity College, Dublin estate *see under* **COUNTY DONEGAL**

COUNTY LONDONDERRY

Bacon estate, Magilligan, Portrush
Lease of 1735 naming 6 tenants in Glenmanus – D/660/1
Rent roll of William Bacon's estate in Ballymaclary and Glenmanus with a list of his debts, 1740 – D/1550/149/1/4
Rental of the late William Bacon's lands in Magilligan, 1785 – D/1514/1/3/2

Clothworkers' Company estate, Dunboe, Killowen
Map of the estate by Thomas Raven, 1622, with information on tenants, printed in *Londonderry and the London Companies*, edited by D. A. Chart (Belfast, 1928)
Current accounts, 1620–1852; selected estate extracts, 1683–1712 – MIC/146/1–15
Rental of the manor of 'Killowen', n.d. [c.1640?] – T/724/1
Rent receipts of tenants on Clothworkers' proportion, 1662 – T/640/92
Chancery bill listing 34 tenants, 1664 – T/808/11342
See also **McClelland/Maxwell estate**

Conolly estate, Bellaghy, Eglinton, Limavady
William Conolly purchased the Limavady estate from the Phillips family in 1697 and in the 18th century his family leased the estates of the Grocers' and Vintners' companies.

Limavady estate and Grocers' estate
Abstracts of leases on the Limavady estate, c.1700–c.1780 – D/2094/58
Rentals and accounts for the manor of Newtownlimavady, the church-lands of Drumachose and the Grocers' proportion, 1718, 1721, 1724–9, including a list of names of tenants who had left their farms for New England in 1718 – T/2825/C/11
Correspondence relating to the Limavady estate, 1718–31 – T/2825/C/27
Rent rolls of the Limavady estate, 1729 – D/2094/26, 27
Rent rolls of the Grocers' proportion, 1729 – D/2094/31, 32
Rentals and surveys of individual farms etc. in Limavady estate, 1781–4 – T/2825/C/15
Map of the manor of Limavady, 1782, naming tenants in some townlands (includes typescript list of named tenants) – T/821/1
Rent roll of the Limavady estate, c.1800 – D/2094/79
Rental of Limavady estate, 1802 – T/2825/C/16/1

Vintners' estate
Rent roll of the Vintners' proportion, 1718 (very detailed) – D/2094/21
Rent rolls of the Vintners' proportion, 1729 – D/2094/29, 30
Rentals of the Vintners' proportion, 1775, 1776 – D/2094/50, 51
Rent accounts of the Vintners' proportion, 1775, 1776 – D/2094/53, 54
Correspondence relating to the Vintners' estate, 1777–1802 – T/2825/C/18
Rentals of the Vintners' estate, 1778, 1781–2, 1786, 1795–1801 – T/2825/C/19
Rentals of the Vintners' proportion, 1788, 1788–90, 1791–3 – D/2094/76, 77, 78

Conyngham estate *see* **Lenox-Conyngham estate**

Dawson estate, Castledawson
Rent roll of Moyola, 1706, including townlands of Anaghmoar, Ballymaguigan, Derrygarave, Leitram, Shanmolagh and Tamniaran – D/1470/6/7
Extracts from manor of Castledawson rental, 1707–45 – T/865/1

Derry (bishopric of) estate, all parishes in the diocese of Derry
Rentals, 1617, 1688, 1708, 1719 – D/683/31, 275, 278, 287
Lease rents of the see of Derry, 1718 – D/683/286
Numerous petitions from tenants of the lands of the bishopric, 1768–1803 – D/2798/3 *passim*
Rental of lands belonging to the bishopric to be let in Clonleigh parish, 1790 – D/2798/3/59

Drapers' Company estate, Moneymore, Ballynascreen, Desertmartin, etc.
Bound typescript volume containing petitions from British inhabitants of Drapers' Plantation for leases, *c.*1610; rent reports, 1613; leases, correspondence, surveys, etc., *c.*1615 onwards; complaint certificates of the Draperstown (Moneymore) inhabitants, 1618; rent rolls for Moneymore, Londonderry and Coleraine, 1728, 1749; map and survey of Moneymore – T/635/1–15

Rentals
Rental, 1614–15 – D/3632/A/30
Rent roll, 1622 – D/3632/A/180
Rental and account, 1622–4 – D/3632/A/184
Rental, 1623 – D/3632/A/190
Rent roll, 1728 (when the estate was leased by William Rowley) – D/3632/K/1
Ledgers, 1750–96 – D/3632
Rent roll, 1790 – D/3632/K/2
Rent roll, 1793 – D/3632/K/3

Maps
Map of the estate by Thomas Raven, 1622, with information on tenants, printed in *Londonderry and the London Companies*, edited by D. A. Chart (Belfast, 1928)
Map and survey of the tenements and parks in Moneymore, 1730 – D/3632/P/5
Maps of the Kilcronaghan and Desertmartin, Ballynascreen, and Moneymore divisions of the estate, 1792–3 – D/3632/P/6–8

Other

Petitions from British inhabitants of the estate for their leases, 1611 – D/3632/A/22

An account of William Conyngham's management of Moneymore proportion, 1690–95, naming tenants by townland – D/1470/3/16

Letters about tenures of leases and rent arrears, 1728–56 – D/3632/A/356

Notes on the holdings of the company's tenants for making out their leases, n.d. [pre-1800] – D/3632/A/340

Fishmongers' Company estate, Ballykelly

Map of the estate by Thomas Raven, 1622, with information on tenants, printed in *Londonderry and the London Companies*, edited by D. A. Chart (Belfast, 1928)

Expired leases etc. relating to the Manor of Walworth, 1613–80 – Guildhall Library, London, Ms 7270

Chancery bill naming 43 tenants in the Manor of Walworth, 1701 – T/808/11309

Map of estate, 1732 (only a few names) – D/519/1

Account book, 1775–6, detailing payments to named tradesmen etc. – T/3990/1

See also R. J. Hunter, 'The Fishmongers' Company of London and the Londonderry Plantation, 1609–41', in G. O'Brien (ed.), *Derry: History and Society* (Dublin, 1999) pp. 205–58.

Gage estate, Magilligan

Survey of part of Magilligan parish belonging to Hodgson Gage, 1768, naming tenants – D/673/56

Survey of part of Magilligan parish belonging to Marcus Gage, 1800, naming tenants – D/673/95A

Goldsmiths' Company estate, New Buildings

Map of the estate by Thomas Raven, 1622, with information on tenants, printed in *Londonderry and the London Companies*, edited by D. A. Chart (Belfast, 1928)

Certificate relating to 1622 Plantation survey listing freeholders, leaseholders and undertenants, over 50 names – MIC/9B/12A

'The severall inhabitants in the Mannor of Goldsmiths which was summoned to appear at a Court Leet held at New Buildings for the said mannor the 19th day of April 1716' – MIC/9B/12A. This lists over 200 names arranged by townland.

Graves estate, Castledawson

18th-century deeds and leases for Castledawson – D/1062/4/B

A list of the leases granted by Admiral Graves to his tenants in the manor of Castledawson, 1768 – D/1062/4/B/15

A list of the tenants and rent payments made for the townlands of Mullaghboy, Aughrim and Drumlamph, 1772–1809 – D/1062/4/C/3

Grocers' Company estate, Eglinton

Map of the estate by Thomas Raven, 1622, with information on tenants, printed in *Londonderry and the London Companies*, edited by D. A. Chart (Belfast, 1928)

In the early 18th century the Grocers' estate was leased by William Conolly: *see* **Conolly estate**

Haberdashers' Company estate, Aghanloo, Dunboe

Rent roll, n.d. [17th century] – T/640/1

Papers relating to the Haberdashers' proportion, c.1614–16, including names of tenants, freeholders from Scotland, and payments to craftsmen – T/520/1

Rent roll, 1623 – T/640/22

Map of the estate by Thomas Raven, 1622, with information on tenants, printed in *Londonderry and the London Companies*, edited by D. A. Chart (Belfast, 1928)

See also McClelland/Maxwell estate

Hervey/Bruce estate, Downhill

This was the personal estate of George Augustus Hervey, earl of Bristol and bishop of Derry (1768–1803).

Rentals of earl of Bristol's lands in Magilligan, c.1780 and 1795 – D/1514/1/3/1, 5

Rental and valuation of the earl of Bristol's lands in Dunboe, c.1780s and c.1790s – D/1514/1/3/3–4

List of workmen, 1780s – D/1514/1/1/41/1

Manuscript valuation book for Magilligan (Tamlaghtard) parish, c.1800 – D/1514/2/4/16

Survey of land taken from undernamed tenants and enclosed with Circular Road and demesne wall, n.d. [late 18th century] – D/2798/3/88. Lands of B'Madakin, Miltown, Ballywoodock, Glebe and Drimagully.

Heyland estate, Coleraine

Rent roll, 1792–5, with names of tenants, dates of leases, observations – D/668/49/1

Irish Society estates, Coleraine, Londonderry

Index to leases, 1616–7; recital of grants, 1617–74; rents, salaries, dividend receipt book, 1683–1712; account book, 1689–1725; description of lands in Londonderry city, 1695 – MIC/9A

Rental of Coleraine, n.d. [c.1640?] – T/724/1

Rent roll of Coleraine, c.1746, names in alphabetical order – T/656/1, no. 60

Rent roll of Londonderry, 1746, names in alphabetical order – T/656/1, no. 61

Rent roll of tenements in Waterside, Coleraine, 1756 – T/656/1, no. 62

Rent roll of Londonderry and Coleraine, 1756 – D/573/1

Rent roll of Londonderry and Coleraine, 1794 – D/573/2

Rent roll of Irish Society's estates in Londonderry and Coleraine, 1782 – D/668/A/13–16

Ironmongers' Company estates, Aghadowey etc.

Map of the estate by Thomas Raven, 1622, with information on tenants, printed in *Londonderry and the London Companies*, edited by D. A. Chart (Belfast, 1928)

Rental of the manor of Agivey, n.d. [c.1640?] – T/724/1

Survey of estate by Isaac Pyke, 1725, containing detailed descriptions of townlands and naming tenants – MIC/145/9

Valuation of estate by John Hood, 1765, naming tenants and with occasional observations on them – MIC/145/8

Rent rolls for, respectively, Mrs Sarah Bryan's part of the estate, John Macky's part and Mr Lecky's part, all c.1765 – MIC/145/8

Jackson estate, Waterside, Coleraine and Articlave
Large collection of 18th-century leases, many of them relating to Aghadowey parish – D/668
Rent roll, 1782, with arrears for 1781 – D/668/A/3
Rent book, 1788 – D/668/A/7. Townlands of Ballyhern, Castletoothery, Kilcranny and Waterside: over 130 names.
Rent rolls of part of George Jackson's estate, 1792, 1793, 1794, 1797 – D/668/A/4, 4A, 4B, 4C
Rent roll, 1798–9 – D/668/A/5
Rent book, 1799–1801 – D/668/A/10
Lists of arrears on estate, 1798, 1799 – D/668/A/9A–B
Rent roll of Joseph Weir's part of the estate, 1796 – D/D/668/A/16. Townlands of Ballyhern, Castletoothery, Kilcranny and Waterside.
Rentals, 1768–74 (rather tattered), 1794 – D/668/A/16

Lenox-Conyngham estate, Springhill
Rental of William Conyngham's estate, 1683–4 – printed in *Analecta Hibernica*, xv (1944), pp. 357–8
Rental of Springhill estate, 1786 – D/1449/3/1
Volume of maps of estate, 1722, naming tenants – D/1449/5/1
18th-century correspondence, some of which relates to estate management – D/1449/12, *passim*
Leases from the 18th century – D/847/6

McClelland/Maxwell estate, Aghanloo, Dunboe, etc.
Rental, 1630 – T/640/31
Leases for farms in Dunboe/Killowen, 1655–6 – T/640/59–60, 62–82
Statements of rents and leases, 1666 – T/640/105
Rent rolls, 1669, 1684 – T/640/108, 138
See also Clothworkers' Company estate and Haberdashers' Company estate.

Maxwell estate see McClelland/Maxwell estate

Mercers' estate, Kilrea
Map of the estate by Thomas Raven, 1622, with information on tenants, printed in *Londonderry and the London Companies*, edited by D. A. Chart (Belfast, 1928)
Rentals and accounts, 1628–33 – Guildhall Library, Ms 3115
Rental of estate, 1714 – MIC/225/2
Rental of the manor of 'Killreagh', n.d. [*c.*1640?] – T/724/1
Account book of Alexander Stewart including rent accounts for Mercer's estate, 1781–90 – D/2784/19

Merchant Taylors' estate, Macosquin
Map of the estate by Thomas Raven, 1622, with information on tenants, printed in *Londonderry and the London Companies*, edited by D. A. Chart (Belfast, 1928)
Rental of Merchant Taylors' estates, post-1729 – T/656/1, no. 52
Printed volume of minutes, 1609–33 – D/2436/1

Phillips estate, Limavady

A 70-page account book, 1684–93 – T/2825/C/5/1

Bundle of documents mainly relating to the Phillips estate at Limavady, 1662–99 including leases, 1682–94 – D/1550/147/1–21. Originals closed, but the calendar provides names of tenants and townlands.

Ponsonby estate, New Buildings

(Formerly Goldsmiths' Company estate)

Survey of the Manor of Goldsmiths, naming tenants, 1771 – D/3482/1

Rowley (including Langford-Rowley) estate, Castleroe, Tobermore

Miscellaneous 17th- and 18th-century papers, including leases MIC/537/1–3

Leases, 1660 onwards – D/1118/3/4

Rentals, valuations and accounts, 1683–1705 – MIC/537/3

Vouchers, 1686–94 – MIC/537/3

Rentals of estate in and around Tobermore with details of building clauses in leases, 1725, 1727 – D/642/H/1–2 (MIC/593/9)

Map of the Tobermore estate, 1724, naming tenants – D/642/G/4 (MIC/593/9)

Map of Derrynoid (Derrynoyd), 1734, naming tenants – D/642/G/6 (MIC/593/9)

Rental and account, 1744–50 – MIC/537/3

See also Drapers' Company estate

Salters' estate, Magherafelt

Map of the estate by Thomas Raven, 1622, with information on tenants, printed in *Londonderry and the London Companies*, edited by D. A. Chart (Belfast, 1928)

Rental of the manor of Magherafelt, n.d. [*c.*1640?] – T/724/1

Petition from the inhabitants of the manor of Sal, *c.*1720, 23 names – D/4108/14G

Rentals of the Salters' estate, 1752, 1766, 1772, 1774, 1783, 1790 – D/4108/15G/1, 16O, 16R, 16Y, 16Z/8, 17B. The rental of 1752 was printed in W. H. Maitland, *History of Magherafelt* (1916, reprinted Moyola Books, 1988 and 1991), pp. 17–19.

List of the inhabitants of the Salters' estate who ought to attend courts leet and baron, 1752, names arranged by townland – D/4108/15F

Skinners' Company estate

Map of the estate by Thomas Raven, 1622, with information on tenants, printed in *Londonderry and the London Companies*, edited by D. A. Chart (Belfast, 1928)

A survey, rental and plans of the Manor of Pellipar, 1792 – Guildhall Library, London, Ms 5202/1–2

Staples estate, Lissan *see under* COUNTY TYRONE

Strafford estate, Bellaghy

Several hundred 18th-century leases relating to lands in County Londonderry – D/1062/1/8A–12

Composition volume of 29 maps and surveys, 1743–*c.*1847 – D/1062/1/14

Vintners' Company estate, Bellaghy

Map of the estate by Thomas Raven, 1622, with information on tenants, printed in *Londonderry and the London Companies*, edited by D. A. Chart (Belfast, 1928)

Rental of the manor of 'Lisneycourt', n.d. [*c.*1640?] – T/724/1

Counterparts of leases issued by Viscount Massereene for the Vintners' estate in 1698 – D/1550/148/1–18. The originals are closed, but the calendar lists the names of the tenants and townlands.

See also **Conolly estate**

COUNTY MONAGHAN

Anketell estate, Trough barony

Rental, 1784–7 – MIC/309/1, printed in *Clogher Record*, xi (1984), pp. 403–20

See also an indexed list of tenants on the Anketell estate, 1784–9 in *Clogher Record* xi (1984), pp. 403–20.

Barrett Lennard estate, Clones

Bundles of 245 leases, 1581–1808 – MIC/170/1

About 400 letters and reports of agents, 1684–1859 – MIC/170/1, 2, 3

Bundles of 247 documents consisting of rentals, accounts and vouchers – MIC/170/3, 4

Map of Clones, 1768, naming tenants – MIC/170/4

Clones rent rolls of the 1630s, 1638, 1640, printed in *Clogher Record*, xvi (1997), pp. 95–100

Clones rent rolls, 1679, 1681, printed in *Clogher Record*, xiii (1988), pp. 126–8

Lease abstracts for the Clones estate, over 200 items from the 17th and 18th centuries, printed in *Clogher Record*, xviii (2003), 53–84

Barton estate, Lough Bawn

Information on tenants in 18th century – printed in *Clogher Record*, xv (1995), pp. 137–45

Bath estate, Farney (formerly Weymouth)

Rent roll, 1732; schedule of leases, *c.*1735; rentals, 1756, 1776, 1778–1810; agents' accounts, 1777–1808 – NLI p. 5894

For additional material relating to this estate *see* **Shirley estate**

Blayney estate, Castleblayney etc.

Rent roll of Lady Blayney's lands in the parishes of Tedavnet and Monaghan, 1790, including details of leases, 1713–99 – T/3729/1

Survey of that part of the Aghnamallow estate belonging to Lord Blayney, 1762 – D/1421/3/4. Lands of Aughnamallow, Ballagh, Cabragh, Cavangarvin, Cloghernaught, Coughin, Creagh, Lisnashanagh and Rusky.

Castleblayney rent book, 1772 – Monaghan County Museum; printed in *Clogher Record*, x (1981), pp. 414–18

Box of miscellaneous estate papers including rentals of 1783 and 1791, and an account book of 1786 containing details of wages paid to gardeners, labourers etc. – D/1421/1/68

Bundles of leases, *c.*1790 onwards – D/1421/2

Brownlow estate, Farney
Rentals of Monaghan estate, 1755–94 – D/1928/R/1 *passim*
Rent roll of Monaghan estate, 1758 – D/1928/A/1/7

Clermont estate, Monaghan
Volume of maps of the estate of the Earl of Clermont, 1791 – MIC/624/1
See also **Rossmore estate**

Clogher (bishopric of) estate *see under* **COUNTY TYRONE**

Crofton estate, Errigal Truagh etc.
Surveys and valuations of the estate, 1719–84 – NLI Ms 20,798
Maps of the estate, 1754–1802 – NLI 26 I 2 (1–8)
Rentals and accounts, 1769, 1783–1814 – NLI Ms 20,783
Rental, 1792 – NLI Ms 8150
Leases mainly for Errigle parish beginning in 1785 – NLI D 26,931–26,956

Dawson (Dartry and Cremorne), Dartrey
Maps
Maps of townlands and farms, 1710 onwards – D/3053/2
Photostat copy of volume of maps, 1768, naming tenants – T/3170
Volume of 20 maps, 1779, naming tenants' estate – NLI Ms 3181

Rentals
Rental, *c.*1780 – NLI Ms 3282
Rental, 1790 – NLI Ms 3184
Rental, 1796–7 – NLI Ms 3674
Rentals, 1800–1 – NLI Mss 3186–7
Survey and rental, n.d. [1802] – D/3053/8/12/1
A list of tenants giving rents and terms of leases, *c.*1800 – NLI Ms 1696

Essex estate, Farney
Lease from the Essex estate, 1624, naming some tenants – printed in *Clogher Record*, xiii (1990),
    pp. 100–14

Evatt estate, Tedavnet
Maps of Corrinshigoe, Aughnacalcuile and Mullytigorrie owned by Humphrey Evatt, 1730 –
    NLI Ms 2794

Forster estate, Killeevan
Volume of maps of Forster estate in counties Monaghan and Tyrone, 1795–1805 – D/1105/2
Rent book of Killeevan estate, 1802–5 – MIC/661/A/1
Typescript rent book of Killeevan estate, 1802–3 – MIC/661/A/6

Hutcheson estate, Donagh
Map of the estate of Alexander Hutcheson in the parish of Donagh, 1788 (later bought by the
    Leslies) – Castle Leslie, G/1/6

Johnston estate, Aghabog etc.
Printed rentals and associated papers, 1750–51 – D/3053/6/10/1–6
See also **Johnston of Gilford estate** *under* **COUNTY DOWN** for more County Monaghan estate material.

Kane estate, Errigal Truagh
Rentals of the Kane estate, 1764 and 1801, and some 18th-century accounts – Monaghan County Museum; printed in *Clogher Record*, xiii (1990), pp. 72–91, with a map of the estate

Ker estate, Newbliss
Information on tenants from estate records, 1790–*c*.1830, printed in *Clogher Record*, xii (1985), pp. 110–26

Leslie estate, Ballybay
Leases arranged by townland, 1780 onwards – D/3406/D/5
Survey of Ballybay estate owened by Rev. Dr Henry Leslie, including maps, 1786 – Monaghan County Museum; over 150 names extracted from it printed in *Clogher Record*, xi (1982), pp. 71–6

Leslie estate, Glaslough
Rental of Glaslough estate, 1751–66 – NLI Ms 5783
Rental of Glaslough and Emly estates, 1765–80, 1802 – NLI Ms 5809
Boxes of leases, 1742 onwards – Castle Leslie, B/1–3
Box of rentals, 1786, 1781–1806 – Castle Leslie, D/1

Madden estate, Hilton Park
Volume of maps of estate in Galloon parish, 1766, naming tenants – D/3465/G/5 (MIC/594/7). Note: due to changes in parish boundaries the area covered by the maps is now in Currin parish.

Massereene estate, Clones etc.
Rentals of the estate in County Monaghan from the early 19th century, but providing details of leases from the mid-18th century – D/1739/3/9, 10
Leases, 1693 onwards – D/4084/1/3/3

Moore estate, Ematris
Rent rolls, 1702–16 – printed in *Clogher Record*, xv (1995), pp. 135–6

Rossmore estate, Monaghan
Leases arranged in bundles by townland starting in the 18th century – T/2929/36
See also **Clermont estate**

Shirley estate, Farney
Rent roll of lands in the barony of Farney, 1695, calendared in full – D/3531/A/4, p. 21
Arrears of rent from tenants in Farney estate, 1708–17 – D/3531/A/4, pp. 23–31
List of tenants on Shirley estate in Farney, 1729, *c*.160 names with a few denominations – D/3531/A/4, p. 107

Rentals, 1726, 1771 – D/3531/R/1/1–2

Survey and abstract of leases granted in the Weymouth estate (east half of Farney), post-1719 – D/3531/S/3/1

Survey of Weymouth estate in Farney, c.1730 – D/3531/S/4/1

Other 18th-century maps and surveys – D/3531/S *passim*

The following Shirley estate material is listed in the PRONI calendar as being in Warwickshire County Record Office:

Farney rentals, 1777, 1800, 1802 – Box 2/1

Farney rentals, 1735–1822 – Box 2/2

Map of the west part of Farney including an inset of Carrickmacross with a key giving tenants' names, 1734 – Item 123/1

Bundles of leases, 1770, 1770; three small boxes of loose leases, 1799; two bundles of leases, 1792–1825, 1729–1829 – Item 222

Singleton estate, Errigal Truagh

Leases calendared individually, 1759 onwards – D/988 *passim*

Verner estate *see under* COUNTY TYRONE

Westenra estate *see* Rossmore estate

Weymouth estate *see* Bath estate

COUNTY TYRONE

Abercorn estate, Strabane

The Abercorn estate was the largest in County Tyrone and one of the most important in Ulster. It owed its origins to the 1st earl of Abercorn, who was granted two manors – Donelong and Strabane – in Strabane barony in 1610. The subsequent history of the Abercorns is complex, but through purchase and inheritance by the beginning of the 18th century the estate comprised four manors in Tyrone – Cloghogall, Derrywoon, Donelong and Strabane – and the manor of Magavelin and Lismochery in County Donegal. The real strength of this archive is the voluminous correspondence that has survived for the 18th century, most of which comprises letters to and from the 8th earl of Abercorn and his Irish agents. Some 20 volumes of typescript calendars containing fairly full transcriptions of most of the letters are available on the open shelves of the Reading Room in PRONI.

Manor of Cloghogall (lands in the parish of Leckpatrick)

Rent roll of Ballymagorry, n.d. [c.1720] – D/623/C/2/1

Rental, 1794–1809, with details of the November 1787 letting of the entire manor – D/623/C/4/2

Maps of the manor of Cloghogall naming tenants, 1777 – D/623/D/1/16/13–33

Valuation of the manor of Cloghogall, 1777 – D/623/D/1/18/1

Manor of Derrywoon (lands in the parish of Ardstraw)
Rental, 1794–1809, with details of the November 1787 letting of the entire manor – D/623/C/4/7
Maps of the manor of Derrywoon naming tenants, 1777 – D/623/D/1/16/61–72
Valuation of the manor of Derrywoon, 1777 – D/623/D/1/19/1

Manor of Donelong (lands in the parish of Donagheady)
Rental, 1794–1809, with details of the November 1787 letting of the entire manor – D/623/C/4/3
Maps of the manor of Donelong naming tenants, 1777 – D/623/D/1/16/1–12

Manor of Magavelin and Lismochery (lands in the parishes of Taughboyne and Raymoghy)
Survey of the manor of 'Magavelin' by Archibald Stewart, 1718 – D/623/D/1/3/1. Names about 30 tenants.
Rental, 1794–1809, with details of the November 1787 letting of the entire manor – D/623/C/4/8
Maps of the manor of Magavelin and Lismochery naming tenants, 1781 – D/623/D/1/16/73–91
Lease book of the Donegal estate from 1782 – D/623/B/11/1

Manor of Strabane (lands in the parishes of Ardstraw, Camus-juxta-Mourne and Urney)
Claims made with regard to the manor of Strabane, 1700–1, published in the *Directory of Irish Family History Research* (2001), pp. 85–6
Printed rental of the manor of Strabane, *c*.1702, published in the *Directory of Irish Family History Research* (2001), p. 86
Rental, 1794–1809, with details of the November 1787 letting of the entire manor – D/623/C/4/1
Maps of the manor of Strabane naming tenants, 1777 – D/623/D/1/16/34–60
Valuation of the manor of Strabane, 1777 – D/623/D/1/17/1

Miscellaneous
Leases, 1614–1734 – D/623/B/13
A muster roll of the Abercorn estate, naming over 200 tenants in possession of firearms, 1745 – printed in the *Directory of Irish Family History Research* 21 (1998). Lists over 200 tenants in the manors of Cloghogall (listed under the parish of Leckpatrick), Derrywoon, Donelong, and Magavelin and Lismochery.
Volume recording tenant right sales in Tyrone and Donegal, *c*.1800 – D/623/B/4

See also: W. H. Crawford, *The Management of a Major Ulster Estate in the Late Eighteenth Century: The Eighth Earl of Abercorn and his Irish Agents* (Dublin, 2001); William Roulston, 'The evolution of the Abercorn estate in northwest Ulster' in *Familia*, 15 (1999), pp. 54–67. Extracts from the Abercorn correspondence were published as *The Abercorn Letters* edited by J. Gebbie (Omagh, 1972).

Auchinleck estate, Omagh
Collection of 18th-century leases relating to Omagh – D/674 *passim*

Belmore estate, Beragh and Sixmilecross
(Records connected with the Lowry family and the manor of Finagh and other Tyrone property; see under County Fermanagh for more Belmore estate material)
Leases arranged by townland, 1740 onwards – D/3007/A/24
Rental of County Tyrone estate, 1777–86 – D/624/1
Rentals of the County Tyrone estate, beginning in 1777 – D/3007/B/3
Vouchers of the County Tyrone estate, beginning in 1777 – D/3007/C/2
Survey and valuation of part of the Belmore estate in County Tyrone, c.1800, including comments on the standard of the tenants – D/3007/D/1/6/1
See also Earl of Belmore, *The History of Two Ulster Manors* (London and Dublin, 1903).

Blessington estate *see* **Mountjoy estate**

Burges estate, Parkanaur
Rentals
Rental, 1794–5 – T/1007/193. Townlands of Stakernagh, Edenacrannon, Terrenew, Tullyallen, Killmoyle, County Tyrone; Annaloist, Derryneskan, Ballyscandal, City of Armagh, County Armagh.
Rental of Tyrone estate, 1797 – T/1007/207
Rental of Armagh and Tyrone estate, 1708–9 – T/1007/216

Maps
Volume of maps with observation on the tenancies, c.1798 – T/2256
Map of Edenacrannon, 1750, naming tenants, with observations of 1799 – T/1007/61
Map of Tullyallen, 1769, naming tenants – T/1007/93
Map of Terrenew, Stakernagh, Edenacrannon, Killmoyle and Tullyallen, 1774, naming tenants – T/1007/108
Map of Tullyallen, 1799, naming tenants – T/1007/224

Miscellaneous
18th-century observations and leases – D/1594
Notebook containing copies of leases and remarks on tenants, c.1700–1902 – T/1085/2
Lists of tenants, 1750–71 – T/1054/2

Cairns estate, Killyfaddy
A list of the counterparts of the tenants' leases for the estate of James Cairns, c.1738–86, calendar names townlands covered – D/2559/1/7
Rent roll and survey of estate, 1780 – D/2559/3/3
Rent rolls of part of the estate to be sold, 1793, 1795 – D/2559/3/3–5
Rent rolls, c.1800 – D/2559/3/8, 10–11
Tenants in Killyfaddy whose rents are raised, c.1800 – D/2559/3/9

Caledon Estate, Caledon
Large collection of 18th-century leases for the Caledon estate in Armagh and Tyrone; calendar names tenants – D/2433/A/1/22 *passim*
Rentals of the estate, 1766, 1796, 1799 – D/2433/A/6/1–3

Draft valuation and rental of the estate, 1774 – D/2433/A/5/1
Letterbooks, 1775–1802 – D/2433/A/3/1–3
Lease book of the estate which provides a summary of leases from 1735 and a statement of the
  position of these leases in the 1770s – D/2433/A/5/3

Castle Stewart estate, Stewartstown and Castlederg
Leases for the manor of Hastings, alias Castlegore, 18th century – D/1618/5/1–2
Leases for Castle Stewart and Forward estates, 17th-18th centuries – D/1618/5/5–10
Leases for Orritor estate, 18th century – D/1618/5/11–12
Originals and typescript copies of mainly 17th-century correspondence and other related papers
  – D/1618/15/1–2 (calendared in full)
Rental of Castle Stewart estate, 1768 – D/476/258A
See **Staples estate, Lissan**, for more Castle Stewart estate material

Charlemont estate, Castlecaulfeild *see under* COUNTY ARMAGH

Clogher (bishopric of) estate, Clogher diocese
Leases of the see of Clogher, Counties Fermanagh, Monaghan and Tyrone, 1746–79
  – NLI 5853

Cooper estate *see under* COUNTY FERMANAGH

Derry (bishopric of) estate *see under* COUNTY LONDONDERRY

Eccles estate, Fintona
Leases etc., 1671 onwards (over 150 pre-1800) – D/526 *passim*
Notebook containing a copy lease book, 1751–1850 – D/1368/1

Erne (Lady) estate, Strabane
List of Lady Erne's rents in Strabane, 1795 – NLI Ms 15,783

Foljambe estate, Newtownsaville
Rentals of the manor of Cecil with the churchlands of Errigal, 1732–3, 1735–8 (rental for 1737
  has observations on tenants) – T/3381/2/1–8
Rentals, accounts and letters, 1783–1811 – T/3381/5/1–63
Leases of farms in the manor of Cecil, 1769, listed in full in the calendar, nearly 100 names in
  total – T/3381/4/1–8
Survey of the manor of Cecil, 1796 – T/3381/9/1
Survey and valuation of the manor of Cecil, 1800 – T/3381/10/1–7
See also Jack Johnston, *Glenhoy: The First 200 Years* (privately published, 1979), which includes
  the rental of the Savile (Foljambe) estate from 1738 and leaseholders in the manor of Cecil
  in 1769.

Forbes estate, Aghintain
Volume of maps of the estate of the Hon. John Forbes at Mount Stewart of Aghintain, 1777,
  naming tenants – T/1132/1

Forster estate, Pomeroy
Rent roll of Lisnagleer and Drumconor, 1786 – D/2469/36
Volume of maps of Forster estate in Counties Monaghan and Tyrone, 1795–1805 – D/1105/2

Gardiner estate *see* Mountjoy estate

Gervais estate, Augher
Household account book, 1767–78 – T/1287

Gorges estate, Clogher and Errigal Keerogue
Rental of part of the estate of Hamilton Gorges sold to John Doherty in trust for Thomas Verner, 1785 – D/847/7/C/1. Covers townland of Millix, Eskermore, Brackagh and Irish Shantavny in the parishes of Errigal Keerogue and Clogher; in very poor condition.

Hall estate, Collermoney, Leckpatrick
Rent roll of Collermoney, 1775 – D/2649/15/3/4

Hamilton estate, Manor Elieston
Rental of estate of Sir Claud Hamilton of Shawfield, 1613–19 – MIC/205, T/544

Huntingdon estate, Castlederg
Rent rolls of the estate in Counties Fermanagh and Tyrone, 1633–66 – Huntington Library, San Marino, California, Hastings Mss, Box 78
Survey of the Countess of Huntingdon's lands, n.d. [*c.*1664] – Huntington Library, San Marino, California, Hastings Mss, Box 76

Knox (Ranfurly) estate, Dungannon
Rentals
Rent rolls of the town and manor of Dungannon, 1745, 1747 – D/235/20, 22
Rent ledger, Dungannon estate, 1781–91 – D/235/159
Rent roll of Dungannon estate, 1795 – D/235/45

Leases
Leases, 1694 onwards, calendared – D/4183/5, 6, 10, 14
Leases from the 18th century onwards, calendared – D/235 *passim*
List of tenants in the town and manor of Dungannon 'whose Minnitts are in Jon Jourdan's hands ...', *c.*1729 – D/235/55
List of lessees and tenants in Dungannon area, 1750–1812, naming lives in leases – D/235/158
Extracts of leases, 1757–1832 – T/953/1

Maps
Map and survey of manor of Dungannon, 1710, naming tenants – D/1018/A/1 (see T/587/1 for another version)
Volume of maps of estate, 1770 – D/1932/7/1

Lindesay estate, Loughrey
Rental of estate, 1745–61 – NLI Ms 5204
Survey of estate, c.1800, naming tenants – NLI Ms 2584

Lowry estate, Clonoe etc.
Collection of leases from second half of 18th century – D/474 *passim*

Lowry estate, Pomeroy
18th-century leases for lands in Pomeroy and Desertcreat parishes, calendar lists names of
    lessees – D/1132/10
Envelope of loose pages of Pomeroy estate rentals, 1767–1803 – D/1132/12/1
Pomeroy estate rental, 1791–4 – D/1132/12/1A
Box of estate maps, 1759–1873 – D/1132/19/1

McCausland estate, Ardstraw
List of tenants in the manor of Ardstraw, 1720s (leased by the McCauslands from the bishop
    of Derry) – printed in the *Directory of Irish Family History Research*, 24 (2001), p. 84

Mervyn estate, Augher, Omagh, Trillick
Rental of the Mervyn estates, 1719 – T/359/1, p. 169. Names tenants in Omagh and Trillick.
Rent book of Colonel Mervyn's estate, 1769–70, covering Augher, Omagh and Trillick estates
    – D/2023/3/1/2

Montgomery estate, Fivemiletown and Derrygonnelly
Rentals
Rent roll of Derrygonelly, 1753 – T/359/1, p. 23
Rent rolls, Derrygonnelly estate, 1759, 1767 – D/464/26, 28
Rent rolls of estates in Fermanagh and Tyrone, 1792–4, 1793–1801, 1797 – D/464/74, 75, 84
Rent roll of Blessingbourne, 1752, 35 tenants – D/627/16
Rental and account books, Blessingbourne, 1769–1810 – D/627/21
Rental of Fivemiletown, 1773 – D/627/23
Receipt book of rents, Fivemiletown, 1783–6 – D/627/37
Rental and survey naming tenants with observations, County Tyrone, 1787–9 – D/627/46
Rentals of estate for most years, 1784–1800 – D/627 *passim*
Rental of c.1810 covering the period 1780–1840, manor of Blessingbourne, County Tyrone
    and manor of Drumcrow, County Fermanagh – D/627/80

Maps, surveys and valuations
Maps of holdings in estate, 1743, 1745, 1750, 1780 – D/482 *passim*
Survey of the manor of Blessingbourne, 1726 – D/627/4
Valuation of Blessingbourne, 1767 – D/627/20
Maps of Timpany, County Tyrone, 1775, naming tenants – D/627/24

Miscellaneous
Account book, 1744–50 – D/627/14
Lists of cattle grazed on Mulnaverl (Mulnavale), County Tyrone, 1777–8, c.1780 – D/627/25, 29

85 names and addresses of men 'ditching in Mulinavel' (Mulnavale), 1779 – D/627/30
Returns of the lives in leases, Blessingbourne, c.1783 – D/627/33–6
Names of 95 freeholders in the manor of Blessingbourne, c.1795 – D/627/56

Mountjoy (Stewart) estate, Newtownstewart (later Gardiner/Blessington estate)
List of tenants in the Mountjoy estate, Newtownstewart, 1734, published in the *Directory of Irish Family History Research*, 24 (2001), p. 84
Collection of c.30 counterpart leases, 1763–6 – NLI Collection List no. 67

Moutray estate, Favour Royal, Augher
Leases, 1714 onwards – D/2023/1
Rental and miscellaneous account books, 1757–63, 1795–1825 – D/2023/3/1/1, 3
Rent account books, 1762–5, 1771–3 – D/1716/16
Notebook listing Favour Royal leases, 1765–1862 – D/2023/1/13
Servants' account book, 1795–1859 – D/2023/4/2/1

Powerscourt estate, Benburb
Leases arranged in bundles alphabetically by town, 1700 onwards – D/1957/2
Index book of leases, 1740–1804 – D/1957/2/46
Letting of lands of Benburb extracted from the counterparts of the tenants' leases, 1739–56 – D/1957/2/48
Survey of the manor of Benburb, 1771 – MIC/280
Register of leases for Powerscourt estate (not just Tyrone) beginning in 1775 – NLI Ms 16,384
Book entitled 'Old leases on Benburb estate', c.1779–c.1801 – D/2634/1. Leases issued by Viscount Powerscourt. PRONI calendar lists townlands covered.

Richardson estate, Drum, Kildress
Rough Drum rental, 1791–2 – D/2002/C/6
Boxes of leases, starting 1636 – D/2002/L/1–2

Speer estate, Rahorran
Map and survey of Rahorran near Fivemiletown owned by John Speer, naming tenants, 1796 – D/847/20/C/1

Staples estate, Lissan
18th-century maps and surveys, calendared in full – D/1567/C *passim*
Envelope containing accounts with Thomas Caulfeild and a rental of the Castle Stewart and Lissan estates, 1767, 1776–8 – D/1567/D/1/1/1–3
Rental of part of W. J. Stephenson's estate in County Tyrone to be sold, 1772 – D/1567/D/1/2/1
Envelope containing rentals of Castle Stewart and Lissan estates, 1786–9 – D/1567/D/1/4/1–3

Stewart estate, Killymoon
Map of estate at Cookstown, 1736, naming tenants (very faint) – D/3/1
Survey of estate, 1767 – NLI Ms 9627
Rentals, 1786–88 – NLI Ms 766

'The survey and estaemation of the sixteen towns or Mannor of Clananise', n.d. but 18th-century – NLI Ms 8734/1

Map of the estate of James Stewart, 1798, naming tenants – D/647/32/1. Townlands of Sherrigrim, Tullaghmore, Ross, Lurgie.

Map of the estate of James Stewart, c.1798, naming tenants – D/647/32/2. Townlands of Allen, Murree, Little Muree, Gortavale, Crossdernot, Mulnagore, Drummond, Carlonen, Moynagh, Annaghquin, Drumballyhugh.

Map of Mulnagore, c.1800, naming tenants – D/647/32/4

Stewart estate, Omagh, Killyman

Valuation of estate of Alexander Stewart near Omagh and in Killyman parish, c.1747, naming tenants – D/3698/2

Survey of Hamilton Stewart's estate in Drumragh parish, 1776 – D/847/21/C/4. Covers the townlands of Creevan, Firreagh, Loughmuck and Gaumy. Names tenants, with an undated list of changes to tenancies at the end of the volume.

Rentals of the Omagh estate, 1788, 1797 – D/847/21/C/6

Stewart estate, Termonmaguirk

Tenants' land reference sheet, estate of Sir John Stewart, c.1800 – D/1021/2

Story estate, Corick

Servants and labourers' account book, 1790–1826; rent book of the Corick estate, 1791–1813 – MIC/42/1

Verner estate, Churchill

Leases etc. relating to lands in counties Armagh and Tyrone beginning in 1641 – D/2538/A *passim*

Large collection of calendared 18th-century leases for Counties Armagh, Monaghan and Tyrone – D/236 *passim*

Rental and valuation of Ballygawley, 1785 – D/236/539

Rental of Tyrone estate, 1788–92 – D/236/487A

APPENDIX 3

Records relating to individual parishes

Introduction

This appendix provides a parish-by-parish breakdown of genealogical sources for early modern Ulster. The main records available for each parish have been categorised under the following headings: *Estate papers, Church records, Census substitutes* and *Corporation records*. Not every parish has entries for all of these categories: a few have no genealogical material of interest at all from this period. After these categories miscellaneous sources of interest are listed individually, followed by any relevant local history publications.

Estate papers

If estate records are available for a particular parish, this is indicated by providing the name of the estate owner. For fuller information on the nature of the estate records available, the reader should refer to Appendix 2, where surviving records are set out in some detail. In some cases a landlord may have been the owner of the greater part of a particular parish. In other instances a landlord's estate in a parish might have extended to only one townland.

It must be pointed out that there is no guarantee that a given townland in a parish will definitely have relevant estate records from the seventeenth or eighteenth century. Researchers should also be aware that the estates frequently changed hands, meaning that some areas will have records available from the archives of more than one owner. For example, lands in the Downpatrick area of County Down were successively part of the Ardglass, Southwell and De Clifford estates, for each of which records are available in PRONI.

Church records

If there are extant church records for a particular parish prior to 1800, the name and denomination of the church concerned is indicated. For fuller information on the nature of the available records (baptisms, marriages, etc.) and the dates covered, the reader should refer to Appendix 1, where surviving church records are set out in full. The use of the word 'see' before the name of a Church of Ireland church indicates that it is not actually in the parish in question. For example, the Anglican inhabitants of the parish of Ballytrustan – where there was no Church of Ireland church – attended church in the neighbouring parish of Ballyphilip.

Census substitutes

For convenience, several categories of sources from the seventeenth and eighteenth centuries have been grouped together as 'census substitutes'. Each of these sources is discussed in more detail in Chapters 4 and 5. The abbreviations used for these 'census substitutes' are as follows.

AC – Agricultural census of 1803
CPH – 'Census of Protestant Householders', 1740
DE – Derry excommunicants, 1667
DP – Dissenters' petition, 1775
FL – Flaxgrowers' list of 1796
FP – Franciscan petition, 1670–71

HMR – Hearth money rolls, 1660s
HSM – Hearts of Steel memorial, 1771–2
PB – Poll book, *c.*1662
RelC – Religious census of 1766
VAA – 'View of the archbishopric of Armagh', 1703

Corporation records
If a parish contains a corporate town with surviving records, this is indicated. For more information, researchers should refer to Chapter 10.2.

Any miscellaneous sources for a parish will then be listed individually. Some publications of potential interest are also listed though this is far from complete and researchers should consult with local libraries for further information. The catalogue of the Linen Hall Library is available online at lh-prism.qub.ac.uk/TalisPrism/.

The parish network in Ulster has been subject to change over the last four centuries, with the result that a number of new parishes have been created. If a parish was formed during the period covered by this book, the year in which this occurred will be given as will the parish or parishes from which it was created. In these cases the researcher should refer to the original parish(es) for further information on source material. For example, Ballybay parish in County Monaghan was formed in 1798 from the parishes of Aughnamullen and Tullycorbet. In addition to the sources listed for Ballybay, researchers should also consult those sources listed under these latter parishes.

PARISHES IN ULSTER

Aghabog parish, County Monaghan
[Aghabog parish was created in 1767 out of Galloon parish.]
Estate papers: Barton estate; Dawson estate; Forster estate; Ker estate; Rossmore estate
Census substitutes: HMR, FL

Aghaderg parish, including the village of Loughbrickland, County Down
Estate papers: Downshire estate; Johnston estate; Meade estate; Whyte estate
Church records: Aghaderg CI; Glascar P
Census substitutes: CPH (Loughbrickland Walk), FL
G. N. Little, *Historical Highlights, Parish of Aghaderg* (Banbridge, 1989) includes inscriptions
    from Aghaderg Church of Ireland graveyard and a list of churchwardens from 1746

Aghadowey parish, County Londonderry
Estate papers: Derry (bishopric of) estate; Ironmongers' Company estate; Jackson estate;
    Mercers' Company estate; Merchant Taylors' Company estate
Church records: Aghadowey CI; Aghadowey P; Killaig P
Census substitutes: HMR, CPH, FL
Thomas H. Mullin, *Aghadowey* (Belfast, 1972) includes muster roll of the Ironmongers' Estate
    of 1630, hearth money roll of 1663, Pyke's survey of 1725, Alsop's survey of 1765,
    flaxgrowers' list of 1796

Aghagallon parish, County Antrim
Estate papers: Conway estate
Census substitutes: HMR

Aghalee parish, County Antrim
Estate papers: Conway estate
Census substitutes: HMR

Aghaloo parish, including the town of Caledon, County Tyrone
Estate papers: Armagh (archbishopric of) estate; Caledon estate
Census substitutes: PB, HMR, FP, VAA, RelC, FL
J. J. Marshall, *History of the Territory of Minterburn and Town of Caledon (formerly Munter Birn, and Kenard, Co. Tyrone)* (Dungannon, 1923)

Aghalurcher parish, including the towns of Lisnaskea and Maguiresbridge, Counties Fermanagh and Tyrone
Estate papers: Brooke estate; Clogher (bishopric of) estate; Erne estate; Montgomery estate
Church records: Aghalurcher CI
Census substitutes: HMR (incomplete), FL

Aghanloo parish, County Londonderry
Estate papers: Derry (bishopric of) estate; Haberdashers' Company estate; McClelland/Maxwell estate
Census substitutes: HMR, CPH, FL
Names of men from Aghanloo parish ordered to appear 'with their best arms' at Limavady, 1666 – T/640/103

Aghanunshin parish, County Donegal
Estate papers: Raphoe (bishopric of) estate
Church records: Aghanunshin CI
Census substitutes: HMR, FL

Aghavea parish, County Fermanagh
Estate papers: Brooke estate; Clogher (bishopric of) estate; Erne estate
Church records: Aghavea CI
Census substitutes: FL

Agivey parish, County Londonderry
Estate papers: Derry (bishopric of) estate; Ironmongers' Company estate
Census substitutes: HMR (under Aghadowey), FL

Ahoghill parish and village, County Antrim
[Ahoghill originally included the present parishes of Craigs and Portglenone.]
Estate papers: Davy estate; Hutchinson estate; O'Neill estate
Church records: Cullybackey P; Gracehill MOR
Census substitutes: HMR, CPH, HSM, FL

All Saints parish, including the village of Newtowncunningham, County Donegal
[This parish was formed out of Taughboyne, date not known.]
Estate papers: Forward estate
Church records: All Saints CI
Census substitutes: FL

Annaclone parish, County Down
Estate papers: Downshire estate; Meade estate; Waring of Ballynafern estate
Census substitutes: FL

Annagelliff parish, County Cavan
Estate papers: Annesley estate; Farmham estate; Lanesborough estate; Saunderson estate
Church records: see Urney CI
Census substitutes: HMR, FL

Annagh parish, County Cavan
Estate papers: Annesley estate; Lanesborough estate; Saunderson estate
Census substitutes: HMR, FL
Corporation records: Belturbet

Annahilt parish, County Down
Estate papers: Downshire estate
Church records: Annahilt CI
Census substitutes: HSM, FL

Antrim parish and town, County Antrim
Estate papers: Donegall estate; Massereene estate
Church records: Antrim CI, Antrim 1st P
Census substitutes: HMR, DP (Antrim Borough and Old Antrim)
Offer of a reward in relation to the burning of a house on the lands of Connor, County Antrim:
    42 names of the principal inhabitants of Antrim – *Belfast Newsletter*, 16 January 1756
List of subscribers from Antrim town offering reward: over 150 names – *Belfast Newsletter*, 27
    January 1761
Certificates of conformity, Antrim parish and town, 1776 – D/207/26
Memorial of the inhabitants of the borough of Antrim – *Belfast Newsletter*, 21–25 August 1778
Borough of Antrim petition in relation to Act of Union – *Belfast Newlstter*, 11 October 1799

Arboe parish, Counties Londonderry and Tyrone
Estate papers: Armagh (archbishopric of) estate; Castle Stewart estate; Drapers' Company estate
Church records: Arboe CI
Census substitutes: HMR, VAA, FL
Survey listing tenants in townlands in Arboe parish, n.d. [?early 18th century]; rental of same,
    n.d. [?late 18th century] – D/668/A/16

Ardclinis parish, County Antrim
Estate papers: Antrim estate
Census substitutes: HMR

Ardglass parish and village, County Down
Estate papers: Fitzgerald estate; Ward estate
Census substitutes: FL, AC

Ardkeen parish, County Down
Estate papers: Savage of Ardkeen estate; Montgomery estate
Church records: Ardkeen CI
Census substitutes: FL, AC
Two lists of inhabitants of the manor of Ardkeen, 1779 and 1783 in a small volume –
D/2223/15/10

Ardquin parish, County Down
Estate papers: Savage-Nugent estate
Church records: see Ballyphilip CI
Census substitutes: FL

Ardstraw parish, including the town of Newtownstewart, County Tyrone
Estate papers: Abercorn estate; Castle Stewart estate; Derry (bishopric of) estate; Huntingdon
estate; McCausland estate; Mountjoy estate
Census substitutes: HMR, DE, FL
John H. Gebbie, *Ardstraw (Newtownstewart): Historical Survey of a Parish, 1600–1900* (Omagh,
1968)
T. P. Donnelly, *A History of the Parish of Ardstraw West and Castlederg* (Strabane, n.d.)
The Parish of Ardstraw East: 1785–1985 (1985)

Armagh parish, including the city of Armagh, County Armagh
Estate papers: Armagh (archbishopric of) estate; Burges estate; Dawson estate; Lenox-
Conyngham estate [*see under* County Londonderry in Appendix 2]; Whaley estate
Church records: Armagh CI; Armagh 1st P; Armagh RC
Census substitutes: HMR, FP, DP, FL
Corporation records: Armagh
Householders in Armagh, 1770 – T/1228/1, T/808/14977

Armoy parish and village, County Antrim
Estate papers: Antrim estate; Macartney estate
Church records: Armoy CI
Census substitutes: HMR, CPH, FL, AC

Artrea parish, Counties Londonderry and Tyrone
Estate papers: Armagh (archbishopric of) estate; Drapers' Company estate; Lenox-Conyngham
estate; Lindesay estate; Salters' Company estate; Stewart of Killymoon estate
Church records: Artrea CI, Woods Chapel CI, Gracefield MOR
Census substitutes: HMR, CPH, RelC, FL
Rental of Ballymilligan [Ballymulligan], 1752 – D/3300/5/1

Aughnamullen parish, County Monaghan
Estate papers: Barton estate; Clogher (bishopric of) estate; Crofton estate; Dawson estate; Leslie of Ballybay estate; Massereene estate
Census substitutes: HMR, FL

Aughnish parish, County Donegal
Estate papers: Raphoe (bishopric of) estate; Stewart of Fortstewart estate
Church records: Aughnish CI
Census substitutes: HMR

Bailieborough parish, County Cavan
Census substitutes: FL

Ballee parish, County Down
Estate papers: De Clifford estate; Fitzgerald estate; Leslie estate; Southwell estate; Ward estate
Church records: Ballee CI; Ballee and Saul RC
Census substitutes: DP (Ballee NSP), FL, AC
View book of the great tithes of the deanery of Down, 1732 – D/1145/D/1

Ballinderry parish, County Antrim
Estate papers: Conway estate
Church records: Ballinderry CI; Ballinderry MOR
Census substitutes: HMR

Ballinderry parish, Counties Londonderry and Tyrone
Estate papers: Armagh (archbishopric of) estate; Drapers' Company estate
Church records: Ballinderry CI
Census substitutes: HMR, CPH, FL

Ballintemple parish, County Cavan
Estate papers: Coyne estate; Farnham estate; Saunderson estate
Census substitutes: FL

Ballintoy parish and village, County Antrim
[Ballintoy was created out of Billy parish in 1670]
Estate papers: Antrim estate; Stewart estate
Church records: Ballintoy CI
Census substitutes: HMR (included under Billy parish), CPH, RelC, FL, AC
George Hill, *The Stewarts of Ballintoy: with notices of other families of the district in the seventeenth century* (Coleraine, 1865, reprinted Ballycastle, 1976)

Ballyaghran parish, including the town of Portstewart, County Londonderry (also known as Agherton)
Estate papers: Bacon estate
Census substitutes: HMR, CPH, FL

Ballybay parish and village, County Monaghan
[Ballybay parish was formed in 1798 out of the parishes of Aughnamullen and Tullycorbet.]
Estate papers: Barton estate; Leslie of Ballybay estate; Massereene estate
Church records: Ballybay P

Ballyclog parish, County Tyrone
Estate papers: Armagh (archbishopric of) estate; Castle Stewart estate; Charlemont estate
Census substitutes: HMR, FL

Ballyclug parish, County Antrim
Estate papers: O'Hara estate
Census substitutes: HMR

Ballycor parish, County Antrim
Estate papers: Donegall estate
Census substitutes: HMR (included under Rashee parish), HSM, DP (Larne, Raloo, Carncastle, Kilwaughter, Glenarm and Ballyeaston)

Ballyculter parish, County Down
Estate papers: De Clifford estate; Fitzgerald estate; Southwell estate; Ward estate
Church records: Ballyculter CI
Census substitutes: FL, AC
View book of the great tithes of the deanery of Down, 1732 – D/1145/D/1
Oaths of the Ballyculter Supplementary Corps, c.1798, 63 names – T/1023/153

Ballyhalbert alias St Andrews parish, County Down
Estate papers: Clanbrassil estate; Blackwood estate
Church records: Inishargy CI (includes Ballyhalbert), Glastry P
Census substitutes: HSM, FL (listed as 'St Andrew')
Petition from inhabitants of Ballywalter and Ballyhalbert in response to the threat of danger from 'our most treacherous enemies the French', 78 names – *Belfast Newsletter*, 13 April 1756
Parish of St Andrews (Ballyhalbert) petition in relation to Act of Union – *Belfast Newsletter*, 31 January 1800

Ballykinler parish, County Down
Estate papers: Downshire estate

Ballylinny parish, County Antrim
Estate papers: Donegall estate
Census substitutes: HMR (included under Ballynure parish)
Subscribers to a reward fund, 1771 – *Belfast Newsletter*, 20 September 1771

Ballymachugh parish, County Cavan
Estate papers: Farnham estate
Census substitutes: FL

Ballymartin parish, County Antrim
Estate papers: Upton estate
Names of tenants in Ballypallady townland, 1784 – *Belfast Newsletter*, 3–6 February 1784

Ballymoney parish, including the town of Ballymena, County Antrim
Estate papers: Antrim estate; Legge estate; Magenis of Dromara estate [*see under* County Down in Appendix 2]; Rowan estate
Church records: Ballymoney P
Census substitutes: HMR, CPH, RelC, HSM, FL, AC
Map of the town of Ballymoney, naming householders, 1734 – T/935/1 (a scanned version of this map is available online at www.ballymoneyancestry.com)
Tithe-payers, 1780–95, giving names and townlands – T/1177/19/16–20 (duplicate at T/1177/17/32–5, but dates given as 1780–85)
Ballymoney applotment, 1795 – T/1177/19/35–8

Ballymore parish, including the town of Tanderagee, County Armagh
Estate papers: Armagh (archbishopric of) estate; De Salis estate; Hamilton estate; Manchester estate; St John estate
Church records: Acton CI; Ballymore CI; Tyrone's Ditches P
Census substitutes: HMR, FP, RelC, DP (Clare congregation), FL
Map of Tandragee naming tenants in town, 1750 – T/1224/1
Subscribers to a reward fund, 1777 – *Belfast Newsletter*, 16–20 May 1777
Landholders and inhabitants in and about Tandragee, County Armagh, petition about Act of Union – *Belfast Newsletter*, 11 February 1800

Ballymyre parish, County Armagh
[This parish was detached from Armagh *c.*1770.]

Ballynascreen parish, County Londonderry
Estate papers: Derry (bishopric of) estate; Drapers' Company estate; Skinners' Company estate
Census substitutes: HMR, CPH, RelC, FL

Ballynure parish, County Antrim
Estate papers: Donegall estate
Census substitutes: HMR, RelC, HSM, DP (plus an Established Church petition)

Ballyphilip parish, including the town of Portaferry, County Down
Estate records: Mount Ross estate; Savage-Nugent estate
Church records: Ballyphilip CI, Portaferry P
Census substitute: FL

Ballyrashane parish, Counties Antrim and Londonderry
Estate papers: Antrim estate; Legge estate
Census substitutes: HMR, CPH, FL, AC
T. H. Mullin, *Families of Ballyrashane* (1969)

Ballyscullion parish, including the village of Bellaghy, County Londonderry
Estate papers: Conolly estate; Derry (bishopric of) estate; Salters' Company estate; Strafford estate; Vintners' Company estate
Census substitutes: HMR, CPH, FL

Ballytrustan parish, County Down
Estate papers: Savage-Nugent estate
Church records: see Ballyphilip CI

Ballywalter parish and village, County Down
Estate papers: Clanbrassil estate; Blackwood estate
Church records: Inishargy CI (includes Ballywalter)
Petition from inhabitants of Ballywalter and Ballyhalbert in response to the threat of danger from 'our most treacherous enemies the French': 78 names – *Belfast Newsletter*, 13 April 1756

Ballywillin parish, including the town of Portrush, Counties Antrim and Londonderry
Estate papers: Antrim estate
Church records: Ballywillin CI
Census substitutes: HMR, CPH, FL, AC
Book of vicarial tithes for the parish of 'Ballywoolen' (Ballywillin), listing tithe-payers by townland, 1783 – D/668/B

Balteagh parish, County Londonderry
Estate papers: Derry (bishopric of) estate
Census substitutes: HMR, DE, CPH, FL
Exchequer Bill naming 12 tenants in the townland of Cloghan, 1727 – T/808/11353

Banagher parish, County Londonderry
Estate papers: Derry (bishopric of) estate; Fishmongers Company estate; Skinners' Company estate
Census substitutes: HMR, CPH, RelC, FL

Bangor parish and town, County Down
Estate papers: Blackwood estate; Clanbrassil estate; Moor estate; Perceval-Maxwell estate
Church records: Bangor CI
Census substitutes: FL
Memorial from inhabitants, 1771 – *Belfast Newsletter*, 25 January 1771
Subscribers to a reward fund – *Belfast Newsletter*, 29 May–2 June 1778
Parish of Bangor petition in relation to Act of Union – *Belfast Newsletter*, 31 January 1800

Barr of Inch or Mintiaghs parish, County Donegal, *see* **Mintiaghs or Barr of Inch**

Belleek parish, County Fermanagh
Estate papers: Caldwell estate
Census substitutes: FL

Billy, County Antrim
Estate papers: Antrim estate; Macartney estate; Wray estate
Census substitutes: HMR, CPH, FL, AC

Blaris parish, including the town of Lisburn, Counties Antrim and Down
Estate papers: Downshire estate; Conway estate; Wallace estate
Church records: Lisburn CI, Lisburn 1st P; Lisburn RSF
Census substitutes: HMR, HSM, DP, FL (one name)
List of tenants of Lisnegarvey (Lisburn), 1630 – T/808/14909
Map of Lisnegarvey (Lisburn) with details of tenements, 1632 – T/343
Collectors' accounts for Lisburn Walk, 1691, over 400 names arranged by place – T/808/14904
    (T/808/14902 is an alphabetical list of these names)
Rent roll of those receiving piped water in the town of Lisburn, 1768 – D/195/1
Subscribers to a reward fund, 1771 – *Belfast Newsletter*, 23 August 1771
Subscribers to a reward fund, 1777 – *Belfast Newsletter*, 1–5 August 1777
H. Bayley, *A Topographical and Historical Account of Lisburn* (Belfast, 1834)

Bodoney parish, County Tyrone
[This parish was divided into Upper and Lower sections in 1774.]
Estate papers: Belmore estate; Derry (bishopric of) estate; Hamilton of Manor Elieston estate
Census substitutes: HMR, DE, FL
Names of masters of families, 1699 – T/542
Miscellaneous 18th-century extracts from the Registry of Deeds – T/808/15112

Boho parish, County Fermanagh
Estate papers: Clogher (bishopric of) estate; Cooper estate; Erne estate
An account of the tithes in the parishes of Devenish and Boho, 1695 (long list of names) –
    printed in W. B. Steele, *The Parish of Devenish, County Fermanagh: Materials for Its History*
    (Enniskillen, 1937), pp. 78–80

Bovevagh parish, County Londonderry
Estate papers: Derry (bishopric of) estate
Church records: Bovevagh CI
Census substitutes: HMR, CPH, RelC, FL

Bright parish, County Down
Estate papers: De Clifford estate; Fitzgerald estate; Lascelles estate; Southwell estate; Ward estate
Church records: Bright CI
Census substitutes: FL, AC
View book of the great tithes of the deanery of Down, 1732 – D/1145/D/1

Burt parish, County Donegal
[This parish was created in 1809 out of Templemore.]
Estate papers: Donegall estate
Church records: Burt P

Camlin parish, including the village of Crumlin, County Antrim
Estate papers: Conway estate; Pakenham estate
Census substitutes: HMR (included under Glenavy parish)

Camus-juxta-Mourne parish, including the town of Strabane, County Tyrone
Estate papers: Abercorn estate; Derry (bishopric of) estate; Erne (Lady) estate
Church records: Clonleigh and Camus RC
Census substitutes: HMR, DP (Strabane), FL
Corporation records: Strabane
Names of inhabitants of the town of Strabane from the Registry of Deeds, 1708–38, published
    in the *Directory of Irish Family History Research* (2001), pp. 83–4
Names of *c.*40 inhabitants of Strabane in a letter by the earl of Abercorn, 1745 – D/623/A/12/5
Petition from inhabitants of Strabane to earl of Abercorn, 1768 (*c.*85 names) – D623/A/38/28
Memorial from the inhabitants of Strabane to the marquess of Abercorn, 1790 (*c.*50 names) –
    D/623/A/151/47

Cappagh parish, County Tyrone
Estate papers: Derry (bishopric of) estate; Huntingdon estate; Mervyn estate; Mountjoy estate
Church records: Cappagh CI
Census substitutes: HMR, DE, FL
Names of masters of families, 1699 – T/542

Carncastle parish, County Antrim
Estate papers: Agnew estate; Antrim estate
Census substitutes: HMR, DP (Larne, Raloo, Carncastle, Kilwaughter, Glenarm and
    Ballyeaston)

Carnmoney parish, County Antrim
Estate papers: Donegall estate; Mussenden estate
Church records: Carnmoney CI, Carnmoney P
Census substitutes: HMR, DP (plus Established Church petition)
Tithe book, Carnmoney parish, listing tithe-payers by parish, 1789 – D/852/1
Robert H. Bonar, *Nigh on three and a half centuries. A history of Carnmoney Presbyterian Church*
    (2004)

Carnteel parish, County Tyrone
Estate papers: Armagh (archbishopric of) estate; Stewart of Killymoon estate; Verner estate
Church records: Carnteel CI
Census substitutes: HMR, RelC
J. J. Marshall, *Annals of Aughnacloy and of the Parish of Carnteel, County Tyrone* (2nd edition,
    Dungannon, 1925)

Carrick parish, County Londonderry
[This parish was created as a perpetual curacy in 1846 out of portions of the parishes of
Balteagh, Bovevagh and Tamlaght Finlagan.]

Carrickfergus parish and town, County Antrim

Estate papers: Brytt estate; Donegall estate; Downshire estate; Kirk estate; Macartney estate; Saunders estate; Vesey estate

Church records: Carrickfergus CI

Census substitutes: HMR, DP

Corporation records: Carrickfergus

Leases etc. for Carrickfergus, starting from 1596 – T/686

List of burgesses and freemen, no date but pre-1706 – D/162/18. Over 250 names, with occupations

McSkimin, *The History and Antiquities of the County of the Town of Carrickfergus* (Belfast, 1811).

Castleboy parish, County Down (also known as St Johnstown)

Estate papers: Savage-Nugent estate

Church records: see Ballyphilip CI

Census substitutes: AC

Castlekeeran or Loughan parish, County Cavan

Estate papers: Plunkett estate

Castlerahan parish, County Cavan

Estate papers: Coyne estate; Farnham estate; Massereene estate

Church records: Castlerahan and Munterconnaught RC

Census substitutes: FL

Castletarra parish, County Cavan

Estate papers: Annesley estate; Lanesborough estate

Church records: Castletara RC

Census substitutes: FL

Cleenish parish, County Fermanagh

Estate papers: Clogher (bishopric of) estate; Enniskillen estate; Erne estate; Hassard estate; Huntingdon estate

Census substitutes: FL

Clogher parish and village, County Tyrone

Estate papers: Clogher (bishopric of) estate; Forbes estate; Gorges estate; Mervyn estate; Montgomery estate; Moutray estate; Speer estate; Story estate

Church records: Clogher CI

Census substitutes: HMR, FL

Corporation records: Clogher

'Clogher parish – some early sidesmen 1662-1734' by Jack Johnston in *Clogher Record* xiv (1991), pp. 89–91

J. J. Marshall, Clochar na Righ *(Clogher of the kings): being a history of the town of and district of Clogher, in the county of Tyrone. Also some account of the parish of Errigal Keeroge, in the county of Tyrone, and the parish of Errigal Truagh, in the county of Monaghan* (Dungannon, 1930)

Jack Johnston, *Glenhoy: The First 200 Years* (privately published, 1979) includes a chapter providing brief biographical notes on the families associated with Glenhoy and appendices including a rental of the Savile (Foljambe) estate from 1738 and leaseholders in the manor of Cecil in 1769

Clogherny parish, County Tyrone
[This parish was created in 1732 out of Termonmaguirk parish.]
Estate papers: Armagh (archbishopric of) estate; Belmore estate
Census substitutes: HMR, FL

Clonallan parish, including the village of Warrenpoint, County Down
Estate papers: Downshire estate; Dungannon estate; Hall estate; Meade estate
Census substitutes: FL

Clonca parish, County Donegal
Estate papers: Derry (bishopric of) estate; Donegall estate
Church records: Clonca CI
Census substitutes: HMR, CPH, FL

Clondahorky parish, County Donegal
Estate papers: Raphoe (bishopric of) estate; Stewart of the Ards estate
Census substitutes: HMR

Clondavaddog parish, County Donegal
Estate papers: Clements estate; Raphoe (bishopric of) estate; Stewart of Fortstewart estate
Church records: Clondevaddock CI
Census substitutes: HMR, FL

Clondermot parish, County Londonderry
Estate papers: Conolly estate; Derry (bishopric of) estate; Goldsmiths' Company estate; Grocers' Company estate; Ponsonby estate
Census substitutes: HMR, DE, CPH, FL
Names of those from the manor of Goldsmiths summoned to appear at a court leet, 1716, over 200 names – MIC/9B/12A

Clonduff parish, including the village of Hilltown, County Down
Estate papers: Annesley estate; Downshire estate; Meade estate
Church records: Clonduff CI
Census substitutes: FL, AC

Clones parish and town, Counties Fermanagh and Monaghan
Estate papers: Barrett Lennard estate; Clogher (bishopric of) estate; Dawson estate; Erne estate; Madden estate; Massereene estate
Church records: Clones CI, Clogh CI
Census substitutes: HMR (listed under 'Ballytraboy or Rosslea' as well as Clones), FL
Map of Clones with a list of tenants, 1768 – MIC/170/4

Resolution of principal inhabitants of Clones concerning danger of invasion and affirming their loyalty, 1796, *c.*170 names of those present at the meeting – MIC/170/5

Clonfeacle parish, including the villages of Benburb, Blackwatertown and Moy, Counties Armagh and Tyrone

Estate papers: Armagh (archbishopric of) estate; Caledon estate; Charlemont estate; Dawson estate; Ker estate; Knox estate; McGeough-Bond estate; Powerscourt estate; Stewart of Killymoon estate; Verner estate
Church records: Clonfeacle CI
Census substitutes: HMR, DP (Benburb), RelC, FL
Map of Moy, 1771, naming tenants – D/291/3

Clonleigh parish, including the town of Lifford, County Donegal

Estate papers: Derry (bishopric of) estate; Erne estate
Church records: Clonleigh CI; Clonleigh and Camus RC
Census substitutes: HMR, DE, FL (listed under 'Lifford')
Corporation records: Lifford
Petition of parishioners of Lifford [*sic*] to the bishop of Derry about the parish schoolmaster, 1664 (80 signatories) – D/683/163 (printed in T. W. Moody and J. G. Simms, *The Bishopric of Derry and the Irish Society of London, 1602–1705* (2 vols, Dublin, 1968–83), i, pp. 380–81)

Clonmany parish, County Donegal

Estate papers: Derry (bishopric of) estate; Donegall estate
Census substitutes: HMR, CPH, FL

Clonoe parish, County Tyrone

Estate papers: Armagh (archbishopric of) estate; Lowry estate
Church records: Clonoe CI
Census substitutes: HMR, FL

Clontibret parish, County Monaghan

Estate papers: Barton estate; Blayney estate; Clogher (bishopric of) estate
Church records: Clontibret CI
Census substitutes: HMR, FL

Coleraine parish and town, County Londonderry

Estate papers: Heyland estate; Irish Society estate
Church records: Coleraine CI; Coleraine 2nd P
Census substitutes: HMR, DP, FL
Corporation records: Coleraine
Collectors' [?] accounts for Coleraine, naming individuals and amounts paid, 1689–91 – T/456/1
Tithes for Coleraine parish, 1690–91 – D/2096/1/13
Map of the town lots of Coleraine, 1758, naming tenants – T/837/1
Some Coleraine residents, 1729, 1783, 1791 – D/4164/A/26

Resolution of inhabitants of Coleraine and Killowen, 1787 – *Belfast Newsletter*, 2–6 February 1787

Tithe book, Coleraine parish, including arrears, 1789–93 – D/668/B

Church cess list, the country part of Coleraine parish, listing names and acreages held, 1792 – D/668/A/16

Coleraine yeomanry, 1796 (116 names) – D/4164/A/12

Notes on the history and genealogy of the Coleraine area – D/4164/A/1–28

T. H. Mullin, *Coleraine in By-gone Centuries* (Belfast, 1976) includes a chapter on 17th–century Coleraine families

T. H. Mullin, *Coleraine in Georgian Times* (Belfast, 1977) has appendices providing brief biographical sketches of Coleraine families

Comber parish and town, County Down

Estate papers: Blackwood estate; Clanbrassil estate; Delacherois estate; Downshire estate; Dungannon estate; Londonderry estate

Church records: Comber CI

Census substitutes: HSM, DP, FL, AC

Connor parish, County Antrim

Estate papers: Massereene estate; O'Hara estate

Church records: Kellswater RP

Census substitutes: HMR

Subscribers to a reward fund (74 names of inhabitants of Kells and Connor) – *Belfast Newsletter*, 16 January 1756

Convoy parish and village, County Donegal

[Convoy was created in 1773 out of a portion of the parish of Raphoe.]

T. H. Mullin, *The Kirk and Lands of Convoy since the Scottish Settlement* (Belfast, 1960) includes names of elders, early vestry appointments (from the Raphoe vestry book), diocesan wills, prerogative wills, 'citizenship' (denization) grants, muster roll of 1631, hearth money roll of 1665 and freeholders in 1768.

Conwal parish, including the town of Letterkenny, County Donegal

Estate papers: Hart estate; Raphoe (bishopric of) estate

Census substitutes: HMR, FL

S. Fleming, *Letterkenny Past and Present* (Ballyshannon, n.d.)

Cranfield parish, County Antrim

Census substitutes: HMR

Creggan parish, County Armagh

Estate papers: Armagh (archbishopric of) estate; Ball estate; McGeough-Bond estate

Church records: Creggan CI; Upper Creggan RC

Census substitutes: HMR, FP, RelC, FL

Petition about Act of Union from Roman Catholic inhabitants of Lower Creggan, County Armagh – *Belfast Newsletter*, 17 January 1800

Crosserlough parish, County Cavan
Estate papers: Farnham estate
Census substitutes: FL

Culdaff parish, County Donegal
Estate papers: Derry (bishopric of) estate; Donegall estate
Church records: Culdaff CI
Census substitutes: HMR, CPH, FL
Cess applotments, 1778, 1782 (published in Amy Young, *Three Hundred Years in Innishowen* (Belfast, 1929) pp. 159–60), *c.*1792, 1800, 1802 – D/3045/7/1/3
Names of parishioners, arranged by families with ages of children given, *c.*1802 – D/3045/7/1/3

Culfeightrin parish, County Antrim
Estate papers: Antrim estate; Boyd estate; Caledon estate; McGildowney estate
Census substitutes: HMR, CPH, FL, AC

Cumber (now Upper and Lower), County Londonderry
Estate papers: Conolly estate; Derry (bishopric of) estate; Fishmongers' Company estate; Goldsmiths' Company estate; Grocers' Company estate; Skinners' Company estate
Census substitutes: HMR, DE, RelC, FL
John Rutherford, *Cumber Presbyterian Church and Parish* (Londonderry, 1939): marriages and baptisms for Cumber parish extracted from the 17th-century registers of St Columb's cathedral in Derry; subsidy roll, 1662; hearth money roll, 1663; Protestant householders, 1740; freeholders' registers, 1761–81, 1791, 1796; flax seed premiums awarded in 1781; Cumber Yeomanry Cavalry, 1797; Cumber wills, 1720–1857; students from Cumber educated at Trinity College, Dublin, Glasgow University and elsewhere

Currin parish, Counties Fermanagh and Monaghan
[This parish was created in 1795 out of Galloon.]
Estates: Dawson estate; Madden estate
Census substitutes: HMR, FL
'Some transactions in Currin parish in the first quarter of the eighteenth century' by P. O Mordha in *Clogher Record* xvi (1997), pp. 162–5 [extracts from the Registry of Deeds]

Denn parish, County Cavan
Estate papers: Annesley estate; Farnham estate; Saunderson estate
Census substitutes: FL

Derryaghy parish, County Antrim
Estate papers: Conway estate
Church records: Derriaghy CI
Census substitutes: HMR
W. N. C. Barr, *Derriaghy: A Short History of the Parish* (Derriaghy, 1974)

Derrybrusk parish, County Fermanagh

Estate papers: Belmore estate; Clogher (bishopric of) estate

Census substitutes: FL

'Cash rec'd by Mr Armar from ye parishioners', 1747–52, covers parishes of Derrybrusk and Enniskillen, gives names and in many cases residences – D/627/14. Volume broken into several sections, with an index of names for one section at the front.

Tithe received by Mr Armar out of Derrybrusk and Enniskillen parishes, *c.*1750; over 140 names, but no residences – D/627/15

Derrykeighan parish, County Antrim

Estate papers: Antrim estate; Legge estate; Macartney estate; Montgomery estate; Moore estate; Rowan estate

Census substitutes: HMR, CPH, FL, AC

Names of parishioners indicating their religion, 1734 – T/808/14905

Thomas Camac, *History of the parish of Derrykeighan for three centuries* (Coleraine, 1908)

Derryloran parish, including the town of Cookstown, Counties Londonderry and Tyrone

Estate papers: Armagh (archbishopric of) estate; Castle Stewart estate; Drapers' Company estate; Lindesay estate; Staples estate; Stewart of Killymoon estate

Church records: Derryloran CI

Census substitutes: HMR, RelC, DP (Cookstown), FL

Miscellaneous extracts from the Registry of Deeds for the Cookstown area – T/808/15103

Derrynoose parish, County Armagh

Estate papers: Armagh (archbishopric of) estate; Irwin estate; Maxwell estate

Church records: Derrynoose CI

Census substitutes: HMR, FP, VAA, CPH, FL

Subscribers to a reward fund, 1784 – *Belfast Newsletter*, 6–9 April 1784

Tithe account, 1785–7, naming tithe-payers by townland – T/636/1, pp. 235–40

Subscribers to a reward fund, 1795 – www.ancestryireland.com

Derryvullan parish, County Fermanagh

Estate papers: Archdale estate; Belmore estate; Clogher (bishopric of) estate; Cooper estate; Enniskillen estate

Church records: Derryvullan CI.

Census substitutes: RelC, FL

Desertcreat parish, County Tyrone

Estate papers: Armagh (archbishopric of) estate; estate; Lindesay estate; Lowry of Pomeroy estate; Moore estate; Stewart of Killymoon estate

Church records: Desertcreat CI

Census substitutes: HMR, FL

Desertegny parish, County Donegal

Estate papers: Derry (bishopric of) estate; Donegall estate

Census substitutes: HMR, CPH, FL

Desertlynn parish, County Londonderry, including the town of Moneymore
Estate papers: Armagh (archbishopric of) estate; Drapers' Company estate; Salters' Company estate
Church records: Desertlynn CI
Census substitutes: HMR, RelC, FL
Names of Moneymore linen drapers, 1796 – www.ancestryireland.com

Desertmartin parish, County Londonderry
Estate papers: Conolly estate; Derry (bishopric of) estate; Drapers' Company estate; Salters' Company estate; Strafford estate; Vintners' Company estate
Church records: Desertmartin CI
Census substitutes: HMR, CPH, FL
Map of Dromore and part of Killymuck, glebe-lands, 1802, with details of tenements – D/360/1

Desertoghill parish, County Londonderry
Estate papers: Derry (bishopric of) estate; Ironmongers' Company estate; Mercers' Company estate
Census substitutes: HMR, CPH, FL

Devenish parish, County Fermanagh
Estate papers: Archdale estate; Clogher (bishopric of) estate; Ely estate; Huntingdon estate; Montgomery estate; O'Brien estate
Church records: Devenish CI
Census substitutes: HMR, RelC, FL
An account of the tithes in the parishes of Devenish and Boho, 1695 (long list of names) – printed in W. B. Steele, *The Parish of Devenish, County Fermanagh: Materials for Its History* (Enniskillen, 1937), pp. 78–80

Donacavey parish, including the town of Fintona, County Fermanagh
Estate papers: Belmore estate; Clogher (bishopric of) estate; Eccles estate; Mervyn estate
Church records: Donacavey CI
Census substitutes: HMR, FL
P. O Gallachair, *Old Fintona* (Monaghan 1974)

Donagh parish, County Donegal
Estate papers: Derry (bishopric of) estate; Donegall estate; Ferguson estate
Church records: Donagh CI
Census substitutes: CPH, FL

Donagh parish, including the village of Glaslough, County Monaghan
Estate papers: Anketell estate; Clogher (bishopric of) estate; Dawson estate; Hutcheson estate; Leslie of Glaslough estate; Rossmore estate; Singleton estate
Church records: Donagh CI
Census substitutes: HMR, FL

Donaghadee parish and town, County Down
Estate papers: Delacherois estate
Church records: Donaghadee CI; Donaghadee 1st P; Ballycopeland P; Millisle P
Census substitutes: AC
Plan of lands near Donaghadee, 1728 – T/2845/11
Subscribers to a reward fund, 1782 – *Belfast Newsletter*, 24–27 December 1782
Notes on occupants, Donaghadee area, *c.*1800 – T/2845/13
Peter Carr, *Portavo: an Irish townland and its people* (Dundonald, 2003)

Donaghcloney parish, including the village of Waringstown, County Down
Estate papers: Clanwilliam estate; Downshire estate; Waring estate
Church records: Donaghcloney CI; Donacloney P
Census substitutes: DP (Seapatrick, Tullylish and Donochclony)
Subscribers to a reward fund, 1779 – *Belfast Newsletter*, 12–15 January 1779
E. D. Atkinson, *An Ulster Parish: Being a History of Donaghcloney (Waringstown)* (Dublin, 1898)

Donaghedy parish, including the village of Dunnamanagh, County Tyrone
Estate papers: Abercorn estate; Belmore estate; Derry (bishopric of) estate; Hamilton of Manor Elieston estate
Church records: Donagheady CI
Census substitutes: PB, HMR, DE, FL
E. T. Dundas, *The History of Donagheady Parish* (privately published, 1979)
William J. Roulston, *The Parishes of Leckpatrick and Dunnalong: Their Place in History* (privately published, 2000)
John Rutherford, *Donagheady Presbyterian Churches and Parish* (Belfast, 1953)

Donaghenry parish, including the town of Stewartstown, County Tyrone
Estate papers: Armagh (archbishopric of) estate; Castle Stewart estate; Charlemont estate; Lindesay estate; Stewart of Killymoon estate
Church records: Donaghenry CI
Census substitutes: HMR, RelC, FL

Donaghmore parish, County Donegal
Estate papers: Conolly estate; Derry (bishopric of) estate; Gage estate; Hamilton estate; McCausland estate; Mansfield estate
Census substitutes: HMR, DE, RelC, FL

Donaghmore parish, County Down
Estate papers: Armagh (archbishopric of) estate; Innis estate; Meade estate
Church records: Donaghmore CI
Census substitutes: FL, AC
J. Davison Cowan, *An Ancient Irish Parish Past and Present Being the Parish of Donaghmore, County Down* (London, 1914)

Donaghmore parish, including the village of Castlecaulfeild, County Tyrone
Estate papers: Armagh (archbishopric of) estate; Burges estate; Charlemont estate; Knox estate; Verner estate
Church records: Donaghmore CI; Carland P
Census substitutes: HMR, VAA, FL
Eamon O Doibhlin, *Domnach Mor (Donaghamore). An Outline of Parish History* (1969), including hearth money roll of 1666 (pp. 160–63)

Donaghmoyne parish, County Monaghan
Estate papers: Bath estate; Clogher (bishopric of) estate; Shirley estate
Census substitutes: HMR, FL

Donegal parish, County Donegal
[This parish was created in 1722 out of Drumholm.]
Estate papers: Conolly estate; Trinity College, Dublin estate
Census substitutes: FL

Donegore parish, County Antrim
Estate papers: Donegall estate
Census substitutes: HMR, DP (Donegore, Kilbride and Nilteen)

Down parish, including the town of Downpatrick, County Down
Estate papers: Ardglass estate; De Clifford estate; Forde estate; Leslie estate; Maxwell estate; Southwell estate; Ward estate
Church records: Down CI, Downpatrick NSP
Census substitutes: FL
Obituaries, Downpatrick area, 1693–1853 – T/684/3–8
A survey of the town carried out in 1708 – D/1759/2A/8. This consists of a list of each of the named premises, giving its size, principal tenant and the half-yearly rent due.
Marriages, Downpatrick area, 1727–1853 – T/684/2, 9
View book of the great tithes of the deanery of Down, 1732 – D/1145/D/1
Subscribers to a reward fund, 1782 – *Belfast Newsletter*, 6–10 December 1782
E. Parkinson, *The City of Downe from Its Earliest Days*, edited by R. E. Parkinson (Belfast and London, 1928) (contains a printed copy of the 1708 survey)
A. Pilson, *Memoirs of Downpatrick and Its Parish Church* (Downpatrick, 1852)
L. A. Pooler, *Down and Its Parish Church* (Downpatrick, 1907)

Dromara parish and village, County Down
Estate papers: Downshire estate; Dungannon estate; Forde estate; Johnston estate; Magenis of Dromara estate; Mathews estate
Church records: Dromara 1st P
Census substitutes: DP, FL, AC

Dromore parish and town, County Down
Estate papers: Clanwilliam estate; Magenis of Dromara estate; Mathews estate
Church records: Dromore CI
Census substitutes: HSM, DP, FL
Map and survey of the town of Dromore, 1790, providing details of tenants – T/2372/1A–C

Dromore parish and village, County Tyrone
Estate papers: Belmore estate; Cooper estate [see under County Fermanagh in Appendix 2]; Huntingdon estate; Mervyn estate
Church records: Dromore CI
Census substitutes: HMR, FL
Names of male Protestants aged 17 and over, 1785 – T/808/15259

Drumachose parish, including the town of Limavady, County Londonderry
Estate papers: Conolly estate; Derry (bishopric of) estate; Phillips estate
Church records: Drumachose CI
Census substitutes: HMR, DE, CPH, RelC, FL
Corporation records: Limavady
Petition of the inhabitants of Limavady, 1796 – *Londonderry Journal*, 18–25 October 1796

Drumballyroney parish, County Down
Estate papers: Annesley estate; Downshire estate; Meade estate
Census substitutes: DP (Drumballyroney and Drumgoolan), FL, AC

Drumbeg parish, Counties Antrim and Down
Church records: Dunmurry NSP
Census substitutes: HMR (portion in County Antrim only, included under heading 'Dunmurry Liberty'), DP (Dunmurry), AC

Drumbo parish, County Down
Estate papers: Downshire estate; Dungannon estate
Church records: Drumbo CI; Drumbo P
Census substitutes: AC

Drumcree parish, including the town of Portadown, County Armagh
Estate papers: Armagh (archbishopric of) estate; Brownlow estate; Burges estate; Jenny estate; Obins estate
Church records: Drumcree CI
Census substitutes: HMR, RelC, FL
Tithe-payers, 1737 – D/2395/9 (another copy at T/808/15298)

Drumgath parish, including the town of Rathfriland, County Down
Estate papers: Annesley estate; Downshire estate; Meade estate
Church records: Rathfriland 1st P
Census substitutes: DP (Rathfriland), FL, AC

Drumglass parish, including the town of Dungannon, County Tyrone
Estate papers: Armagh (archbishopric of) estate; Knox estate
Church records: Drumglass CI; Dungannon 1st P
Census substitutes: HMR, RelC, DP (Dungannon town and neighbourhood + Dungannon barony), FL
Corporation records: Dungannon

Drumgooland parish, County Down
Estate papers: Annesley estate; Meade estate
Church records: Drumgooland CI
Census substitutes: DP (Drumgooland + Drumballyroney and Drumgoolan), FL, AC

Drumgoon parish, County Cavan
Estate papers: Coote estate
Church records: Cootehill RSF
Census substitutes: FL

Drumhome parish, County Donegal
Estate papers: Conolly estate; Hamilton of Brownhall estate; Raphoe (bishopric of) estate;
    Trinity College, Dublin estate
Church records: Drumhome CI
Census substitutes: HMR, FL

Drumkeeran parish, County Fermanagh
[This parish was created out of Magheraculmoney in 1774.]
Estate papers: Archdale estate; Barton estate; Lenox estate
Church records: Drumkeeran CI
Census substitutes: FL

Drumlane parish, County Cavan
Estate papers: Annesley estate; Farnham estate; Lanesborough estate
Census substitutes: FL

Drumlumman parish, County Cavan
Estate papers: Annesley estate; Coyne estate; Farnham estate
Census substitutes: FL

Drummaul parish, including the town of Randalstown, County Antrim
Estate papers: O'Neill estate
Census substitutes: HMR, CPH
Subscribers to a reward fund, 1772 – *Belfast Newsletter*, 7 April 1772

Drummully parish, Counties Fermanagh and Monaghan
See the note under Galloon parish for more information.
Estate papers: Clogher (bishopric of) estate; Dawson estate
Census substitutes: FL

Drumragh parish, including the town of Omagh, County Tyrone
Estate papers: Derry (bishopric of) estate; Huntingdon estate; Mervyn estate; Stewart estate
Church records: Drumragh CI
Census substitutes: HMR, FL
Masters of families, 1699 – T/542
Publication of a loyal resolution by the Roman Catholics of Omagh and its vicinity, dated 14
    June 1798, indicating their willingness to join the Volunteers or Supplementary Yeomanry,

*c.*60 names, printed in Brendan McEvoy, *The United Irishmen in County Tyrone* (Armagh, 1998), p. 90

Drumsnat parish, County Monaghan
Estate papers: Blayney estate; Clogher (bishopric of) estate; Evatt estate
Census substitutes: HMR, FL

Drung parish, County Cavan
Estate papers: Annesley estate
Church records: Drung CI
Census substitutes: FL

Dunaghy parish, County Antrim
Estate papers: Antrim estate; Moore estate; O'Hara estate; Rowan estate
Church records: Dunaghy CI
Census substitutes: HMR, CPH, HSM, FL

Dunboe parish, including the village of Articlave, County Londonderry
Estate papers: Bruce estate; Clothworkers' Company estate; Derry (bishopric of) estate; Jackson estate; McClelland/Maxwell estate; Merchant Taylors' Company estate
Church records: Dunboe CI
Census substitutes: CPH, FL

Dundonald parish and town, County Down
Estate papers: Clanbrassil estate; Londonderry estate; Ross of Portavoe estate
Church records: Dundonald P
Census substitutes: DP, FL
Peter Carr, *'The most unpretending of places': a history of Dundonald, County Down* (Belfast, 1988)

Duneane parish, County Antrim
Estate papers: O'Neill estate
Census substitutes: HMR, CPH

Dungiven parish and town, County Londonderry
Estate papers: Derry (bishopric of) estate; Skinners' Company estate
Church records: Dungiven CI
Census substitutes: HMR, DE, CPH, RelC, FL

Dunluce parish, including the town of Bushmills, County Antrim
Estate papers: Antrim estate; Montgomery estate
Church records: Dunluce CI
Census substitutes: HMR, CPH, FL, AC

Dunsfort parish, County Down
Estate papers: Fitzgerald estate; Hall of Ballyhornan estate; Ward estate
Census substitutes: FL, AC

Eglish parish, County Armagh
[This parish was created out of Armagh parish in 1720.]
Estate papers: Armagh (archbishopric of) estate; Charlemont estate; Houston estate; Johnston estate; Ker estate; McGeough-Bond estate; Whaley estate

Ematris parish, County Monaghan
[This parish was created c.1730 out of the parish of Galloon.]
Estate papers: Clogher (bishopric of) estate; Dawson estate; Moore estate
Church records: Ematris CI
Census substitutes: HMR, FL

Enniskeen parish, County Cavan
Estate papers: Pratt estate
Census substitutes: FL
List of Protestant inhabitants, 1802 – *The Irish Ancestor* (1973)

Enniskillen parish and town, County Fermanagh
Estate papers: Belmore estate; Clogher (bishopric of) estate; Cooper estate; Enniskillen estate; Erne estate; Lendrum estate; Montgomery estate; Tennant estate
Church records: Enniskillen CI
Census substitutes: HMR, FL (also listed under 'Tempo')
'Account of the losses of the inhabitants of Enniskillen delivered to me [Sir Michael Cole] by the Provost, July 1705' – D/1702/12/1 (printed in W. C. Trimble, *The History of Enniskillen* (3 vols, Enniskillen, 1919–21), iii, pp. 747–8). This comprises a long list of names and losses following the devastating fire in Enniskillen in 1705.
'Cash rec'd by Mr Armar from ye parishioners', 1747–52, covers parishes of Derrybrusk and Enniskillen, gives names and in many cases residences – D/627/14. Volume broken into several sections, with an index of names for one section at the front.
Tithe received by Mr Armar out of Derrybrusk and Enniskillen parishes, c.1750; over 140 names, but no residences – D/627/15
Map of Enniskillen, 1772; names tenements, not tenants – D/53/1
W. H. Bradshaw, *Enniskillen Long Ago* (Dublin, 1878)
W. H. Dundas, *Enniskillen, parish and town* (Dundalk and Enniskillen, 1913)
W. C. Trimble, *The History of Enniskillen* (3 vols, Enniskillen, 1919–21)

Errigal parish, including the town of Garvagh, County Londonderry
Estate papers: Derry (bishopric of) estate; Ironmongers' Company estate; Merchant Taylors' Company estate
Church records: Garvagh 1st P
Census substitutes: HMR, CPH, FL

Errigal Keerogue parish, County Tyrone
Estate papers: Armagh (archbishopric of) estate; Gorges estate; Verner estate
Church records: Errigal Keerogue CI
Census substitutes: HMR, FP, RelC, FL

J. J. Marshall, *Clochar na Righ (Clogher of the kings): being a history of the town of and district of Clogher, in the county of Tyrone. Also some account of the parish of Errigal Keeroge, in the county of Tyrone, and the parish of Errigal Truagh, in the county of Monaghan* (Dungannon, 1930)

Errigal Trough parish, Counties Monaghan and Tyrone
Estate papers: Anketell estate; Barton estate; Clogher (bishopric of) estate; Crofton estate; Dawson estate; Kane estate; Leslie of Glaslough estate; Massereene estate; Mervyn estate; Moutray estate; Singleton estate; Verner estate
Church records: Errigal Trough CI
Census substitutes: HMR, FL
Names of male Protestants aged 17 and over, 1785 – T/808/15259
J. J. Marshall, *Clochar na Righ (Clogher of the kings): being a history of the town of and district of Clogher, in the county of Tyrone. Also some account of the parish of Errigal Keeroge, in the county of Tyrone, and the parish of Errigal Truagh, in the county of Monaghan* (Dungannon, 1930)

Fahan Upper and Lower parishes, County Donegal
Estate papers: Derry (bishopric of) estate
Church records: Fahan CI
Census substitutes: HMR, CPH, FL

Faughanvale parish, including the village of Eglinton, County Londonderry
Estate papers: Derry (bishopric of) estate; Fishmongers' Company estate; Grocers' Company
Church records: Faughanvale CI
Census substitutes: HMR, DE, CPH, FL

Finvoy parish, County Antrim
Estate papers: Magenis of Dromara estate [see under County Down in Appendix 2]; Rowan estate; Stewart of Finvoy estate
Church records: Finvoy CI
Census substitutes: HMR, CPH, FL

Forkill parish, County Armagh
[This parish was created in 1771 out of Loughgilly, with an addition made to it in 1773 from Killevy.]
Estate papers: Armagh (archbishopric of) estate; Jackson estate

Galloon parish, County Fermanagh
The present bounds of the parish of Galloon were determined in the early 19th century. Prior to this the parish of Galloon was almost entirely within County Monaghan (now the parishes of Aghabog, Currin, Ematris and Killeevan) and the area now covered by Galloon corresponded roughly to the parish of Drummully. For this reason research in Galloon is not without its difficulties. Researchers should also consult the records for the following parishes: Aghabog, Currin, Drummully, Ematris and Killeevan.
Estate papers: Clogher (bishopric of) estate; Erne estate; Lanesborough estate; Madden estate
Church records: Galloon CI (Newtownbutler)

Gartan parish, County Donegal
Estate papers: Raphoe (bishopric of) estate
Census substitutes: HMR, FL

Garvaghy parish, County Down
Estate papers: Waring of Garvaghy estate
Census substitutes: FL, AC

Glenavy parish, County Antrim
Estate papers: Conway estate
Church records: Glenavy CI
Census substitutes: HMR

Glencolumbkille parish, County Donegal
Estate papers: Murray of Broughton estate; Raphoe (bishopric of) estate
Census substitutes: HMR

Glenwhirry parish, County Antrim
Estate papers: Mountcashell estate
Census substitutes: HMR (included under Racavan)

Glynn parish, County Antrim
Estate papers: Donegall estate
Census substitutes: HMR (included under heading 'Parish of Magheramorne')

Grange parish, County Armagh
[This parish was created out of Armagh parish in 1776.]
Estate papers: Armagh (archbishopric of) estate; Charlemont estate; Ker estate; McGeough-
    Bond estate
Church records: Grange CI

Grange of Ballyrobert, County Antrim
Estate papers: Donegall estate

Grange of Ballyscullion, County Antrim
Estate papers: Massereene estate
Church records: Antrim or Grange RSF
Census substitutes: HMR

Grange of Ballywalter, County Antrim
Estate papers: Donegall estate

Grange of Doagh, including the town of Ballyclare, County Antrim
Estate papers: Agnew estate; Donegall estate
Census substitutes: HMR (included under Rashee parish), DP (Ballyclare)

Grange of Drumtullagh, County Antrim
Estate papers: Antrim estate
Census substitutes: HMR (included under Armoy parish)

Grange of Dundermot, County Antrim
Estate papers: Antrim estate
Census substitutes: HMR (included under Dunaghy parish)

Grange of Inispollan, County Antrim
Estate papers: Antrim estate
Census substitutes: HMR (included under Layd parish)

Grange of Killyglen, County Antrim
Census substitutes: HMR (included under Carncastle)

Grange of Layd, County Antrim
Estate papers: Antrim estate; Edwards estate
Census substitutes: HMR (included under Layd parish)

Grange of Mallusk, County Antrim
Estate papers: Donegall estate; Pakenham estate

Grange of Muckamore, County Antrim
Estate papers: Massereene estate
Census substitutes: HMR

Grange of Nilteen, County Antrim
Estate papers: Donegall estate
Census substitutes: HMR (included under Donegore parish), DP (Donegore, Kilbride and Nilteen)

Grange of Shilvodan, County Antrim
Estate papers: O'Neill estate
Census substitutes: HMR

Greyabbey parish, County Down
Estate papers: Londonderry estate; Montgomery estate
Church records: Greyabbey CI

Hillsborough parish, County Down
Estate papers: Downshire estate
Church records: Hillsborough CI, Annahilt P
Census substitutes: FL
Corporation records: Hillsborough
Subscribers to a reward fund, 1770 – *Belfast Newsletter*, 24 April 1770
J. Barry, *Hillsborough: A Parish in the Ulster Plantation* (Belfast, 1962)

Holywood parish, County Down
Estate papers: Clanbrassil estate; Ross of Portavoe estate; Ward estate
Census substitutes: FL

Inch parish, County Donegal
[This parish was created in 1809 out of Templemore.]
Estate papers: Donegall estate
Census substitutes: RelC, FL

Inch parish, County Down
Estate papers: Ardglass estate; De Clifford estate; Perceval Maxwell estate; Southwell estate
Church records: Inch CI
Census substitutes: FL
Receipts for guns and bayonets to be used in Robert Maxwell's troop of militia, 1746 –
    D/1556/16/15/1–14
Men in the parish of Inch who have subscribed towards finding substitutes for the militia, 1793,
    c.150 names – T/1023/139
Return of 23 inhabitants of the parish, 1793 – T/1023/140
Signatures in relation to the formation of a yeomanry corps in the parish, 1797, around 200
    names – T/1023/144–5
List of names by townland in Inch parish, c.1798, over 190 names – T/1023/162
Names of those proposing to form a cavalry unit to act with the Inch infantry and to be known
    as Inch Legion, c.1798, 18 names – T/1023/163
Names of men who have sworn that they are not United Irishmen, c.1798 – T/1023/164
M. Donnelly, *Inch Abbey and Parish* (Privately published, 1979)

Inishargy parish, County Down
Estate papers: Clanbrassil estate
Church records: Inishargy CI, Kircubbin P

Inishkeel parish, County Donegal
Estate papers: Murray of Broughton estate; Raphoe (bishopric of) estate
Church records: Inishkeel CI
Census substitutes: HMR

Inishkeen parish, Counties Louth and Monaghan
Estate papers: Bath estate; Clogher (bishopric of) estate
Census substitutes: HMR, FL

Inishmacsaint parish, Counties Donegal and Fermanagh
Estate papers: Archdale estate; Clogher (bishopric of) estate; Conolly estate; Ely estate;
    Montgomery estate
Church records: Inishmacsaint CI
Census substitutes: HMR (Donegal portion only), FL (Fermanagh portion listed under
    'Churchill')

Inver parish, County Antrim
Estate papers: Donegall estate
Church records: Inver CI
Census substitutes: HMR (included under heading 'Parish of Magheramorne'), HSM

Inver parish, County Donegal
Estate papers: Murray of Broughton estate; Raphoe (bishopric of) estate
Church records: Inver CI
Census substitutes: HMR, FL

Island Magee parish, County Antrim
Estate papers: Donegall estate; Dungannon estate
Census substitutes: HMR, HSM
List of lands and tenants of Lord Dungannon on Island Magee – *Belfast Newsletter*, 13 February 1770
Dixon Donaldson, *Historical, traditional, and descriptive account of Islandmagee* (1927)

Jonesborough parish, County Armagh
[This parish was created in 1760 out of Killevy]
Church records: Jonesborough CI
Petition of Protestant inhabitants, *c.*1785 – DIO/4/32/J/1/4/1

Keady parish and village, County Armagh
[This parish was created out of Derrynoose parish in 1773.]
Estate papers: Armagh (archbishopric of) estate; Charlemont estate; Irwin estate
Church records: Keady CI
Census substitutes: FL
F. X. McCorry, *Parish Registers: Historical Treasures in Manuscript* (Lurgan, 2004) (includes information from the Keady CI registers)

Kilbarron parish, including the town of Ballyshannon, County Donegal
Estate papers: Conolly estate; Folliott estate; Raphoe (bishopric of) estate; Trinity College, Dublin estate
Church records: Kilbarron CI
Census substitutes: HMR, FL
Hugh Allingham, *Ballyshannon: Its History and Antiquities* (Londonderry, 1937)

Kilbride parish, County Antrim
Estate papers: Agnew estate; Donegall estate
Census substitutes: HMR (included under Donegore parish), DP (Donegore, Kilbride and Nilteen)

Kilbride parish, County Cavan
Estate papers: Coyne estate; Farnham estate
Census substitutes: FL

Kilbroney parish, including the village of Rostrevor, County Down
Estate papers: Hall estate; Kilmorey estate; Ross of Rostrevor estate
Church records: Kilbroney CI
Census substitutes: CPH, RelC, FL
W. H. Crowe, *Village in Seven Hills, the Story and Stories of Rostrevor, Co. Down* (Dundalk, 1972)

Kilcar parish, County Donegal
Estate papers: Murray of Broughton estate; Raphoe (bishopric of) estate
Census substitutes: HMR, FL

Kilclief parish, County Down
Estate papers: Leslie estate; Ward estate
Census substitutes: FL, AC

Kilclooney parish, County Armagh
Estate papers: Armagh (archbishopric of) estate; Charlemont parish; Gosford estate; McGeough-Bond estate
Census substitutes: HMR, FP, VAA

Kilcoo parish, County Down
Estate papers: Annesley estate; Downshire estate; Mathews estate
Church records: Kilcoo CI
Census substitutes: FL, AC

Kilcronaghan parish, including the village of Tobermore, County Londonderry
Estate papers: Derry (bishopric of) estate; Drapers' Company estate; Rowley estate; Salters' Company estate; Vintners' Company estate
Church records: Kilcronaghan CI
Census substitutes: HMR, CPH, FL

Kildallan parish, County Cavan
Estate papers: Annesley estate; Craige estate; Farnham estate; Stanford estate
Church records: Killeshandra CI
Census substitutes: HMR, FL

Kildollagh parish, County Londonderry
Church records: see Coleraine CI
Census substitutes: HMR (listed with Ballyrashane)

Kildress parish, County Tyrone
Estate papers: Armagh (archbishopric of) estate; Castle Stewart estate; Richardson estate; Stewart of Killymoon estate
Church records: Kildress CI
Census substitutes: HMR, VAA, CPH, RelC, FL

Kildrumsherdan parish, County Cavan
Estate papers: Clements estate; Coote estate
Church records: Killersherdoney CI
Census substitutes: FL

Kilkeel parish and town, County Down
Estate papers: Anglesey estate; Kilmorey estate; Mathews estate
Census substitutes: FL, AC

Killagan parish, County Antrim
Estate papers: Antrim estate; Hamilton estate; Wray estate
Census substitutes: HMR (included under Dunaghy)

Killaghtee parish, County Donegal
Estate papers: Murray of Broughton estate; Raphoe (bishopric of) estate
Church records: Killaghtee CI
Census substitutes: HMR, FL

Killaney parish, County Down
Estate papers: Downshire estate
Church records: Boardmills 1st P

Killanny parish, County Monaghan
Estate papers: Bath estate; Clogher (bishopric of) estate; Shirley estate
Census substitutes: HMR, FL

Killea parish, County Donegal
Church records: Killea CI
Census substitutes: FL

Killead parish, County Antrim
Estate papers: Massereene estate; Owens estate; Pakenham estate
Census substitutes: HMR, HSM
Tithe roll for townlands of Ballyrobin, Ballysculty, Ballymather and Kilcross, 1776 – D/2624/5
Subscribers to a reward fund, 1776 – *Belfast Newsletter*, 6–10 December 1776

Killeeshil parish, County Tyrone
Estate papers: Armagh (archbishopric of) estate; Stewart of Killymoon estate; Verner estate
Census substitutes: HMR (included under Aghaloo and Carnteel), VAA, FL

Killeevan parish, County Monaghan
[This parish was created in 1795 out of Galloon.]
Estate papers: Barton estate; Clogher (bishopric of) estate; Forster estate; Ker estate; Leslie of
    Glaslough estate; Massereene estate; Rossmore estate
Census substitutes: HMR, FL

Killelagh parish, County Londonderry
Estate papers: Conolly estate; Derry (bishopric of) estate; Mercers' Company estate; Strafford estate; Vintners' Company estate
Census substitutes: HMR, CPH, FL

Killeshandra parish, County Cavan
Estate papers: Craige estate; Farnham estate; Gosford estate
Church records: Killeshandra CI
Census substitutes: HMR, FL

Killesher parish, County Fermanagh
Estate papers: Enniskillen estate; Erne estate
Church records: Killesher CI
Census substitutes: FL

Killevy parish, County Armagh
Estate papers: Armagh (archbishopric of) estate; Charlemont estate; Hall estate; Johnston of Drumbanagher estate; Stewart estate
Census substitutes: HMR, FP, VAA, FL

Killinagh parish, County Cavan
Census substitutes: HMR

Killinchy parish, County Down
Estate papers: Blackwood estate; Clanbrassil estate; Londonderry estate; Macartney estate [see under County Antrim in Appendix 2]; Pollock estate
Church records: Killinchy CI; Killinchy NSP
Census substitutes: HSM, FL, AC

Killinkere parish, County Cavan
Estate papers: Farnham estate; Saunderson estate
Church records: Killinkere RC
Census substitutes: HMR, FL

Killowen parish, County Londonderry
Estate papers: Clothworkers' Company estate; Derry (bishopric of) estate; Jackson estate; McClelland/Maxwell estate
Church records: Killowen CI
Census substitutes: HMR, CPH, DP (Coleraine and Killowen), FL
Tithe book, Killowen parish, 1785 – D/668/B
Resolution of inhabitants of Coleraine and Killowen, 1787 – *Belfast Newsletter*, 2–6 February 1787
Rev. Robert Hezlet's tithe and rent book, Killowen parish, 1788 – D/668/B

Killybegs parish, County Donegal
Estate papers: Murray of Broughton estate; Raphoe (bishopric of) estate
Church records: Killybegs CI
Census substitutes: HMR, FL

Killygarvan parish, including the village of Rathmullan, County Donegal
Estate papers: Raphoe (bishopric of) estate; Stewart of Fortstewart estate
Census substitutes: HMR, FL

Killyleagh parish, County Down
Estate papers: Blackwood estate; Clanbrassil estate; De Clifford estate; Forde estate; Maxwell estate; Southwell estate
Church records: Killyleagh P
Census substitutes: DP, FL, AC

Killyman parish, Counties Armagh and Tyrone
Estate papers: Armagh (archbishopric of) estate; Stewart of Omagh estate; Verner estate
Church records: Killyman CI
Census substitutes: HMR, VAA, FL

Killymard parish, County Donegal
Estate papers: Murray of Broughton estate; Raphoe (bishopric of) estate
Census substitutes: HMR, FL

Kilmacrenan parish, County Donegal
Estate papers: Clements estate; Raphoe (bishopric of) estate
Census substitutes: HMR, FL

Kilmegan parish, County Down
Estate papers: Annesley estate; Downshire estate; Forde estate; Mathews estate
Census substitutes: FL, AC

Kilmood parish, County Down
Estate papers: Blackwood estate; Downshire estate; Londonderry estate
Church records: Kilmood CI
Offer of reward from inhabitants of Ballymonistrogh and Tullynagee, Kilmood parish, County Down; 29 names – *Belfast Newsletter*, 29 June 1756

Kilmore parish, County Armagh
Estate papers: Armagh (archbishopric of) estate; De Salis estate; Johnston of Gilford, County Down, estate, Magenis of Dromara estate [see under County Down in Appendix 2]; Manchester estate; Sachervell estate; Verner estate
Church records: Kilmore CI; Ballyhagen RSF; Richhill and Grange RSF
Census substitutes: HMR, FP, VAA, RelC, FL
Subscribers to a reward fund, Richhill, 1763 – *Belfast Newsletter*, 5 August 1763
Manors of Richhill and Mullalelish petition in relation to Act of Union – *Belfast Newsletter*, 20 December 1799

Kilmore parish, County Cavan
Estate papers: Annesley estate; Farnham estate; Story estate
Church records: Kilmore CI
Census substitutes: FL

Kilmore parish, County Down
Estate papers: Delacherois estate; Maxwell estate
Census substitutes: FL
Subscribers to a reward fund, 1771 – *Belfast Newsletter*, 11 June 1771

Kilmore parish, County Monaghan
Estate papers: Barton estate; Blayney estate; Clogher (bishopric of) estate; Dawson estate; Leslie of Glaslough estate; Rossmore estate
Census substitutes: HMR, FL

Kilraghts parish, County Antrim
Estate papers: Agnew estate; Antrim estate; Magenis of Dromara estate [see under County Down in Appendix 2]; Montgomery estate
Census substitutes: HMR, CPH, FL, AC
S. Alexander Blair, *Kilraughts: A Kirk and Its People* (Privately published, 1973)

Kilrea parish and town, County Londonderry
Estate papers: Derry (bishopric of) estate; Mercers' Company estate
Church records: Kilrea CI
Census substitutes: HMR, CPH, FL
Loyal declaration by the inhabitants of Kilrea and Tamlaght O'Crilly, 1745–6 (over 130 names) – MIC/1/55

Kilroot parish, County Antrim
Census substitutes: HMR

Kilskeery parish, County Tyrone
Estate papers: Clogher (bishopric of) estate; Cooper of Rossfad estate [see under County Fermanagh in Appendix 2]; Mervyn estate
Church records: Kilskeery CI
Census substitutes: HMR (listed under Magheracross), FL

Kilteevoge parish, County Donegal
[This parish was created out of Stranorlar in 1773.]
Estate papers: Styles estate
Census substitutes: FL

Kilwaughter parish, County Antrim
Estate papers: Agnew estate
Church records: see Larne and Kilwaughter NSP
Census substitutes: HSM, DP (Larne, Raloo, Carncastle, Kilwaughter, Glenarm and Ballyeaston)

Kinawley parish, County Fermanagh
Estate papers: Crofton estate; Enniskillen estate; Erne estate
Church records: Kinawley CI; Swanlinbar CI
Census substitutes: RelC, FL

Kirkinriola parish, including the town of Ballymena, County Antrim
Estate papers: Adair estate
Church records: Kirkinriola CI
Census substitutes: HMR, CPH (listed as Ballymena), DP (Ballymena), FL (one name)
Map of the Adair estate, 1747, listing tenants with holdings in the Town Parks of Ballymena –
    T/1333/1
Memorial of inhabitants of the town and neighbourhood of Ballymena – *Belfast Newsletter*,
    20 April 1773

Knockbreda parish, County Down
Estate papers: Clanbrassil estate; Downshire estate; Dungannon estate
Church records: Knockbreda CI; Gilnahirk P
Census substitutes: FL (listed under 'Castlereagh'), AC
Petition from parishioners, 1763 – *Belfast Newsletter*, 1 July 1763
W. P. Carmody, *History of the Parish of Knockbreda* (Belfast, 1929)

Knockbride parish, County Cavan
Church records: Coronary P
Census substitutes: FL

Lambeg parish, Counties Antrim and Down
Estate papers: Conway estate
Census substitutes: HMR
Subscribers to a reward fund, 1779 – *Belfast Newsletter*, 16–20 July 1779

Larah parish, County Cavan
Estate papers: Annesley estate; Saunderson estate
Census substitutes: FL

Larne parish and town, County Antrim
Estate papers: Agnew estate; Antrim estate
Church records: see Inver CI; Larne and Kilwaughter NSP
Census substitutes: HMR, HSM, DP (Larne, Raloo, Carncastle, Kilwaughter, Glenarm and
    Ballyeaston)
Map of the 'Old Town of Lairn als Gardenmore' of 1735 listing nearly 80 tenants' names –
    D/2977/36/2/1 (see also T/982/1 for a list of names extracted from this map)

Lavey parish, County Cavan
Estate papers: Annesley estate; Saunderson estate
Census substitutes: RelC (Protestants), FL

Layd parish, County Antrim
Estate papers: Antrim estate; Edwards estate; Rowan estate
Census substitutes: HMR, FL
Subscribers to a reward fund, 1772 – *Belfast Newsletter*, 14 April 1772

Learmount parish, County Londonderry
[This parish was created in 1831 out of Banagher and Cumber.]

Leck parish, County Donegal
Estate papers: Raphoe (bishopric of) estate
Census substitutes: HMR, RelC (Protestants), FL

Leckpatrick parish, County Tyrone
Estate papers: Abercorn estate; Derry (bishopric of) estate; Hall estate
Census substitutes: HMR, FL
William J. Roulston, *The Parishes of Leckpatrick and Dunnalong: Their Place in History* (Privately
   published, 2000)

Lettermacaward parish, County Donegal
Estate papers: Raphoe (bishopric) estate
Census substitutes: HMR

Lisnadill parish, County Armagh
[This parish was created out of Armagh parish in 1772.]
Estate papers: Armagh (archbishopric of) estate; Charlemont estate; McGeough-Bond estate;
   Whaley estate

Lissan parish, Counties Londonderry and Tyrone
Estate papers: Armagh (archbishopric of) estate; Drapers' Company estate; Staples estate
Church records: Lissan CI
Census substitutes: HMR, CPH, FL

Longfield parish, County Tyrone
Estate papers: Castle Stewart estate; Derry (bishopric of) estate; Huntingdon estate; Mervyn
   estate
Census substitutes: HMR, FL
Subscribers to a reward fund relating to Longfield – *Belfast Newsletter*, 4 December 1770

Loughan parish, County Cavan *see* **Castlekeeran**

Loughgall parish, County Armagh
Estate papers: Armagh (archbishopric of) estate; Charlemont estate; Cope estate; Molyneux
   estate; Verner estate
Church records: Loughgall CI.
Census substitutes: HMR, FP, VAA, CPH, FL
Subscribers to a reward fund, 1778 – *Belfast Newsletter*, 1–4 September 1778
Pat Reilly, *Loughgall: A Plantation Parish* (Loughgall, 1995), includes a muster roll of the estate
   of Antony Cope, 1630 (pp. 177–9), hearth money roll, 1664–5 (pp. 180–85),
   churchwardens, 1773–1995 (pp. 165–73), inhabitants of Loughgall to whom money was
   owed by Camboon's regiment in King William's Army, 1689–96 (p. 186) and seatholders in
   the parish church, 1775 and 1803 (pp. 189–90).

Loughgilly parish, County Armagh
Estate papers: Armagh (archbishopric of) estate; Charlemont estate; Magenis estate, Dromara [see under County Down in Appendix 2]; Stewart estate
Church records: Loughgilly CI; Tullyallen P
Census substitutes: HMR, FP, VAA, FL

Loughguile parish, County Antrim
Estate papers: Antrim estate; Legge estate; Macartney estate
Church records: Loughguile CI
Census substitutes: HMR, CPH, FL, AC

Loughinisland parish, County Down
Estate papers: Forde estate; Ker estate; Rawdon estate
Church records: Loughinisland CI; Clough NSP; Clough P
Census substitutes: FL

Lurgan parish, County Cavan
Estate papers: Farnham estate; Plunkett estate
Church records: Lurgan RC
Census substitutes: HMR, RelC (Protestants), FL

Macosquin parish and village, also known as the parish of Camus-juxta-Bann, County Londonderry
Estate papers: Clothworkers' Company estate; Derry (bishopric of) estate; Jackson estate; Merchant Taylors' Company estate
Census substitutes: HMR, CPH, FL
Names of some inhabitants of the parish, 1675 – printed in T. W. Moody and J. G. Simms, *The Bishopric of Derry and the Irish Society of London, 1602–1705* (2 vols, Dublin, 1968–83), ii, pp. 10–11

Maghera parish, County Down
Estate papers: Mathews estate
Census substitutes: FL, AC

Maghera parish and town, County Londonderry
Estate papers: Conolly estate; Derry (bishopric of) estate; Mercers' Company estate; Strafford estate; Vintners' Company estate
Church records: Maghera CI
Census substitutes: HMR, CPH, FL

Magheracloone parish, County Monaghan
Estate papers: Brownlow estate; Clogher (bishopric of) estate; Shirley estate
Census substitutes: HMR, FL
Names of male Protestants aged 17 and over, 1785 (Protestants and Presbyterians listed separately) – T/808/15259

Magheracross parish, Counties Fermanagh and Tyrone
Estate papers: Clogher (bishopric of) estate; Conolly estate; Lendrum estate; Mervyn estate
Census substitutes: HMR, FL

Magheraculmoney parish, County Fermanagh
Estate papers: Archdale estate; Clogher (bishopric of) estate
Church records: Magheraculmoney CI
Census substitutes: FL

Magheradrool parish, County Down
Estate papers: Annesley estate; Forde estate; Ker estate; Rawdon estate
Church records: Ballynahinch P
Census substitutes: HSM, FL
Subscribers to a reward fund, 1775 – *Belfast Newsletter*, 8–12 December 1775

Magherafelt parish and town, County Londonderry
Estate papers: Armagh (archbishopric of) estate; Dawson estate; Salters' Company estate; Vintners' Company estate
Church records: Magherafelt CI; Magherafelt 1st P
Census substitutes: HMR, VAA, CPH, RelC, HSM, FL
Subscribers to a reward fund, 1769 – *Belfast Newsletter*, 18 April 1769
W. H. Maitland, *History of Magherafelt* (1916, reprinted Moyola Books, 1988 and 1991)

Magheragall parish, County Antrim
Estate papers: Conway estate; Rawdon estate [see under County Down in Appendix 2]
Church records: Magheragall CI
Census substitutes: HMR, HSM

Magheralin parish, County Down
Estate papers: Clanwilliam estate; Downshire estate; Rawdon estate
Church records: Magheralin CI
Census substitutes: FL
F. X. McCorry, *Parish Registers: Historical Treasures in Manuscript* (Lurgan, 2004) (includes information from the Magheralin CI registers)

Magherally parish, County Down
Estate papers: Downshire estate
Church records: Magherally CI; Magherally P
Census substitutes: FL

Magheramesk parish, County Antrim
Estate papers: Conway estate
Census substitutes: HMR

Magheross parish, including the town of Carrickmacross, County Monaghan
Estate papers: Bath estate; Clogher (bishopric of) estate; Essex estate; Shirley estate
Church records: Magheross CI
Census substitutes: HMR, FL

Names of male Protestants aged 17 and over, 1785 – T/808/15259
Some Protestant inhabitants of Carrickmacross in 1777 – printed in *Clogher Record*, vi (1966), pp. 119–25

Magilligan parish, County Londonderry (also known as Tamlaghtard)
Estate papers: Bruce estate; Derry (bishopric of) estate; Gage estate
Church records: Tamlaghtard CI
Census substitutes: HMR, CPH, FL
Names of men from Magilligan parish ordered to appear 'with their best arms' at Limavady, 1666 – T/640/103

Mevagh parish, County Donegal
Estate papers: Clements estate; Raphoe (bishopric of) estate
Census substitutes: HMR, FL

Mintiaghs or Barr of Inch parish, County Donegal
Estate papers: Donegall estate; Ferguson estate

Moira parish and town, County Down
[This parish was created in 1722 out of Magheralin.]
Estate papers: Downshire estate; Rawdon estate
Church records: Moira CI
Subscribers to a reward fund, 1779 – *Belfast Newsletter*, 2–5 November 1779

Monaghan parish and town, County Monaghan
Estate papers: Barton estate; Blayney estate; Clermont estate; Clogher (bishopric of) estate; Dawson estate; Rossmore estate; Verner estate
Census substitutes: HMR, FL
List of tenants in Monaghan Town, 1791 – MIC/426/1

Moville parish, County Donegal
Estate papers: Alexander estate; Derry (bishopric of) estate; Donegall estate
Church records: Lower Moville CI
Census substitutes: HMR, CPH, FL

Muckno parish, including the town of Castleblayney, County Monaghan
Estate papers: Blayney estate; Clogher (bishopric of) estate
Census substitutes: HMR, FL

Muff parish, County Donegal
[This parish was created in 1809 out of Templemore.]
Estate papers: Donegall estate; Hart estate

Mullagh parish, County Cavan
Estate papers: Plunkett
Church records: Mullagh CI
Census substitutes: HMR

Mullaghbrack parish, County Armagh

Estate papers: Armagh (archbishopric of) estate; Charlemont estate; Gosford estate; Hamilton of Hamilton's Bawn estate

Church records: Mullaghbrack CI

Census substitutes: HMR, FP, VAA, CPH, FL

Commonplace book of Rev. Squire Barker, *c*.1750–*c*.1770 – D/943/1. This contains much information about the inhabitants of the parish as well as marriage banns relating to Mullaghbrack.

Munterconnaught parish, County Cavan

Estate papers: Plunkett estate

Church records: Castlerahan and Munterconnaught RC

Census substitutes: HMR, RelC (Protestants), FL

Newry parish and town, Counties Armagh and Down

Estate papers: Anglesey estate; Downshire estate; Kilmorey estate

Church records: Newry CI; Newry NSP

Census substitutes: DP (plus Established Church petition), FL, AC

Map of Ballywholan [Ballyholland], 1776 plus a list of holdings in 1792 – T/1101/10/1

Newtowncrommelin parish, County Antrim

[This parish was formed *c*.1830 out of Dunaghy.]

Newtownards parish and town, County Down

Estate papers: Londonderry estate

Census substitutes: FL

Corporation records: Newtownards

Map of the town of Newtownards, 1720, naming tenants, but very faded – D/952/1

Subscribers to a reward fund, 1782 – *Belfast Newsletter,* 27–31 December 1782

Newtownhamilton parish and town, County Armagh

[This parish was created in 1773 out of Creggan parish.]

Census substitutes: FL

Pomeroy parish and town, County Tyrone

[This parish was created in 1775 out of Donaghmore.]

Estate papers: Forster estate; Lowry of Pomeroy estate; Stewart of Killymoon estate

Portglenone parish and town, County Antrim

[This parish was created in 1840 out of Ahoghill parish.]

Racavan parish, County Antrim

Estate papers: Mountcashell estate; O'Neill estate

Census substitutes: HMR, FL

Raloo parish, County Antrim
Estate papers: Dungannon estate; Neale estate
Church records: Inver CI (includes Raloo)
Census substitutes: HMR (included under heading 'Parish of Magheramorne'), HSM, DP
    (Larne, Raloo, Carncastle, Kilwaughter, Glenarm and Ballyeaston)
Map of Raloo parish, naming tenants, 1770 – D/1954/6/1

Ramoan parish, including the town of Ballycastle, County Antrim
Estate papers: Antrim estate; Boyd estate; McGildowney estate
Census substitutes: HMR, CPH, FL, AC

Raphoe parish and town, County Donegal
Estate papers: Abercorn estate; Abraham estate; McClintock estate; Raphoe (bishopric of) estate
Church records: Raphoe CI
Census substitutes: HMR, RelC (Protestants), FL

Rasharkin parish, County Antrim
Estate papers: Antrim estate
Census substitutes: HMR, CPH, FL

Rashee parish, County Antrim
Estate papers: Donegall estate
Census substitutes: HMR

Rathlin parish, County Antrim
Estate papers: Antrim estate; Gage estate
Church records: Rathlin CI
Census substitutes: HMR, CPH, AC
'Book of Rathlin' recording sales of household goods, meal and seed to the islanders, 1783–94
    (index at front of volume to islanders: over 200 names) – D/1375/11/1
Mrs Gage, *A history of the island of Rathlin* (1851)

Rathmullan parish, County Down
Estate papers: Leslie estate; Ward estate
Census substitutes: FL, AC

Raymoghy parish, County Donegal
Estate papers: Abercorn estate; Forward estate; Raphoe (bishopric of) estate
Census substitutes: HMR, FL

Rossorry parish, County Fermanagh
Estate papers: Clogher (bishopric of) estate; Enniskillen estate; Huntingdon estate
Church records: Rossorry CI
Census substitutes: RelC, FL
M. Rogers, *A Short History of Rossory Parish* (privately published, n.d.)

Saintfield parish and town, County Down

Estate papers: Clanbrassil estate; Downshire estates; Hutcheson estate; Maxwell estate; Price estate

Church records: Saintfield CI

Census substitutes: HSM, FL, AC

M. C. Perceval-Price, *Saintfield Parish under the Microscope* (n.d.)

Saul parish, County Down

Estate papers: Ardglass estate; De Clifford estate; Leslie estate; Southwell estate; Ward estate

Church records: see Down CI

Census substitutes: FL, AC

Scrabby parish, County Cavan

Estate papers: Gosford estate

Seagoe parish, including the town of Portadown, County Armagh

Estate papers: Brownlow estate; Burges estate; Magenis of Dromara estate [see under County Down in Appendix 2]

Church records: Seagoe CI

Census substitutes: HMR, FL

F. X. McCorry, *Parish Registers: Historical Treasures in Manuscript* (Lurgan, 2004) (includes information from the Seagoe CI registers)

Seapatrick parish, including the town of Banbridge, County Down

Estate papers: Downshire estate; Dungannon estate; Whyte estate

Church records: 1st Banbridge NSP

Census substitutes: CPH, RelC, DP (Seapatrick, Tullylish and Donochclony), FL

R. Linn, *A History of Banbridge*, edited by W. S. Kerr (Banbridge, 1935)

Shankill parish, including the city of Belfast, County Antrim

Estate papers: Donegall estate; Legg estate; Saunders estate

Church records: St Anne's CI, Belfast; All Souls NSP, Belfast; Rosemary St NSP, Belfast; Rosemary St P, Belfast; St Patrick's RC, Belfast

Census substitutes: HMR, DP

Names of inhabitants of Belfast extracted from Donegall estate leases, 17th and 18th centuries – D/509 (listed in calendar)

List of names of lessees on the Donegall estate in Belfast, 1750–1815, arranged by occuation with nearly 400 names in all – T/1641

List of free and independent inhabitants of Belfast: *c.*120 names – *Belfast Newsletter*, 26 February 1754

Names of merchants, traders and inhabitants of Belfast, 1774, *c.*60 names – *Belfast Newsletter*, 26–29 July 1774

List of Belfast inhabitants who subscribed to a request for information on missing artillery pieces, *c.*151 names – *Belfast Newsletter*, 5 June 1798

George Benn, *The History of the Town of Belfast* (Belfast, 1823)

Jean Agnew, *Belfast Merchant Families in the Seventeenth Century* (Dublin, 1996)

Shankill parish, including the town of Lurgan, Counties Armagh and Down
Estate papers: Brownlow estate
Church records: Shankill CI, Lurgan P, Lurgan RSF
Census substitutes: HMR, CPH, HSM
List of tenants in the manor of Brownlow's-Derry, c.1670–1799 (572 names plus occupations
    and residences) – published in *Familia* no. 16 (2000), pp. 51–60
Lurgan Free School records, 1786 – D/1928/S
F. X. McCorry, *Lurgan: An Irish Provincial Town, 1610–1970* (Lurgan, 1993)
F. X. McCorry, *Parish Registers: Historical Treasures in Manuscript* (Lurgan, 2004) (includes
    information from the Shankill CI registers and Lurgan Quaker records)

Shercock, County Cavan
Estate papers: Fitzherbert estate

Skerry, County Antrim
Estate papers: O'Neill estate
Census substitutes: HMR, FL

Slanes, County Down
Church records: see Ballyphilip CI

Stranorlar parish and village, County Donegal
Estate papers: McCausland estate; Raphoe (bishopric of) estate
Census substitutes: HMR, FL

Tamlaght parish, Counties Londonderry and Tyrone
Estate papers: Armagh (archbishopric of) estate; Drapers' Company estate; Lenox-Conyngham
    estate
Census substitutes: HMR, CPH, DP (Coagh), FL

Tamlaght Finlagan parish, including the village of Ballykelly, County Londonderry
Estate papers: Conolly estate; Derry (bishopric of) estate; Fishmongers' Company estate;
    Grocers' Company estate; Phillips estate
Church records: Tamlaght Finlagan CI, Ballykelly P
Census substitutes: HMR, DE, CPH, FL
Freeholders from Tamlaght Finlagan parish, 1774 (136 names and addresses) – D/2094/46

Tamlaght O'Crilly parish, County Londonderry
Estate papers: Conolly estate; Derry (bishopric of) estate; Mercers' Company estate; Strafford
    estate; Vintners' Company estate
Census substitutes: HMR, CPH, HSM, FL
Loyal declaration by the inhabitants of Kilrea and Tamlaght O'Crilly, 1745–6, over 130 names
    – MIC/1/55

Tartaraghan parish, County Armagh
Estate papers: Armagh (bishopric of) estate; Atkinson estate; Charlemont estate; Verner estate
Census substitutes: HMR, VAA, RelC, FL

Taughboyne parish, including the village of St Johnstown, County Donegal
Estate papers: Abercorn estate; Forward estate; Raphoe (bishopric of) estate
Church records: Taughboyne CI
Census substitutes: HMR, FL

Tedavnet parish, County Monaghan
Estate papers: Blayney estate; Clogher (bishopric of) estate; Crofton estate; Evatt estate; Rossmore estate
Church records: Ballyalbany P
Census substitutes: HMR, FL

Tehallan parish, County Monaghan
Estate papers: Clogher (bishopric of) estate; Leslie of Glaslough estate
Church records: Tyholland CI
Census substitutes: HMR, FL

Templecarn parish, including the village of Pettigo, Counties Donegal and Fermanagh
Estate papers: Caldwell estate; Clogher (bishopric of) estate; Lenox estate; Leslie estate
Church records: Templecarn CI
Census substitutes: HMR, FL

Templecorran parish, including the village of Ballycarry, County Antrim
Estate papers: Edmonstone estate
Church records: Ballycarry NSP
Census substitutes: HMR (included under heading 'Brode Island Parish')

Templecrone parish, County Donegal
Estate papers: Murray of Broughton estate; Raphoe (bishopric of) estate
Church records: Templecrone CI
Census substitutes: HMR
Protestant householders, 1799, published in *The Irish Ancestor* (1984).

Templemore parish, including the city of Londonderry, Counties Donegal and Londonderry
[Until the nineteenth century Templemore covered what are now the parishes of Burt, Inch and Muff in County Donegal.]
Estate papers: Derry (bishopric of) estate; Irish Society estate
Church records: St Columb's Cathedral (CI)
Census substitutes: HMR, CPH, DP (Londonderry plus Established Church petition), FL
Corporation records: Londonderry
'A particular of the howses and familyes in London Derry', 15 May 1628 – D/683/42 (MIC/517/1) (printed in T. W. Moody and J. G. Simms, *The Bishopric of Derry and the Irish Society of London, 1602–1705* (2 vols, Dublin, 1968–83), i, pp. 154–60)
Parish cess lists, 1751–6 – T/1020/1
Inhabitants of the city of Londonderry who subscribed to a petition in relation to the proposed legislative union of Great Britain and Ireland, 1799, published in the *Directory of Irish Family History Research*, 24 (2001), pp. 87–9

Second half of a list of names and addresses of people living in or near Londonderry, n.d. [late 18th century], over 80 names – D/2798/3/87

Templepatrick parish and village, County Antrim
Estate papers: Upton estate
Church records: Lylehill P; Templepatrick NSP; Templepatrick P
Census substitutes: HMR
Names of tenant farmers – *Belfast Newsletter*, 26 July 1768, 15 November 1768, 28 March 1769

Templeport parish, County Cavan
Estate papers: Annesley estate
Census substitutes: HMR, RelC

Termonamongan parish, County Tyrone
Estate papers: Castle Stewart estate; Derry (bishopric of) estate; Huntingdon estate
Census substitutes: HMR, FL
List of suspected United Irishmen to be apprehended, 1798, over 40 names mainly from Termonamongan parish, printed in Brendan McEvoy, *The United Irishmen in County Tyrone* (Armagh, 1998), pp. 37–8

Termoneeny parish, County Londonderry
Estate papers: Conolly estate; Derry (bishopric of) estate; Vintners' Company estate
Census substitutes: HMR, DE, CPH, FL

Termonmaguirk parish, County Tyrone
Estate papers: Armagh (archbishopric of) estate; Mervyn estate; Stewart of Termonmaguirk estate
Church records: Termonmaguirk CI
Census substitutes: PB, HMR, FP, VAA, FL
Volume containing a list of the names of 'housekeepers' in 'Termont' (Termonmaguirk), 1780 – DIO/4/32/T/4/4/1. This lists 524 householders in all by townland: 414 Roman Catholic, 58 Presbyterian and 52 Church of Ireland.

Tickmacrevan parish, including the town of Glenarm, County Antrim
Estate papers: Antrim estate, Agnew estate
Church records: Tickmacrevan (Glenarm) CI
Census substitutes: HMR, DP (Larne, Raloo, Carncastle, Kilwaughter, Glenarm and Ballyeaston)
J. Irvine, 'A map of Glenarm – 1779' in *The Glynns*, no. 9 (1981), pp. 52–61 – names tenants in Glenarm
F. McKillop, *Glenarm: A Local History* (1987)

Tomregan parish, Counties Cavan and Fermanagh
Estate papers: Annesley estate
Church records: Tomregan CI
Census substitutes: HMR

Trory parish, County Fermanagh
[This parish was created out of Devenish c.1779.]
Estate papers: Archdale estate; Clogher (bishopric of) estate; Huntingdon estate
Census substitutes: FL
Names of male Protestants aged 17 and over, 1785 – T/808/15259

Tullaghobegley parish, County Donegal
Estate papers: Raphoe (bishopric of) estate
Census substitutes: HMR

Tullyaughnish parish, County Donegal *see under* Aughnish

Tullycorbet parish, County Monaghan
Estate papers: Barton estate; Clogher (bishopric of) estate; Dawson estate; Massereene estate
Church records: Tullycorbet CI; Cahan P
Census substitutes: HMR (included with Aghnamullen), FL

Tullyfern parish, County Donegal
Estate papers: Clements estate, Raphoe (bishopric of) estate
Census substitutes: HMR, FL

Tullylish parish, County Down
Estate papers: Clanwilliam estate; Downshire estate; Johnston estate; Lawrence estate
Church records: Tullylish CI
Census substitutes: DP (Seapatrick, Tullylish and Donochclony), FL
Names of 90 persons excommunicated by Church of Ireland diocese of Dromore between 1725 and 1740 – T/426/1, pp. 47–8
Marriage licences (28 entries), 1734–56, providing names and addresses – T/426/1, pp. 95–7
Resolution of linen drapers, freeholders and inhabitants of the Gilford area, 1772 – *Belfast Newsletter*, 29 May 1772

Tullynakill parish, County Down
Estate papers: Clanbrassil estate; Downshire estate

Tullyniskan parish, County Tyrone
Estate papers: Armagh (archbishopric of) estate; Castle Stewart estate
Church records: Tullyniskan CI
Census substitutes: HMR, VAA, RelC, FL

Tullyrusk parish, County Antrim
Estate papers: Conway estate
Census substitutes: HMR (included under Glenavy parish)

Tynan parish and village, County Armagh
Estate papers: Armagh (archbishopric of) estate; Houston estate; Maxwell estate
Church records: Tynan CI
Census substitutes: HMR, FP, VAA, CPH, FL
Thomas Hughes, *The History of Tynan Parish, County Armagh* (Dublin, 1910)
Seamus Mallon, *Historical Sketches of the Parish of Tynan and Middletown* (Tynan, 1995)
J. J. Marshall, *History of the Parish of Tynan in the County of Armagh* (Dungannon, 1932)
F. X. McCorry, *Parish Registers: Historical Treasures in Manuscript* (Lurgan, 2004) (includes
    information from the Tynan CI registers)

Tyrella parish, County Down
Estate papers: Downshire estate; Ward estate
Census substitutes: FL, AC
View book of the great tithes of the deanery of Down, 1732 – D/1145/D/1

Urney parish, including the town of Cavan, County Cavan
Estate papers: Annesley estate; Farnham estate; Lanesborough estate; Saunderson estate
Church records: Urney CI
Census substitutes: HMR, FL
Corporation records: Cavan
Index from Registry of Deeds for Cavan Town, 1708–38 – T/808/14142

Urney parish, including the town of Castlederg, Counties Donegal and Tyrone
Estate papers: Abercorn estate; Castle Stewart estate; Derry (bishopric of) estate; Gage estate;
    Huntingdon estate
Census substitutes: HMR, FL
T. P. Donnelly, *A History of the Parish of Ardstraw West and Castlederg* (Strabane, n.d.)

Warrenpoint parish, County Down
[This parish was formed *c.*1840 out of Clonallan.]

Witter parish, County Down
Estate papers: Savage-Nugent estate
Church records: see Ballyphilip CI
Census substitutes: FL, AC

APPENDIX 4

Archives and libraries

The following repositories have material of interest to those conducting research on the seventeenth and eighteenth centuries.

ARMAGH PUBLIC LIBRARY
Abbey Street
Armagh, BT61 7DY
Northern Ireland

Telephone: (028) 3752 3142; Fax: (028) 3752 4177
E-mail: ArmROBLib@aol.com
Website: www.armaghrobinsonlibrary.org

BELFAST CENTRAL LIBRARY
Royal Avenue
Belfast, BT1 1EA
Northern Ireland

Telephone: (028) 9050 9150; Fax: (028) 9033 2819
E-mail: info@libraries.belfast-elb.gov.uk
Website: www.belb.org.uk

BODLEIAN LIBRARY
Broad Street,
Oxford OX1 3BG
England

Telephone: 01865 277180; Fax: 01865 277105
Email: admissions@bodley.ox.ac.uk
Website: www.bodley.ox.ac.uk

CAMBRIDGE UNIVERSITY LIBRARY
West Road,
Cambridge,
CB3 9DR

Telephone: 01223 333000
Email: library@lib.cam.ac.uk
Website: www.lib.cam.ac.uk

CAMBRIDGESHIRE COUNTY RECORD OFFICE
Grammar School Walk
Huntingdon
Cambridgeshire
PE18 6LF

Telephone: 01480 375842; Fax: 01480 375842
Email: county.records.hunts@cambridgeshire.gov.uk

CASTLE LESLIE
Glaslough
County Monaghan
Ireland

Telephone: 00 353 47 88109 Fax: 00 353 47 88256
Email: info@castleleslie.com
Website: www.castleleslie.com/

DONEGAL COUNTY ARCHIVES SERVICE
Donegal County Council
Three Rivers Centre
Lifford, Co. Donegal
Ireland

Telephone: (074) 72490; Fax: (074) 41367
E-mail: nbrennan@donegalcoco.ie
Website: www.donegal.ie/dcc/arts/archive.htm

GRAND LODGE OF FREEMASONS OF IRELAND: LIBRARY, ARCHIVES AND MUSEUM
Freemasons' Hall
17 Molesworth Street
Dublin 2
Ireland

Telephone: (01) 676 1337; Fax: (01) 662 5101
E-mail: library@freemason.ie

GUILDHALL LIBRARY
Aldermanbury,
London EC2P 2EJ

Telephone: 020 7332 3803; Fax: 020 7600 3384
E-mail: search.guildhall@corpoflondon.gov.uk
Website: www.history.ac.uk/gh

HISTORICAL LIBRARY, RELIGIOUS SOCIETY OF FRIENDS
Swanbrook House
Bloomfield Avenue
Dublin 4
Ireland

Telephone: (01) 668 7157
Website: www.quakers-in-ireland.org

HUNTINGTON LIBRARY
1151 Oxford Road
San Marino, CA 91108
United States of America

Telephone: 626-405-2100
Email: publicinfo@huntington.org
Website: www.huntington.org

JOHN RYLANDS LIBRARY
150 Deansgate
Manchester
M3 3EH

Telephone: 0161-275 3764
Email: special.collections@man.ac.uk
Website: rylibweb.man.ac.uk/

LINEN HALL LIBRARY
17 Donegall Square North
Belfast, BT1 5GD
Northern Ireland

Telephone: (028) 9032 1707; Fax: (028) 9043 8586
E-mail: info@linenhall.com
Website: www.linenhall.com

MONAGHAN COUNTY MUSEUM
1-2 Hill Street
Monaghan Town, Co. Monaghan
Ireland

Telephone: (047) 82928; Fax: (047) 71189
E-mail: comuseum@monaghancoco.ie
Website: www.monaghan.ie/museum

NATIONAL ARCHIVES OF IRELAND
Bishop Street
Dublin 8
Ireland

Telephone: (01) 407 2300; Fax: (01) 407 2333
E-mail: mail@nationalarchives.ie
Website: www.nationalarchives.ie

NATIONAL ARCHIVES OF SCOTLAND
H M General Register House
2 Princes Street
Edinburgh
EH1 3YY

Telephone: 0131 535 1334
E-mail: enquiries@nas.gov.uk
Website: www.nas.gov.uk

NATIONAL LIBRARY OF IRELAND
Kildare Street
Dublin 2
Ireland

Telephone: (01) 603 0200; Fax: (01) 676 6690
E-mail: info@nli.ie
Website: www.nli.ie

OFFICE OF THE CHIEF HERALD/GENEALOGICAL OFFICE
2–3 Kildare Street
Dublin 2
Ireland

Telephone: (01) 603 0230; Fax: (01) 662 1061
E-mail: herald@nli.ie
Website: www.nli.ie/new_office.htm

PRESBYTERIAN HISTORICAL SOCIETY
26 College Green
Belfast, BT7 1LN
Northern Ireland

Telephone: (028) 9072 7330
E-mail: phsilibrarian@pcinet.org
Website: www.presbyterianhistoryireland.com

PUBLIC RECORD OFFICE *see* **THE NATIONAL ARCHIVES**

PUBLIC RECORD OFFICE OF NORTHERN IRELAND
2 Titanic Boulevard
Titanic Quarter
Belfast
BT3 9HQ
Northern Ireland

Website: www.proni.gov.uk

REGISTRY OF DEEDS
Henrietta Street
Dublin 1
Ireland

Telephone: (01) 8716533; Fax: (01) 8716536
E-mail: declan.ward@prai.ie
Website: www.landregistry.ie

REPRESENTATIVE CHURCH BODY LIBRARY
Braemor Park
Churchtown, Dublin 14
Ireland
Telephone: (01) 492 3979; Fax: (01) 492 4770
E-mail: library@ireland.anglican.org
Website: www.ireland.anglican.org

ROYAL IRISH ACADEMY
19 Dawson Street
Dublin 2
Ireland

Telephone: (0) 676 2570, (01) 676 4222; Fax: (01) 676 2346
E-mail: library@ria.ie
Website: www.ria.ie

SCOTTISH RECORD OFFICE see **NATIONAL ARCHIVES OF SCOTLAND**

THE NATIONAL ARCHIVES (formerly the PUBLIC RECORD OFFICE)
Kew
Richmond
Surrey TW9 4DU

Telephone: 020 8876 3444
Email: enquiry@nationalarchives.gov.uk
Website: www.nationalarchives.gov.uk

TRINITY COLLEGE DUBLIN LIBRARY – MANUSCRIPTS DEPARTMENT
College Green
Dublin 2
Ireland

Telephone: (01) 698 1189; Fax: (01) 671 9003
E-mail: mscripts@tcd.ie
Website: www.tcd.ie/Library

ULSTER HISTORICAL FOUNDATION
49 Malone Road
Belfast, BT9 6RY
Northern Ireland

Telephone: (028) 9066 1988; Fax: (028) 9066 1977
E-mail: enquiry@uhf.org.uk
Websites: www.ancestryireland.org.uk
          www.booksireland.org.uk

UNION THEOLOGICAL COLLEGE – GAMBLE LIBRARY
108 Botanic Avenue
Belfast, BT7 1JT
Northern Ireland

Telephone: (028) 9020 5093
Fax: (028) 9058 0040
E-mail: librarian@union.ac.uk
Website: www.union.ac.uk/library.htm

APPENDIX 5

Glossary of administrative divisions

Barony. A unit used in Ireland between the sixteenth and nineteenth centuries for administrative (census, taxation, and legal) purposes. Often drawn on pre-existing Gaelic divisions, baronies consisted of large groupings of townlands within a county. The 1891 census is the last to use the barony as an administrative unit.

County. The county system as a form of territorial division was introduced into Ireland shortly after the Norman Conquest in the late twelfth century. The creation of counties or shires was gradual, however, and the present arrangement of county boundaries was not finalised in Ulster until the early seventeenth century. In 1898 local councils based on county divisions were created. County councils remain the principal administrative body of local government in the Republic of Ireland but were abolished in Northern Ireland in 1973. The counties in Ulster are: Antrim, Armagh, Cavan, Donegal, Down, Fermanagh, Londonderry, Monaghan and Tyrone. Of these, Cavan, Donegal and Monaghan are in the Republic of Ireland, with the rest in Northern Ireland.

Diocese. A diocese is an area controlled by a bishop and composed of a group of parishes. The number of parishes in a diocese varies considerably. In the diocese of Connor, there were over seventy parishes, while in the diocese of Clogher there were approximately thirty-five parishes. The network of dioceses was created in the medieval period and continues to be used by both the Church of Ireland and Roman Catholic Church with only minor alterations. The dioceses in Ulster are Armagh (covering all or part of counties Armagh, Londonderry and Tyrone), Clogher (Donegal, Fermanagh, Monaghan and Tyrone), Connor (Antrim, Down and Londonderry), Derry (Donegal, Londonderry and Tyrone), Down (Down), Dromore (Antrim, Armagh and Down), Kilmore (Cavan and Fermanagh) and Raphoe (Donegal).

Manor. The manor was introduced to Ireland by the Normans in the twelfth century. In the early seventeenth century grantees in the Ulster Plantation were given power to 'create manors'. The manor provided the basic legal framework within which an estate could be managed and was vital to its successful development. The lord of the manor was enabled to hold courts leet and baron to regulate the affairs of his estate. The manor courts also provided an arena where tenants could settle their disputes (see Chapter 6.3.8 for more information on manor courts).

Parish. This territorial division refers to both civil and ecclesiastical units. Civil parishes largely follow the pattern that was established in medieval times. Ecclesiastical parishes do not always coincide with civil parish boundaries, however. Following the Reformation in the sixteenth century, the Church of Ireland more or less maintained the pre-Reformation arrangement. Church of Ireland parishes are, therefore, largely coterminous with civil parishes. When the Catholic Church began its institutional re-emergence in the late eighteenth and nineteenth centuries, it constructed a new network of parishes which did not follow the civil parish network.

Province. Provinces are composed of groups of counties. There are four provinces in Ireland: Ulster in the north, Leinster in the east, Munster in the south, and Connacht or Connaught in the west.

Townland. This is the smallest administrative territorial unit in Ireland, varying in size from a single acre to over 7,000 acres. Originating in the older Gaelic dispensation, townlands were used as the basis of leases in the estate system, and subsequently to assess valuations and tithes in the eighteenth and nineteenth centuries. They survive as important markers of local identity.

APPENDIX 6

County Maps of Ulster

The following maps of the counties of Ulster are taken from S. Lewis, *Atlas of the counties of Ireland* (London, 1837). These show the general location of parishes within each county. For more detailed maps showing parish boundaries, researchers should visit www.ancestryireland.com/database.php?filename=civilparishmaps.

COUNTY ANTRIM

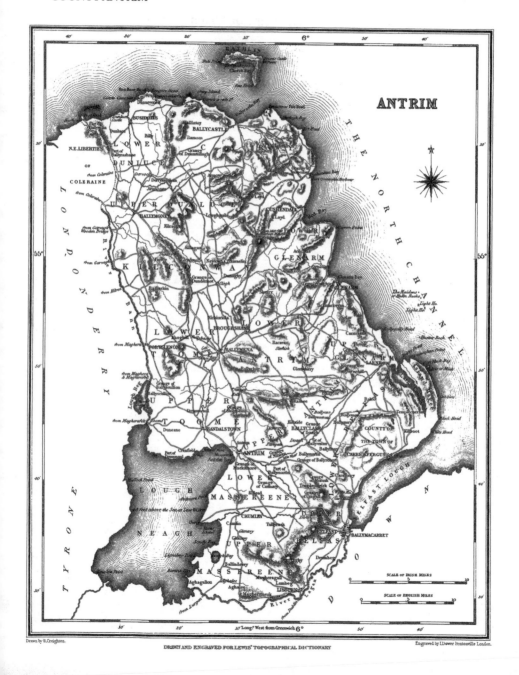

COUNTY ARMAGH

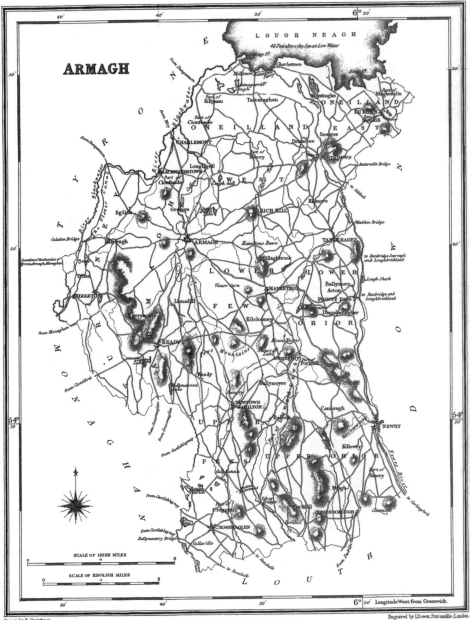

COUNTY CAVAN

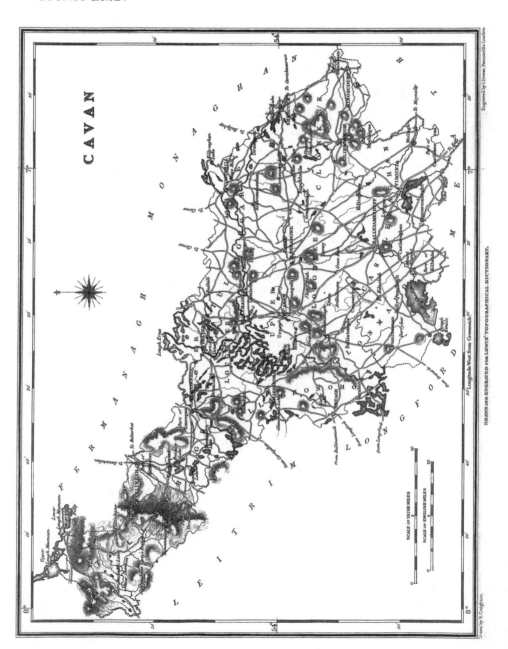

COUNTY DONEGAL

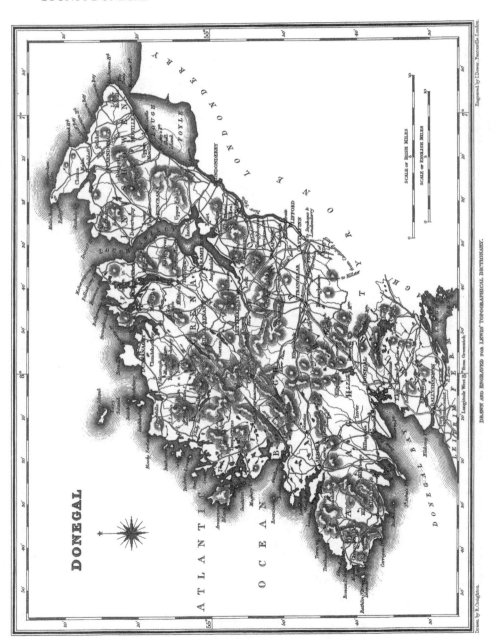

COUNTY DOWN

Drawn by R.Creighton.

DRAWN AND ENGRAVED FOR LEWIS' TOPOGRAPHICAL DICTIONARY.

Engraved by J.Dower,Pentonville London.

COUNTY FERMANAGH

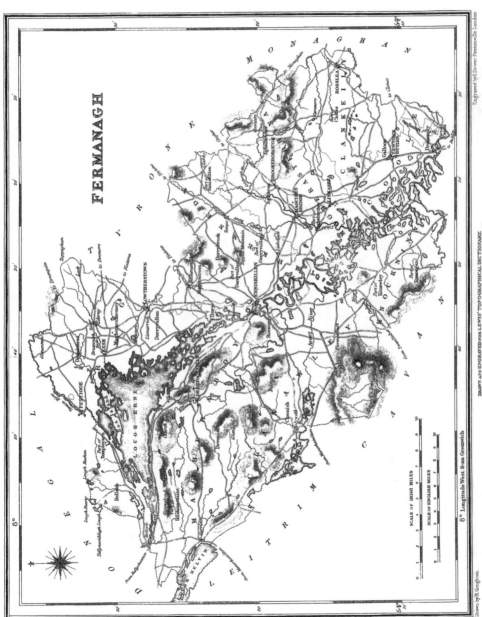

COUNTY LONDONDERRY

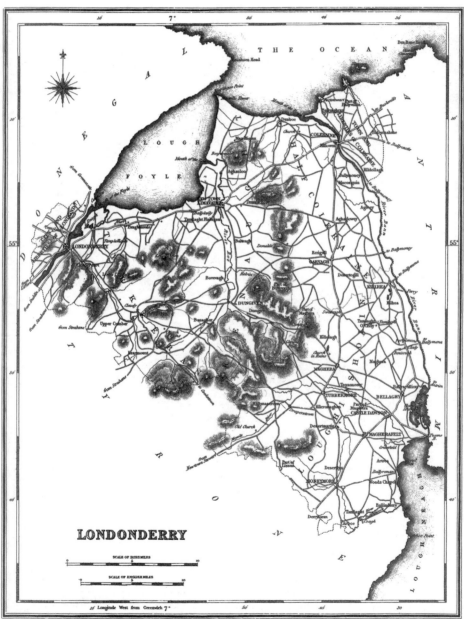

COUNTY MONAGHAN

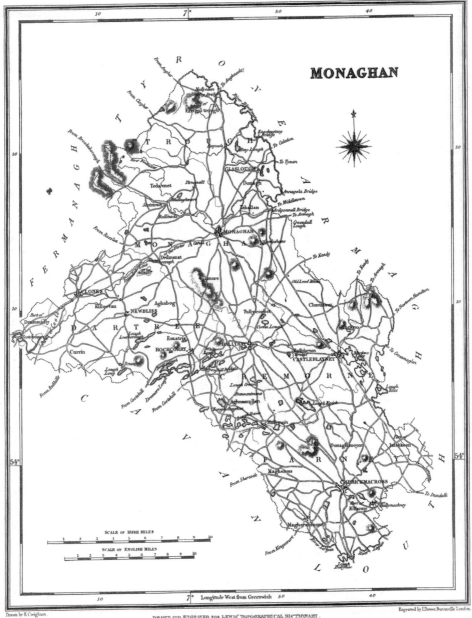

COUNTY TYRONE

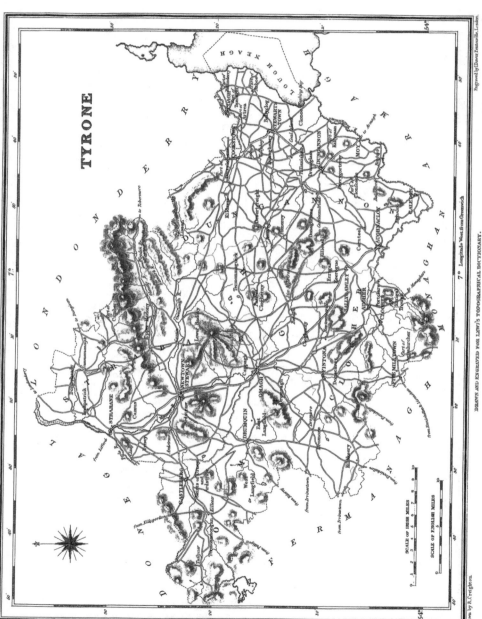

INDEX

Limavady, County Londonderry, corporation
of, 95
Lisburn, County Antrim, 103
Local government records, 91-6
Lodge Manuscripts, 53
Loghtee barony, County Cavan, 58
Londonderry, County Londonderry,
corporation of, 95
Londonderry Journal, 101-03
Londonderry muster roll, 1622, 57
Londonderry, marquess of, 67
Loughinsholin Militia, 100
Loughrey Infantry, 100
Lurgan Free School, 107

McCausland, Robert, 17
McCrea, William, linen buyer, 107
MacDonnell, Randal, 3
McKenna, Charles, will of, 84
McMahon, Bishop Hugh, 10
Magennis family, 3
Magilligan, County Londonderry, 100
Manor court records, 74-5
Maps, 72
Marriage licence bonds, 39
Marriage registers, 27
Marriage settlements, 79
Mellifont, Treaty of, 1
Methodist Church, 36-7
Military records, 97-100
Militia, 98
Moira and Lisburn Associate Presbytery, 35
Monaghan, County Monaghan, 107
Monaghan Secession records, 35
Moneymore, County Londonderry, 107
Montgomery, Hugh, 3
Moravian Church, 37
Mortgages, 79
Mourne Volunteers, 100
Mullalelish, County Armagh, manor of, 66
Munro, Major-General Robert, 6
Muster rolls, 50-51, 97, 99-100

National Covenant, 5, 13, 35
Newry Journal, 101
Newry Volunteers, 99

Newry, 89, 105, 108
Newspapers, 101-03
Newtownards, County Down, corporation
of, 95
Newtownards Volunteers, 99
Newtownstewart, County Tyrone, 107
Nine Years' War, 1
Non-Subscribing Presbyterian Church, 12-
13, 35
Northern Star, 101, 103

O'Donnell, Hugh and Rory, 1
O'Neill, Con, 3
O'Neill, Hugh, earl of Tyrone, 1
O'Neill, Owen Roe, 6
O'Neill, Sir Phelim, 6
Omagh, County Tyrone, 16, 107
Orange Order, 109

Penal Laws, 12, 62, 79
Personal Names Index, PRONI, 25
Petitions of Protestant Dissenters, 65
Plantation in Ulster, 2-3
Plantation surveys, 2, 47-8
Plunkett, Archbishop Oliver, 7-9
Poll books, 87-9
Portadown, County Armagh, 88, 103
Prerogative wills, 84-5
Presbyterian Church, 5, 8, 12-13, 31-2
Presbyterian ministers, 34-5
Presbytery records, 32-3
Presentments, 91-3
Public Record Office, Dublin, destruction of,
xi
Pue's Occurrences, 103

Quit rent rolls, 70

Raphoe marriage licence bonds, 39
Raven, Thomas, 72
Rawdon, Sir George, 7
Reas of Magheraknock, 19-21
Rebellion of 1641, 6
Rebellion of 1798, 17-18, 66
Rebellion Papers, 66
Reformed Presbyterian Church, 13, 35-6

ULSTER HISTORICAL FOUNDATION

The Ulster Historical Foundation is a not-for-profit educational charity (No. XN48460) which was founded in 1956. It exists to promote a knowledge of, and interest in, Irish history and genealogy with particular reference to the historic province of Ulster and to make information about the documentary sources in these fields more readily available. For almost half a century the Ulster Historical Foundation has been the premier genealogical research agency in Northern Ireland. In that time it has completed over 12,500 searches for clients with Irish and Scots-Irish roots. We have also published a broad range of books looking at different aspects of Irish history and genealogy and organise conferences, family history workshops and lectures tours. The register of our membership organisation, the Ulster Genealogical and Historical Guild, has topped the 12,000 mark. Guild members get free access to numerous online genealogical databases.

If you would like to find out more about the work of the Ulster Historical Foundation and how we can help you trace your ancestors, you can contact us at the address below:

Ulster Historical Foundation
49 Malone Road
Belfast, BT9 6RY
Northern Ireland
Telephone: +44 (0)28 9066 1988
Fax: +44 (0)28 9066 1977
Email: enquiry@uhf.org.uk
Websites:
www.ancestryireland.com
www.booksireland.org.uk
www.historyfromheadstones.com